Quality of Life in the Soviet Union

About the Book and Editor

"Quality of life" is a difficult concept to define, and particularly so when referring to the Soviet Union because Westerners have many preconceptions about Soviet living conditions. This volume goes a long way toward illuminating the realities of daily Soviet life and stands as an important contribution to our understanding of the Soviet Union. Contributors focus primarily on the relation of quality of life to living conditions but also discuss the quality and availability of state-provided services such as education, health care, and housing. Of special interest is their coverage of problems in Soviet society, including working conditions in factories, living conditions in rural areas, alcohol abuse, and the status of the elderly. Together these essays show that although the Soviet government has made great strides in improving the living conditions of its citizens, Soviet living standards and services are relatively poor by Western standards and several important social problems continue to burden the Soviet people.

Horst Herlemann is an associate professor of political science at Würzburg University, Federal Republic of Germany.

A SPECIAL STUDY OF THE
KENNAN INSTITUTE
FOR
ADVANCED RUSSIAN STUDIES

WOODROW WILSON INTERNATIONAL CENTER FOR SCHOLARS

THE
WILSON
CENTER

KENNAN
INSTITUTE
*For Advanced
Russian Studies*

Quality of Life
in the Soviet Union

edited by Horst Herlemann

Westview Press / Boulder and London

A *Special Study of the Kennan Institute for Advanced Russian Studies, Woodrow Wilson International Center for Scholars*

Published in 1987 in the United States of America by Westview Press, Inc.; Frederick A. Praeger, Publisher; 5500 Central Avenue, Boulder, Colorado 80301

Library of Congress Cataloging-in-Publication Data
Main entry under title:
   Quality of life in the Soviet Union.
   1. Quality of life—Soviet Union—Congresses.
2. Soviet Union—Social conditions—1970-   .—
Congresses.   I. Herlemann, Horst.
HN524.Q35 1987   305′.0947   85-10679
ISBN 0-8133-0191-2

Composition for this book was created by conversion of the editor's word-processor disks. This book was produced without formal editing by the publisher.

Printed and bound in the United States of America

⊚ The paper used in this publication meets the requirements of the American National Standard for Permanence of Paper for Printed Library Materials Z39.48-1984.

6   5   4   3   2

Contents

Tables

Foreword

It was a special pleasure for me to host a conference on the quality of life in the Soviet Union during my tenure as secretary of the Kennan Institute. In part, this was because many of the conference papers were presented by scholars from the Federal Republic of Germany. Those familiar with German scholarship in the field of Soviet studies recognize that it is enormously impressive both in quality and quantity, yet the substantial portion of it published only in German is missed by many American specialists, not to mention the general reader. The conference provided an opportunity for a large group of Soviet specialists from Washington, D.C., and from other parts of the United States to read and discuss the work of an important group of German scholars.

The theme of the conference was significant and rewarding. Focusing on the broad question of the quality of life in the Soviet Union—a concept that Horst Herlemann and Robert Belknap present in the opening chapters of this volume—enabled the conference group to draw together a wide range of subjects on which there has been a good deal of research and to view them in a new light. Among specialists on such topics as Soviet living standards, consumer goods and services, housing, and medical care, it is well known that simple statistics, including statistical comparisons with Western nations, do not capture the reality of life in the Soviet Union. One must be aware of the quality of consumer goods and services, the quality of housing, medical care, education, and other aspects of Soviet life. Each of the papers at the conference was designed to emphasize the theme of "quality." The collective product provides the reader with a broad picture of the quality of life in the contemporary Soviet Union, which is difficult to find in any other single volume.

Gertrude E. Schroeder shows that the Soviet standard of living is still far below prevailing Western and East European levels. In 1976, for example, the Soviet standard of living was one-third the American level and somewhat less than half the level of France and the Federal Republic of Germany. Dr. Schroeder cites several comparative studies showing that the relatively low standard of living in the Soviet Union can be traced to the fact that the Soviet government spends a considerably smaller share of its gross national product (GNP) on consumption than do most Western and East European nations. The Soviet Union has traditionally neglected its consumer sector, and this has resulted in chronic shortages of consumer goods, services, and food supplies. Moreover, Soviet wage scales require consumers to devote about two-thirds of their earnings to basic necessities such as food and clothing. Thus, not only is the Soviet standard of living relatively low as compared to the West, but Soviet consumption patterns resemble those of developing nations more closely than those of industrialized nations.

Wolfgang Teckenberg stresses that the Soviet Union maintains a "shortage economy," where consumption is restricted in favor of investment. As a result, Soviet consumers often find it difficult to purchase the items they want regardless of their disposable income. The Soviet Union has made progress in the distribution of certain consumer items, especially during the late 1970s, but as Dr. Teckenberg emphasizes, Soviet consumers still lag behind their Western counterparts as regards the purchase of most consumer goods and services. More importantly, per capita consumption levels have fallen since the late 1970s, and governmental expenditures on state-provided social services have also decreased in recent years. Social services such as health care and education are provided by the state, ostensibly free, but through taxes and other hidden charges, Soviet consumers pay for almost half of all "free" services. For the foreseeable future, it seems that the Soviet Union will remain a production-oriented society that underinvests in consumer goods and services.

While acknowledging that all nations contain a large number of poor people, Mervyn Matthews reveals that the Soviet poverty sector is surprisingly large given the USSR's concern with its image as a socialist welfare state. Using Soviet estimates of minimum family income requirements, it appears that the average family in 1965 existed in a state of poverty. A large number of surveys conducted during the 1960s revealed that as many as a quarter to a third of the urban working class lived below the poverty line, and because rural wages are about 10 percent lower than urban wages and rural inhabitants account for about 35 percent of the Soviet population, Dr. Matthews estimates that the total number of "poor" people in the Soviet Union was perhaps 40 percent of the entire population. Although industrial workers are among the best-paid employees in Soviet society, available statistics indicate that almost a third of them do not rise above the poverty threshold.

Mark G. Field, who shows that the Soviet health care system is highly stratified, emphasizes that there remains a wide gulf between the promises and realities of the system. The Soviet medical system is divided into a series of "networks" that serve different segments of the population according to one's position in Soviet society. Special clinics and hospitals exist throughout the Soviet Union for the benefit of the elite, but most Soviet citizens must make do with the much lower quality of the general health care system. Though the Soviet Union has the world's largest number of hospital beds per person, its medical system is over-bureaucratized and routinized and is plagued by chronic shortages of most health care materials, from high-technology equipment to bandages. Dr. Field notes that these shortages stem from continued underinvestment in the health care sector, illustrated by the fact that the proportion of the Soviet GNP allocated to health care is only one-third of the American level. Furthermore, Soviet spending on health care has declined significantly since the early 1970s.

Friedrich Kuebart, while recognizing the introduction of universal 10-year secondary education to be an admirable achievement, describes the reasons why the secondary school system is lacking in quality. General education in the Soviet Union is to be mastered by all students, irrespective of their individual abilities, and it is left to Soviet teachers to ensure that all students complete their studies successfully. As a result, Dr. Kuebart points out, most teachers have relaxed their grading practices so that few students fail. Still, there were 129,000 grade repeaters in 1981, accounting for 0.33 percent of the student population. Efforts to reform the school system are continually underway, but the practice of inflating grades will not be diminished easily, as the universal completion of secondary education in the Soviet Union is primarily a political issue.

Henry W. Morton notes that one of the Soviet Union's most impressive consumer achievements has been the creation of 2.2 million housing units per year since 1957. Yet despite this tremendous amount of construction, Dr. Morton emphasizes that the demand for new housing far exceeds supply. Soviet citizens still suffer from the poorest housing conditions of any industrialized nation, primarily because many families do not have private apartments. The wait for a new apartment can last up to 10 years or more if one is not "sponsored" by an influential organization or cannot find another family willing to engage in a housing exchange. Moreover, housing has become increasingly stratified, and identifiable "housing classes" have emerged. The upper classes live in or near the city centers, where transportation and shopping is readily available, and the lower classes live on the outskirts of major cities, where urban amenities are few. Soviet citizens spend very little on housing compared to Westerners, as rents are heavily subsidized by the government, but quality housing is available to only a small portion of the population.

According to Soviet ideology, the socialist economic system should have put an end to poor working conditions and the alienation of labor. However, Anna-Jutta Pietsch describes how Soviet working conditions leave much to be desired, even according to Soviet sources. Working conditions are generally best in production-oriented sectors of the economy because scarce resources tend to be concentrated in large-scale endeavors. Soviet workers generally receive low wages and are becoming increasingly dissatisfied with organizational problems, such as "intrashift down time," that negatively affect their earning possibilities.

Stephen Sternheimer posits that as a result of demographic changes, such as the increasing nuclearization of urban families, older Soviet women are being deprived of their traditional role as *babushki*, or grandmother-child minders. Most pension-age Soviet women are not eager to assume the *babushka* role after retirement anyway, and they tend not to work after they reach retirement age. As many are widowed, a large proportion probably find themselves in a position of economic hardship, being solely dependent on state pensions. Soviet pensions are largely inadequate because they are tied to past wages, and the wages of Soviet women are considerably lower than those of Soviet men. Thus Dr. Sternheimer shows that Soviet *babushki* can be considered an underprivileged group, insufficiently cared for by the Soviet state.

In analyzing alcohol abuse and alcoholism in the Soviet Union, Vladimir G. Treml demonstrates that the magnitude and severity of the problem is unique. Soviet consumers drink over 17 liters of pure alcohol equivalent per person each year, and the Soviet Union ranks first in the world in per capita consumption of strong alcoholic beverages such as vodka. More striking, Soviet consumption of hard liquor has increased by approximately 4.5 percent per year over the last 25 years. Dr. Treml notes that, according to Soviet social scientists, heavy drinking is an important factor contributing to overall mortality rates in the USSR. The number of deaths attributed to acute alcohol poisoning was estimated at over 50,000 in 1978. Furthermore, Soviet economists have estimated that alcohol abuse decreased Soviet labor productivity by about 10 percent during the early 1970s. But the government depends on alcohol sales for a large share of its budgetary revenues, and alcoholic beverages, unlike most other consumer items, were continually available in the Soviet Union until General Secretary Gorbachev's anti-alcohol campaigns began in 1985.

Dr. Herlemann points out that no other nation has as large a rural population as the Soviet Union, and no other nation employs so many people in its agricultural sector. But consistent with its underinvestment in the consumer sector, the Soviet Union also neglects the cultural life of its rural inhabitants. Consumer items such as televisions exist in abundance in the Soviet countryside, but no real rural culture has emerged among the peasant classes. To the contrary, Dr. Herlemann holds that those who are able to do so emigrate to the cities in search of better living conditions. Although the Soviet village of the 1980s might have the material resources to organize a rural culture, this might no longer be possible as the expectations of the rural population continue to rise.

Modern communism is ultimately a scheme for the revolutionary transformation of society undertaken on the promise that the result will be a better life for the citizens of the new order. In the Soviet case, the costs have been enormous—the cost of establishing the communist monopoly of political power in revolution and civil war, the cost of transforming an economic and social system, and the sacrifice of freedom and living standards required to sustain that system through a seemingly endless process of mobilized economic expansion. To outsiders, especially those from Western nations, it has often seemed that the sacrifices outweighed the rewards and that the fulfillment of the revolution's promise was unconscionably slow. This book does not change that impression, and it will add much to the understanding of the quality of life in the Soviet Union.

Herbert J. Ellison
Henry M. Jackson School of International Studies
University of Washington
Seattle, Washington

Acknowledgments

The papers that make up this volume were presented before a conference on the quality of life in the Soviet Union held on April 12–13, 1984, at the Kennan Institute for Advanced Russian Studies of the Woodrow Wilson International Center for Scholars, Smithsonian Institution, Washington, D.C. The conference was cosponsored by the Kennan Institute; Volkswagenstiftung (Volkswagen Foundation); the National Council for Soviet and East European Research; the William and Mary Greve Foundation; Queens College, New York; and the U.S. Department of State.

The conference, which was initiated by the former secretary of the Kennan Institute, Herbert J. Ellison, and myself, brought together several leading German and American specialists on the Soviet Union, who proved that German-American scholarly cooperation has much to explore on Earth before it turns to space. Although the quality of life in the Soviet Union is difficult to quantify, the assumption that Western specialists have accumulated enough data to begin making judgments on this once-neglected topic encouraged us to proceed with both the conference and this volume.

For their assistance in bringing this project to fruition, I would like to thank Westview Press and the entire staff of the Kennan Institute. Special thanks go to Herbert J. Ellison for his encouragement of and enthusiasm for this project. I am also grateful to Kennan Institute staff members Bradford P. Johnson for organizing the conference and Evan A. Raynes for editing the conference materials. Needless to say, I am also grateful to the contributors to this volume for allowing their conference papers to be published in this form.

In addition to the scholars who formally presented papers at the conference, the conference organizers are indebted to the following panel discussants, who added a wide range of insightful commentary to the proceedings: Marjorie Mandelstam Balzer of Harvard University; Igor Birman of *Russia* magazine; Keith Bush of Radio Free Europe; Murray Feshbach of Georgetown University; Hans·Hermann Hohmann of the Federal Institute for East European and International Studies, Cologne; Peter Juviler of Barnard

College; Bernice Madison of San Francisco State University; Stephen Rapaway of the U.S. Department of Commerce; Seymour Rosen of the U.S. Department of Education; Jack Underhill of the U.S. Department of Housing and Urban Development; and Frank Wallick of the United Auto Workers.

Horst Herlemann
Universität Würzburg
Federal Republic of Germany

Horst Herlemann

1. What Is and Why Do We Study the Quality of Life in the Soviet Union?

When in 1789 Friedrich Schiller for the first time ascended the rostrum of Jena University, his lecture bore the title, *"Was ist und zu welchem Zweck studieren wir Universalgeschichte?"*—"What is and Why do we Study Universal History?" To define the object of study and the purpose of inquiry still seems the best way to start a scientific project, particularly if the topic is one that everybody should understand and be concerned with, such as the quality of life in the Soviet Union.

In preparing the conference from which this volume derives, I asked a colleague to write a paper on social conditions in Soviet factories. How many hot showers are available per capita? What kind of cafeterias can one have lunch in? And what about personal facilities, work clothes, and safety devices? His answer was that he would prefer to comment on the basic question "What is the quality of life?" rather than count restrooms. This shows that even empirically inclined social scientists prefer to talk about definitions, to play the overture, so to speak, instead of pulling the curtain.

When I tried to convey the idea of an investigation of the quality of life in the Soviet Union to a colleague in Moscow, his immediate reply was, "This is only another attempt to slander the achievements of socialism." Thus it seems appropriate to explain the purpose of this inquiry. By asking for a qualitative description of Soviet life, we hope to arrive at a better understanding of contemporary Soviet society. We also hope to advance the level of comparative research by departing from GNP and industrial growth rates as the only way to measure social change and compare different economic systems. There is, however, no intention to give up quantification, exact measurement, or calculation. The introduction of the term "quality of life" is first and foremost meant to be a program of social research that aims at a description of individual lives and of factors that influence personal well-being. Instead of calculating the number of kilometers of newly-built railroad, we would rather like to know if access to railroad transportation is still limited in the Soviet countryside. Knowing how many million tons of steel the Soviet Union produces, we would still like to know under what conditions they are produced. How crowded is the streetcar that carries the average steel worker home? What is the quality of the air that steel workers breathe if they live in the vicinity of a steel mill? To understand the principal direction of our inquiry, it might be helpful to recall the development of the concept "the quality of life" in affluent societies.

The term gained recognition in the late 1960s when many people discovered that their lives and the development of their society were not what they should be. The negative side effects of affluence could not be gleaned from statistical yearbooks, but were nonetheless visible, audible, and to be experienced in many different ways. Books were published that questioned the costs of economic growth and discussed questions such as "bigger vs. better" at length.[1] Spurious measures of progress and goal attainment were seen as one of the reasons for this increasing dissatisfaction. Many people began to ask what an ever-increasing GNP meant in relation to their personal lives. It was their general conclusion that progress had been measured inadequately in relation to the genuine needs of human beings.

Attempts to use GNP as a yardstick to measure welfare and progress have long been criticized. Most reproaches have been based on the fact that GNP is concerned only with the exchange of goods on the market. The more goods that are produced and exchanged, the higher the GNP, and the better the state of the society one lives in. If one spends time playing the violin, this will lower the GNP no matter how much satisfaction the player receives from doing so. On the other hand, every device to increase productivity, no matter what impact it might have on the environment or on the people who use it, increases the GNP—the incarnation of progress. Such criticisms are now common knowledge. Discussions of the future of our industrial and commercial behavior have turned to new horizons, but 20 years ago they led to the search for alternatives in evaluating progress and in defining the goals of modern society.

Members of the scholarly community concerned with Soviet studies also took part in those discussions. For example, excerpts from the diary of George F. Kennan read like a modern accusation of unfettered industrial growth and illustrate the perspicacity of this farsighted scholar.[2]

One serious attempt to remedy the shortcomings of using GNP to address the quality of life was made by Japanese scholars who in the late 1960s replaced it with a measure called net national welfare (NNW). The most interesting aspect of this measurement was that leisure time and activities outside the marketplace were considered to have value. Therefore, housework, the costs of spoiling the environment, and increasing urbanization were quantified and became part of a new yardstick of development.[3]

Another instrument to describe and measure the state of society is the "social indicator." The pioneer step in this direction was a report by R. A. Bauer published in 1966.[4] In 1969, the U.S. Department of Health, Education and Welfare released a study entitled *Toward a Social Report* that used Bauer's newly-developed indicators. "Thus, while the first strategy to develop more adequate welfare measure [involved] efforts to restructure the system of economic accounts, especially by incorporating non-market activities . . . a second strategy was the establishment of a regular system of social reporting matching economic reporting. Social indicators were conceived of as qualitative measures to evaluate benefits and disbenefits in major areas of social concern. They ought to indicate, directly and in non-monetary terms, changes in the individual's quality of life."[5]

One approach to establishing meaningful indicators of the quality of life was to focus on certain aspects of well-being that could be subsumed under one index figure. Another was to define goals of societal development and then create indicators to measure the attainment of those goals. In both cases, however, there were elements of arbitrariness. Later studies by the Organization of Economic Cooperation and Development (OECD) aimed at minimizing such elements by systematically defining the goals a welfare policy could possibly strive for.

The OECD's definition contained nine basic social goals—health, education, occupation and quality of work, spare time, income and consumption, environment, security, family life, and social equality and mobility. The all-embracing character of these goals led to the definition of 22 "fundamental social concerns," 74 "sub-concerns," and 177 "sub-sub-concerns."[6] Evidently, the imagination of a bureaucracy as to what should happen is unlimited, particularly if it has modern statistical methods at its disposal. The OECD's main interest in this project was to define as many social concerns as possible in order to provide politicians with a set of goals for societal improvement or with material to illustrate the quality of their policies.

For many observers, the main deficiency of such social indicators remained their disregard of personal satisfaction, which might not depend on any identifiable indicator. Social statistics are seldom concerned with individual satisfaction and subjective well-being, yet the quality of life depends on personal happiness, which might be considered a state of mind totally independent from material living conditions and the social environment that one lives in. Such happiness occurs only in individual cases. Elsewhere in this volume, Robert Belknap discusses the interdependencies between material and spiritual well-being. The social sciences have established various ways to determine the relationship between subjective satisfaction and objective circumstances. Two of them have gained a certain significance and have been used in several comparative studies.

The first proceeds from the degree of "needs satisfaction," the other from "command over resources." The latter was elaborated by the Scandinavian sociologist S. Johansson, who defined welfare as being "the individual's command over resources such as money, possessions, knowledge, mental and physical energy, social relations, security, etc., with which the individual can control and consciously direct his living conditions."[7] In Johansson's view, the individual stands out as an active being who shapes his or her own life.

One of the problems with defining the quality of life in terms of resources is that it defines the concept too narrowly and disregards dependencies regarding the unuseability of certain resources. If, for example, one has sufficient mental and physical energy at one's disposal, but is without a job or generally lacking the chance to make use of it according to one's wishes, then this "resource" is evidently useless. In other words, one must contend with prerequisites that one does not control. These prerequisites are the determinants of the actual command that individuals might have over their resources.[8]

The other approach to the relationship between subjective satisfaction and objective circumstances was developed by E. Allardt.[9] Allardt defined the "level of living" as "the extent to which the overall needs of a given population are satisfied." In classifying human needs, he used the traditional categories of Abraham Maslow, who in 1943 defined three levels of need— "having, loving, and being."[10] "Having" is related to the individual's physical needs and security requirements, which grant existence and survival. "Loving" is related to the needs of affection and appreciating, and concerns both personal and social interaction. "Being" has to do with the individual's need for self-realization. The main problem posed by a definition of the quality of life in terms of needs satisfaction is the difficulty of finding out just how content people really are. Under what circumstances are people satisfied? The answer depends not only on objective circumstances, but also on one's personal aspirations and one's assessment of one's rightful due. Such factors depend on earlier experiences and are open to manipulation.

One must use sophisticated methods of empirical research to study individual satisfaction. Without such methods, the categories of "loving" and "being" remain a matter of conjecture. Given the quality of Soviet sociology, the degree of individual satisfaction in the Soviet Union also remains a matter of speculation.

It seems an understandable concern in an affluent society to inquire into individual perceptions of the quality of life. It also seems natural to have a powerful minority maintain that material well-being is the smallest part of personal happiness. Under circumstances where food and shelter are merely a matter of further sophistication—when they are simply "structural problems" for most people—some people naturally discover that the quality of life is no longer a function of the production of consumer goods.

For most Soviet citizens, these questions are completely irrelevant. Very few Soviet needs are consistently satisfied, and for almost all Soviet citizens, "more is more" and "better is better." The Soviet government shares this attitude, and official statistics provide ample proof that everything is becoming "bigger and better." There is no dearth of information about the number of washing machines or televisions, or about the number of doctors, hospitals, and recreation facilities available to the population. Each is increasing, and will continue to increase. Questions as to the quality of household machinery, television programs, and medical care are sometimes discussed, but if problems are identified, most believe that they can be solved by greater numbers.

Thus it seems worthwhile to try to assess certain aspects of Soviet life with reference to quality. What does the number of doctors per capita mean for the quality of medical care? What does it mean to be poor or old in the Soviet Union while the GNP is continually increasing? How does alcohol abuse affect the quality of life in the Soviet Union? And what of life in the Soviet countryside?

Obviously, there are aspects of Soviet life deserving attention that are not discussed in this volume—for example, personal mobility and the limits of personal communication. Thus it remains the hope of all the contributors to the conference and this volume that their efforts will encourage further studies on the quality of life in the Soviet Union. We share this hope and our basic intentions with our Soviet colleagues. As the Soviet scholar A. Salai said in 1980, "Today, as mankind has enormous scientific-technical, industrial and economic capacities at its disposal to satisfy the material needs of the people, the investigation of the quality of life becomes important. Research about this problem, including comparative studies, supports the social progress of mankind and improves mutual understanding between different countries."[11]

Notes

1. E. J. Mishan, The Costs of Economic Growth (London: Staples Press, 1967); and Donella H. Meadows et al., The Limits of Growth: A Report for the Club of Rome's Project on the Predicament of Mankind (New York: Universe Books, 1972).

2. George F. Kennan, Memoirs, 1950–1963 (New York: Pantheon Books, 1972), p. 84.

3. S. Loercher, "Lebensqualität" Japan (Bremen, 1975).

4. R. A. Bauer (ed.), Social Indicators (Cambridge: M.I.T. Press, 1966).

5. Department of Health, Education and Welfare, *Toward a Social Report* (Washington, D.C., 1969).

6. Organization of Economic Cooperation and Development, *List of Social Concerns Common to Most OECD Countries* (Paris, 1973).

7. S. Johansson, *Om Levnadsnivaundersoekingen* (Stockholm, 1970), p. 25. English summary, "The Level of Living Survey," *Acta Sociologica* 16, no. 3 (1973).

8. R. Erikson, "Welfare as a Planning Goal," *Acta Sociologica* 17, no. 2 (1974).

9. E. Allardt, *A Frame of Reference for Selecting Social Indicators* (Helsinki, 1972; Commentationes Scientarum Socialium).

10. Abraham Maslow, "A Theory of Human Motivation," *Psychological Review* 50 (1943), pp. 370-396.

11. A. Salai, "Kachestvo zhizni kak sotsiologicheskaya kategoriya," *Sotsiologicheskie issledovaniia*, 1982, no. 2, p. 13.

2. On Quantifying Quality

Much of this volume uses modern analysis of modern data for a 19th-century task—the study of the quality of life in measurable terms that have been so dear to positivist thinkers. Positivism, however, developed in the presence of a puzzle that has frustrated utilitarians for many years. If we are to pursue the greatest good for the greatest number of people, where is the "hedonometer," the measure of pleasure that will tell whether Plato enhances the quality of one's life enough to compensate for the less widespread appeal of, for example, pinball? This epistemological problem shapes much American and Soviet propaganda and decisionmaking today. Both governments boast of their culture, technology, and attentions to the sick and ignorant, but in their councils they debate whether to devote finite resources to educating the young or hospitalizing the old, whether to allocate steel to highways or subways, and whether to use grain for meat or alcohol. In both nations, the decisions and the propaganda rest on the assumption that while more of one element may produce greater benefits than more of another, more is still better.

This assumption, of course, has not gone unquestioned. Beyond the argument that "more" is simply dangerous or impossible, there stand three great challenges—minimalism, perversity, and delayed gratification. Diogenes exemplified the minimalist challenge. "One day, observing a child drinking out of his hands, he cast away the cup from his wallet with the words, a child has beaten me in plainness of living."[1] This pure belief in simplicity tends to appear in rich cities, and it has played a smaller part in Russian art, architecture, costume, cuisine, or literature than it has in the West in this century.

A less austere form of minimalism—the pastoral—has flourished in Russia from the days of the Slavophiles, or even Karamzin's *Poor Liza*, to those of the village writers of our time. When Tolstoy's Levin prefers simple kasha to an elaborate French meal, or Solzhenitsyn urges the Soviet leaders to abandon pomp and empire, they are writing in a tradition older than Longus, Theocritus, or the Psalms, which sees the life of shepherds as simpler, purer, and therefore happier and more complete than the rich, sophisticated life of urban writers and their urban readers. In the second book of Plato's *Republic*, Socrates advocates the pastoral life. "They will feed on barley and wheat, baking the wheat and kneading the flour, making noble puddings and loaves; these they will serve up on a mat of reeds or clean leaves, themselves reclining the while upon beds of yew or myrtle boughs."[2] His interlocutor, who has a 19th century mind, compares this diet to that of well-fed pigs, but the mere existence of this competing vision of well-being suggests that it is hard to find statistics that represent the quality of life and distinguish poverty from pastoral life.

The challenge of perversity makes a more basic attack on the doctrine that more is better. Dostoevsky, the most eloquent Russian enemy of utilitarianism, enunciated this challenge most clearly and savagely in *The Underground Man*.

> Why are you so firmly, so triumphantly convinced that just one thing is positive and normal: in a word, that only well-being is good for man? Isn't reason wrong about the good? Perhaps man doesn't love well-being alone. Perhaps he loves suffering just as much. Perhaps suffering is just as good for him as well-being.[3]

This perverse standard drives the underground man to stick his tongue out at the Crystal Palace, which for the purposes of this study symbolizes the quantifiable component of the quality of life—technology and wealth applied intelligently to human needs. Mies offers the minimalist challenge to "more is better" by saying "less is more." Here the Underground Man is making a far more basic, more perverse, and equally paradoxical attack on "more is better." He is saying "less is better."

Delayed gratification—the third great challenge to the assumption that more is better—comes in three forms. The first form is familiar in America, where many people diet as austerely as Diogenes, but unlike him believe the macrobiotic or the Scarsdale minima damage the quality of life at the moment, but are a means to better looks and better health. In a poorer country such selfish sacrifices occur less often. Those who trudge to work do not jog.

The second form of deferred gratification is that of the religious ascetic, whose consumption of worldly goods may be less than those of Diogenes, but for a very different reason. A minimalist denies the excellence of luxury, but a religious ascetic rejects luxury or even sufficiency for the sake of a future reward. Minimalists might or might not share the tastes of Lucullus, but one overriding concern outweighs the excellence of this world in their conception. Russia has a rich tradition of asceticism dating from the starving and self-flagellating monks of the Kiev catacombs a millennium ago, but in general Russian Orthodoxy probably asserts the excellence of this created world more than Western Christianity does. In *The Brothers Karamazov*, for example, the sadistic madman Ferapont lives on mushrooms in the wilderness while the holy elder Zosima lives in a cheerful room, urges Alyosha to go out into the world, and has his apotheosis in a dream about a wedding feast which sanctifies food and wine and sex.

The third type of delayed gratification remains the most interesting for studying the quality of life in the Soviet Union. Long before the Russian revolution, Anatoly Lunacharsky, later the first Soviet Commissar of Culture, wrote a rather bad play in which a revolutionist dying in prison has a vision of the future.

You see the garden filled with joy,
Timeless and without a bound
The azure waves of the canals
And marble palace tops around? . . .
You hear the distant music chiming,
Chorusing earth's dismal past?
It has approached: before us climbing
Rise a thousand people massed
On piles of steps, a mighty crowd.
What faces theirs are! Clean and proud,
Their eyes ablaze, and to their breast
Rich waves of golden hair are tressed.

. . . they sing . . .
We shall be gods and daunt the world;
We shall uproot woe and pain,
And dying, we shall rise again . . .
The world shall be like a holy crown
Of spotless, godlike glory shown
Sleep soft, grandfathers; your day
Of rising is not far away . . .[4]

Unlike the dieter or the religious ascetic, here the hero genuinely rejoices in the quality of a life that he has no hope of seeing in this or any other world. Instead of being deferred until a later date or an afterlife, his gratification is deferred until another person's life. Such altruism can enhance the quality of a person's life that is abysmal in every measurable way. Since Chernyshevsky's hero Rakhmetov first slept on his bed of nails, Russian literature and Russian life have produced many such secular ascetics who sacrificed not just the quality of their lives, but often life itself for the sake of a glowing future that they would not see. Like Christian ascetics they rejoiced in their sacrifice, and unlike Diogenes they felt that they were sacrificing the good things of this world. One can be cynical from afar and say that Marxism is the opium of the masses, but any serious study of the quality of life must distinguish between the citizen denied good things and the citizen who altruistically and perhaps proudly sacrifices them. With every Soviet generation, this distinction becomes less clear because the press, official fiction, the agitation and propaganda network, and other instruments of institutionalized hypocrisy become more shameless.

Taken together, minimalism, perversity, and deferred gratification offer a serious challenge to the positivist idea of quantifying the quality of life. But even altruistic sacrifice depends on two elements that border on the measurable—"solidarity" and "hope." If one gives up a good without reward—whether present or future, in this world or any other—one does so because the beneficiary of the sacrifice in some sense remains oneself. Such solidarity with family members, friends, or benefactors seems so common that sociobiologists have sought Darwinian explanation for it. In the Soviet Union, solidarity with one's work brigade seems to function as it does on the squad level in many armies.

On a larger scale, Soviet society has achieved solidarity by floundering through a series of crises. While the two world wars, the civil war, and Stalin's economic, administrative, and political upheavals were costing the Soviet people millions of lives and untold treasure, the measurable quality of life in the Soviet Union remained low, but broad segments of the population made sacrifices for comrades whose identity overlapped with their own because they shared a fearsome problem or an awesome enemy. Now that the Soviets have learned to build apartment houses with more efficiency than heroism, to buy grain from the United States to feed their cattle, to reduce the population of political prisoners substantially, and to influence allies such as Cuba, Libya, and Vietnam instead of China, Indonesia, and Egypt, the measurable quality of life has risen, and widespread solidarity has retreated from real life to the propaganda world. The loss of solidarity with comrades beyond one's immediate circle is impossible to measure without polling techniques that cannot be used in the Soviet Union, but it correlates impressively with the quantitative patterns described in this book.

Well-being demands a certain minimum below which only saints and heroes can live happy and fulfilling lives. The papers in this book suggest that in recent years, virtually nobody outside of the penal network died directly or indirectly of hunger or exposure, and that most Soviet citizens had access to refrigerators, televisions, 10 years of free education, and medical resources that were better than any in the world a century ago. Moreover, without taking some political action, it is hard to lose one's job or one's pension. Thus at the level of minimum objective need, the Soviet quality of life suffices. At any level above that, we measure the good life against some standard. In modern times, that standard is often numerical. For example, this volume discusses income levels and the number of square feet of living space that Soviet sociologists and economists have prescribed at various times. One curious feature of these prescribed norms is their closeness to the proclaimed average. Because these figures in every case lie above the survival level, it seems probable that the authorities have simply prescribed what most people already have. When analyzed statistically, this process is social science; when done by millions of individuals, it is "envy"—one of the most important political forces throughout history.

The quality of one's life depends not merely on the quantity of goods and services one uses, but also on what others have and do. Envy is the displeasure that one derives from the prosperity of another; solidarity produces the pleasure that one derives from the prosperity of a person not completely apart from oneself. Envy craves level statistics more than favorable ones, but the reverse is true of solidarity.

The papers in this volume treat the special hospitals, special stores, special vehicles, housing, schools, and other unpublicized privileges of the Soviet leadership. But for a proper "envy-solidarity index," one might also compare the homes of Stalin, Khrushchev, Andropov, and Gorbachev with those of Louis XIV and other potentates who held less power over smaller, poorer, and weaker nations. The restraint of Soviet rulers as to their personal ostentation serves the same purpose as limiting access to information about the quality of life abroad. This isolation of the public from the enviable at home and abroad reinforces propaganda efforts to promote solidarity and administrative efforts to improve the measurable side of the quality of life.

If much of the quality of life is comparative rather than absolute, once starvation has been prevented, the central object of comparison can shift from one's leaders and foreigners to the past. A sense of progress matters at least as much as the level of consumption that has been achieved. In this regard, the Soviets seem to have achieved something extraordinary in recent years. Since the early 1960s, there has been genuine progress in many areas of consumption, such as urban housing, transportation, and electrification, but with virtually no general sense of progress among much of the population. Soviet propaganda might be counterproductive in this regard, for it is far easier to surpass the achievements of yesteryear than to surpass the claims made for them. As a result, grandiose claims encounter cynicism.

A sense of progress does much to govern the greatest of the unquantifiable elements in the quality of life—hope. A utopian vision like the one in Lunacharsky's play may occasionally arouse envy, but Lunacharsky uses words like "grandfather" to increase solidarity with future blessed beings.

Yet even this perfect future life would remain unfulfilling without hope for further progress. Lunacharsky's future people sing about their future deeds, including a resurrection that will eventually reward the dying revolutionary who will not see the first utopia. There is no quantitative index for hope and felt progress in the Soviet Union, but the quality of life remains unknowable without it. As with solidarity, its obverse may be more detectable. The absence of hope probably varies more or less in proportion to escapism. This book quantifies chemical escapism in its chief Soviet form—alcoholism—but it eschews the task of separating escapism from other Soviet uses of alcohol, such as male bonding ceremonies and expressions of machismo. Literary escapism is also prevalent in the Soviet Union, but quantification remains difficult in a system where publication figures do not reflect demand.

One way to arrive at an index of the thirst for literary escapism might be to focus on the stridency of demands for optimism in the Writers' Union and *Literaturnaia gazeta*. An objective count could be calculated from the number of lines devoted to optimism and the recurrence of certain key words that would carry different weightings of importance in different decades. Such an analysis would flaunt its impression in a salutary manner. Hope and solidarity shape the quality of life and will remain barely measurable. Minimalism, perversity, and deferred gratification will always cloud our basic understanding of the quality of life. And yet, although we cannot quantify the quality of life in its entirety, the effort to do so makes it harder for us to talk nonsense with impunity. The best doctors ply their profession in the fullest recognition of mortality. Likewise, social scientists should ply theirs in full recognition of the limitations as to what they can quantify. The human condition confines but does not vitiate our enterprise.

Notes

1. Diogenes Laertius, *Lives of Eminent Philosophers*, vol. 2, trans. R. D. Hicks (Cambridge: Loeb Classical Library, 1950), p. 39.

2. Plato, *The Republic*, trans. Benjamin Jowett (New York: Vintage Books, 1877), p. 194.

3. F. M. Dostoevsky, *Notes from Underground*, in *Polnoe sobraniie sochinenii*, vol. 5 (Leningrad, 1973), p. 119.

4. A. V. Lunacharsky, *Gosti v Odinochke*, in *Idei v Maskakh* (Moscow, 1912), pp. 207–221.

Gertrude E. Schroeder

3. Soviet Living Standards in Comparative Perspective

Spokesmen for the Soviet communist party and government have long maintained that their economic system—centrally planned socialism—would be able to produce such fast economic growth that the USSR would catch up with the capitalist West within a relatively short period of time. Even in the late 1920s and early 1930s, Stalin and others spoke of catching up with the West in terms of per capita consumption in 10 to 15 years. In 1960, Nikita Khrushchev declared that by 1965 the USSR would surpass the most highly-developed nations of Western Europe in the consumption of "many important consumer goods." He further claimed that "soon" the Soviet Union would attain levels of per capita consumption equal to those of the United States "as regards all consumer goods that are really needed by the people."[1] The following year, the Soviet communist party adopted a grand program to achieve communism "in the main" by 1980, when the Soviet people would have "the highest living standard in the world."[2] However, Khrushchev's successors have been quite reticent as regards this aspect of the "race" with capitalism. Instead, they usually speak of achieving "rational" levels of consumption for the Soviet people. Soviet writers often inveigh against manifestations of "consumerism" and the people's evident penchant for acquiring material goods.

Instead of having achieved communism, the Soviet Union of the early 1980s is experiencing a painful time of troubles. Living standards are rising at a much slower pace than in the past two decades; consumer markets are in severe disequilibrium; and there is widespread dissatisfaction with the quality, style, and mix of consumer goods and services as well as the pace at which matters are improving.[3] Given this state of affairs and the Soviet leadership's concern about the USSR's image as a socialist welfare state, an analysis of how present living standards in the Soviet Union compare with those of other industrialized nations, both East and West, seems to be in order.

Comparisons with Western Capitalist Countries

The best overall measure of the standard of living of a given country is the quantity of goods and services consumed by the population on a per capita basis. This measure, derived from national product accounts, is the sum of private consumption expenditures and government non-invest-ment expenditures on health, education, and related consumer-oriented services. In order to conduct an international comparison of living standards, each nation's consumption expenditures must be expressed in terms of a common currency. The standard procedure is to calculate purchasing power parities for the various components of consumption expenditures by collecting prices of a representative sample of comparable goods and services in each nation. The relative price ratios thus obtained can then be used to convert each country's expenditures into another's prices. Almost invariably, a country's relative position will look more favorable when the comparison uses another country's prices. Although, theoretically, both comparisons (index numbers) are equally valid, a single, overall ratio using both percentage comparisons is commonly used.

In 1975, comparisons of this kind were made for 34 nations representing a wide range of developmental levels. The results of this study have been published as Phase III of the United Nations International Comparisons Project (ICP).[4] A comparable study has been done comparing levels of consumption in the Soviet Union and the United States in 1976.[5] As both studies used common statistical procedures to the extent that this was feasible, their results can be used to provide an idea of how living standards in the Soviet Union compare with those of the nations included in the ICP study. Table 3.1 uses percentage comparisons in terms of international prices for seven industrialized market economies and the United States; it also uses a binary comparison between the Soviet Union and the United States with a geometric mean comparison as the basis for comparison. While this procedure leaves much to be desired from a theoretical standpoint, a wide variety of related evidence suggests that the results are probably not too far off the mark. Certainly, they are not biased against the Soviet Union. Indeed, they probably overstate the standard of living in the USSR relative to the West.

Relative Levels of Per Capita Consumption

Table 3.1 compares the level of per capita consumption in the Soviet Union with that of the United States, Japan and six West European nations.

TABLE 3.1
Relative Levels of Per Capita Consumption for the USSR and Eight Capitalist Nations, 1975-76

	U.S.	FRG	France	Austria	U.K.	Spain	Japan	Italy
				USSR as a Percentage of Each Nation				
Total Consumption	34	46	46	50	54	57	59	65
Food, Beverages, Tobacco	58	65	54	56	70	50	69	59
Clothing, Footware	47	52	79	46	76	72	68	81
Rent, Fuel	17	27	28	28	30	36	43	43
Household Expenditures	19	16	17	21	32	42	42	44
Transportation, Communications	12	23	24	30	34	46	36	37
Recreation	30	38	46	54	38	75	42	86
Education	80	136	101	141	144	141	121	152
Health Care	33	33	34	40	40	54	39	62
Other Expenditures	32	57	48	35	42	52	53	75

Sources: For percentages for Western Europe and Japan relative to the United States, see Irving B. Kravis, Alan Heston, and Robert Summers, *World Product and Income: International Comparisons of Real Gross Product* (Baltimore: Johns Hopkins University Press, 1982), pp. 182–183. For percentages for the USSR relative to the United States, see Gertrude E. Schroeder and Imogene Edwards, *Consumption in the USSR: An International Comparison,* U.S. Congress, Joint Economic Committee (Washington, D.C., 1981), p. 20. A geometric mean comparison was used in that study. The values given for "food, beverages, tobacco," "recreation," and "other expenditures" were revised to achieve comparability with International Comparisons Project data for 1975. The adjustments entailed the transfer of expenditures on restaurants and cafes from "food, beverages, tobacco" to "other expenditures," and the transfer of expenditures on "hotels and lodging" from "recreation" to "other expenditures."

Percentages are given for total consumption and for nine major categories of consumption. Although the underlying expenditure data for the USSR pertain to 1976 and those for the other countries are for 1975, the difference is of little significance because the overall growth rates of each nation changed little between 1975 and 1976. As the data indicate, the Soviet Union has a long way to go to catch up with the standards that prevail in major Western nations. In 1976, the living standard of the Soviet people was roughly one third that of the United States; less than half that of France, West Germany, and Austria; over half that of the United Kingdom, Spain, and Japan; and about two-thirds that of Italy. Similar relationships prevailed in 1982 because per capita consumption grew at roughly the same rate in all of these nations except Spain.

Large lags in Soviet living standards can be found in all major categories of consumption except education. With respect to food, beverages, and tobacco, Soviet per capita consumption ranges from 50–70 percent of Western levels. Moreover, the quality of the Soviet people's diet is poor by Western standards. It contains a much larger share of grain products and potatoes, and a much smaller share of meat, dairy products, fruits, and vegetables. In 1976, for example, Soviet consumers obtained 46 percent of their daily calories from bread and potatoes, and only 8 percent from meat and fish. In the United States, the comparative figures were 22 percent and 20 percent.[6] The Soviet position would look even less favorable if restaurants and cafes were included in the calculations.

Soviet per capita expenditures on clothing and footwear are well below those of other nations, but compared with food expenditures, the variability is greater. Soviet expenditures range from 46–81 percent of the level of other nations. As both foreign visitors and the Soviet press testify, the style, variety, and general appearance of Soviet attire is far inferior to what is available in the West. Such considerations cannot be fully captured by quantitative comparisons.

Housing is the area where the gap between Soviet and Western living standards is perhaps greatest. Soviet per capita expenditures on housing and related household operations are less than one-fifth of those in the United States. Soviet expenditures are well under half those of Spain, Japan, and Italy, and under one-third of those in most other nations. Housing is probably the area of greatest frustration for the Soviet people. Most urban residents pay low, heavily-subsidized rents and live in small apartments in large, crowded, and poorly-maintained buildings. Housing is rationed, and one-fifth of all families must share kitchen and bath facilities with other families. Per capita living space in cities did not reach the nine square meter minimum standard for health and decency until 1983, though this standard was set by the Soviet government in 1928. Although most rural housing is privately owned, much of it lacks modern amenities, though electricity is now available almost everywhere. For the Soviet Union to improve housing conditions relative to the West would require huge and sustained increases in investment and the provision of a commensurate flow of related household furnishings and maintenance services.

Soviet transportation and communication services are inadequate relative to conditions in the West. Soviet consumers spend large amounts of money relative to the West on public transportation and minuscule amounts on private automobiles. According to Soviet data, only about one Soviet family in 10 owned a car in 1980, whereas car ownership is almost universal among American families and overwhelmingly predominant among families in Western Europe and Japan. The fact that Soviet citizens tend to spend their vacations in state-run vacation resorts and spas is in part a reflection of the Soviet Union's lack of private cars. Roughly only one out of seven urban families has a private telephone, whereas most Western families have at least one home telephone. Home telephones are exceedingly rare in rural Russia.

The availability of recreational goods and services in the Soviet Union is well below the Western level, though the size of the gap varies rather widely among various nations. The Soviet level approximates that of Spain and Italy. Over nine-tenths of all Soviet families reportedly have television sets, and color sets are rapidly coming into general use.

Soviet consumers also spend much less than their Western counterparts on miscellaneous goods and services as is evident from the data in Table 3.1. The largest component of this category consists of expenditures on restaurants and lodging places. Both of these services are much less abundant in the Soviet Union than in the West. While restaurant sales account for about one-sixth of all retail food and beverage sales in the Soviet Union, the share is larger in Western nations. Moreover, most Soviet public dining establishments are attached to factories, collective farms, and offices, and are not open to the general public. This was true of 73 percent of the total number of restaurants and 79 percent of the total number of lodging places in 1980.[7] Miscellaneous expenditures also include a wide variety of goods and services for personal care, such as cosmetics, hairdressers, and barbers. Expenditure lags in this area are comparable to those for recreation because of the Soviet government's neglect of the personal service sector. The relatively favorable Western showing in the "other expenditures" category reflects the fact that a wide variety of financial, legal, and similar services are available in the West, whereas such services are provided in minuscule amounts or not at all in the Soviet Union.

Health and education services are distributed almost entirely as public goods in the Soviet Union, that is, without direct charge to the recipient. This is true of health care in the United Kingdom, and Western governments in general now pay for a large part of the cost of both health care and education. As previously noted, these data include both private and government expenditures. Despite the Soviet Union's repeated boast of having more doctors and hospital beds per capita than any other country, the data in Table 3.1 show that per capita expenditures on health care are only about one-third of those in the United States, France, and West Germany, and only about two-fifths of those of Austria, the United Kingdom, and Japan. The Soviet level is nearest that of Italy and Spain.

This is partially due to the fact that the Soviet Union's health care system uses much more labor and far fewer materials than is common in the West. Moreover, wages paid to Soviet health care personnel are very low relative to the West. Among the major branches of the Soviet economy, they are next to the lowest. Medical care is rationed in the Soviet Union, and widely-varying levels of service are provided to different groups. Large numbers of "closed" facilities cater only to selected clienteles. Judging from a wide variety of testimony, the general quality of Soviet health care is quite inferior by Western standards, especially in rural areas—a situation that might have something to do with the recent decline in life expectancy in the Soviet Union.[8]

In sharp contrast to its poor showing in all of the above areas, the Soviet Union leads all nations except the United States in per capita expenditures on education. Per capita expenditures in the Soviet Union are about equal to those of France, and are well above those of other nations. This reflects the Soviet government's longstanding effort to raise educational levels in order to create a skilled labor force to man a rapidly expanding and modernizing economy. Although general secondary education is now compulsory and nearly universal, access to full- time higher education is strictly limited by the government's estimated need for trained manpower. Less than one-fifth of all Soviet highschool graduates are permitted to enroll in full-time colleges, and college graduates account for only 10 percent of the Soviet labor force. In the United States, over two-fifths of all highschool students go to college, and 25 percent of all American workers are college graduates. In light of the Soviet Union's low per capita GNP, one might venture the hypothesis that the Soviet government has overinvested in human capital formation relative to its ability to use its educated manpower in a productive manner, especially as education is regarded as primarily utilitarian rather than a universal good in itself. In terms of overall efficiency, the government might have been better advised to shift resources to upgrade its health care system and improve the population's lot by investing more in housing, retail trade, and personal service facilities.

Patterns of Consumption

The distribution of consumption expenditures in the Soviet Union differs markedly from that in the United States, Japan, and Western Europe. The relevant data for 1975–76 are given in Table 3.2. As can be seen, the Soviet Union devotes a far larger share of its total consumption expenditures to food, beverages, and tobacco than the United States, France, West Germany, and Austria. This is consistent with Engel's law, which holds that the share of such expenditures tends to decline as incomes rise. However, while the Soviet Union's per capita GNP approximates that of Italy, the United Kingdom, and Japan, and is much larger than that of Greece and Spain, it devotes a far larger share of its consumption expenditures to food, beverages, and tobacco than all of these nations. It also devotes a much larger share of its total outlays to alcoholic beverages, especially hard liquor. Similarly, larger relative shares of consumption go to clothing and footwear than in other nations. With close to two-thirds of all consumption expenditures devoted to food and clothing, the Soviet Union displays consumption patterns similar to those exhibited by developing countries.

Only about one-tenth of the Soviet Union's total consumption expenditures go to housing and related outlays. The share in most other nations is about one-fifth. The proportion devoted to transportation and communications is well below the Western level, but the proportion of Soviet and Western expenditures devoted to recreational goods and services is roughly similar. The proportion devoted to education is about average for the nations compared, but the proportion that the Soviet Union devotes to health is the lowest of any nation. The Soviet level is even below that of Greece, which has a per capita GNP of only about two-thirds of the USSR's.

These comparative consumption patterns illustrate another dimension of the Soviet Union's quest to catch up with the West. Not only is the Soviet Union's standard of living far below Western levels; its pattern of consumption is quite backward as well. Moreover, Soviet consumption patterns have been changing at a glacial pace relative to the changes that have been occurring in the West in recent decades. Finally, the Soviet Union devotes an extraordinarily small share of its consumption expenditures to services—a share that has changed little in the past 25 years. In 1976, expenditures on goods comprised almost four-fifths of the total, while expenditures on services accounted for the remaining fifth. The respective shares in the United States were 45 and 55 percent.

Trends in Per Capita Consumption

The Soviet Union's record with regard to improving the standard of living of its population has been mixed, but on the whole not particularly impressive.[9] Table 3.3 displays average annual growth rates of per capita private consumption during the postwar period in the USSR and a number of capitalist nations. From 1953–1970, per capita private consumption in the Soviet Union rose nearly twice as fast as in the United States, but since 1970 growth has slowed markedly, remaining about the same as in

TABLE 3.2
Consumption Patterns in the USSR and Nine Capitalist Nations, 1975–76

	U.S.	FRG	France	Austria	U.K.	Spain	Japan	Italy	Greece	USSR
Total Consumption	100	100	100	100	100	100	100	100	100	100
Food, Beverages, Tobacco	20	23	28	31	30	35	31	38	44	47
Clothing, Footware	6	9	8	10	8	10	7	8	11	17
Rent, Fuel	17	15	14	11	17	12	14	12	12	5
Household Expenditures	7	10	10	8	6	8	6	6	8	5
Transportation, Communications	13	12	11	12	12	10	9	10	10	6
Recreation	6	7	6	6	8	5	7	5	3	5
Education	9	6	6	5	7	4	7	6	4	6
Health Care	13	13	11	9	6	8	9	8	5	4
Other Expenditures	9	5	6	8	6	8	10	7	3	5

Sources: Percentages for all capitalist nations except Greece are based on data from Kravis, Heston, and Summers, *World Product and Income*, pp. 253, 258, 259, 264, 266, 278, and 282. In each case, expenditures in restaurants and cafes were removed from "other expenditures" and included in "food, beverages, tobacco." The required data are on pp. 206–207. Data on restaurant sales for the United States were obtained from U.S. Department of Commerce publications. Data for the USSR were taken from Schroeder and Edwards, *Consumption in the USSR*, pp. 20 and 29. Percentages for Greece were calculated from an Organization of Economic Cooperation and Development study, *National Accounts, 1952–1981*, vol. 2 (Paris: OECD, 1982).

TABLE 3.3
Growth of Per Capita Private Consumption in the USSR and Fifteen Capitalist Nations, 1953-1981

	1953-70	1970-81	1975-81
	Average Annual Rates of Growth		
Soviet Union	4.1	2.6	1.9
United States	2.2	2.0	2.2
Austria	4.8	3.2	2.5
Belgium	2.7	2.9	2.3
Denmark	3.5	1.2	1.0
Finland	5.1	2.7	1.7
France	6.5	3.3	3.0
West Germany	7.2	2.5	2.5
Greece	6.2	2.9	1.9
Italy	8.6	2.2	2.5
Netherlands	7.2	1.9	1.6
Norway	2.7	2.8	2.6
Portugal	4.4	2.2	0.5
Spain	9.2*	2.3	0.6
Sweden	2.8	1.5	0.5
United Kingdom	2.1	1.8	1.7
Japan	7.6	3.0	2.4

Note: *1954-1970

Sources: Growth rates for the USSR were calculated from the index numbers in USSR: Measures of Economic Growth and Development, 1950-1980, U.S. Congress, Joint Economic Committee (Washington, D.C., 1982), pp. 367-368. Rates of growth for capitalist nations are from National Accounts, 1952-1981 (Paris: OECD, 1982).

the United States. Indeed, the Soviet-American "consumption gap" actually widened after 1975. The USSR fares even less well in comparison to Western Europe. From 1953-70, living standards rose more rapidly in nine West European nations than in the Soviet Union, generally by wide margins. Since 1970, however, the Soviet Union has improved its standard of living faster than eight of these nations. Overall, living standards have improved more rapidly in the USSR than in "welfare states" such as the Scandinavian nations and the United Kingdom, and considerably less rapidly than in France, West Germany, Austria, Finland, Italy, Japan, Greece, and Spain. Of the countries compared, the most rapid gains were made by Japan, which not only managed to catch up with the Soviet Union, but to leave it far behind.

These comparisons refer to relative rates of growth in per capita private consumption expenditures that comprise the vast bulk of total expenditures in all nations. The other major component consists of government outlays on health, education, and similar services. A lack of available data precludes their inclusion for most of the countries in our comparison. Such outlays have increased more slowly than private consumption expenditures in the Soviet Union. Since 1970, per capita government outlays on health and education have risen by 15 percent, while private expenditures have increased by 33 percent. In the United States and Western Europe, government expenditures on such services apparently have risen at least as fast as private consumption outlays. Clearly, this has been the case in the United States and the United Kingdom, and probably also in Italy and Scandinavia. In most of the nations surveyed, government outlays for such services account for about one-tenth of all consumption outlays.

Comparisons with the Communist Nations of Eastern Europe

The International Comparisons Project and other recent research permit us to address the question of how living standards in the Soviet Union compare with those of the communist nations of Eastern Europe. The ICP study includes data for Hungary, Poland, Romania, and Yugoslavia. The work of the Research Project on National Income in East Central Europe has produced measures of consumption growth rates for East European nations, excluding Yugoslavia, comparable with those used in the West. These measures provide an alternative to the misleading indexes published by East European governments. As all of these nations, except Yugoslavia, have centrally planned economies, these data add an interesting dimension to our assessment of comparative living standards. Moreover, several of these nations are geographically contiguous to the USSR, and this provides Soviet citizens with a basis for comparing their own living standards with those of other communist nations. It should also be emphasized that all of the above-mentioned caveats concerning comparisons between the Soviet Union and Western nations also apply to Soviet-East European comparisons.

Table 3.4 provides data for four communist nations comparable to the data on capitalist nations in Table 3.1. As the data indicate, in 1976 per capita consumption in the Soviet Union was roughly three-quarters of the Hungarian level in 1975 and about four-fifths of Poland's. The Soviet level was about the same as Yugoslavia's, but exceeded Romania's by about one-fifth. Although Czechoslovakia and East Germany were not included in the ICP study, a variety of evidence indicates that living standards in these

TABLE 3.4
Relative Levels of Per Capita Consumption for the USSR and Four East European
Communist Nations, 1975-76

	Hungary	Poland	Romania	Yugoslavia
	USSR as a Percentage of Each Nation			
Total Consumption	74	80	119	101
Food, Beverages, Tobacco	70	77	107	96
Clothing, Footware	102	94	126	128
Rent, Fuel	86	52	56	77
Household Expenditures	43	42	102	54
Transportation, Communications	83	102	216	85
Recreation	52	75	197	97
Education	140	113	182	161
Health Care	46	53	87	73
Other Expenditures	63	111	180	112

Sources: Same as Table 3.1.

nations are the highest in Eastern Europe. They are well above the level
in the Soviet Union, but still generally below the level in most West
European nations. As for Bulgaria, the evidence is mixed. One might hazard
the guess that Bulgarian living standards are roughly equivalent to those
in Yugoslavia. The average Hungarian or Polish citizen consumes considerably
more food and clothing than the average Soviet citizen, but the reverse is
the case for Romanians and Yugoslavs. All four nations enjoy more housing
and housing-related goods and services than the Soviet Union, but exhibit
considerable differences with regard to other types of household expenditures.
The Soviet Union apparently spends considerably more on education and
much less on health care than any East European nation.

Table 3.5 provides data on the pattern of consumption expenditures in
the four East European nations and the USSR. As might be expected,
consumption patterns in the Soviet Union are much more akin to those
in Eastern Europe than those in the West. The Soviet pattern most closely
resembles that of Romania. In both nations, expenditures on food and
clothing account for nearly two-thirds of all consumption outlays. This is
quite high even for developing countries and substantially higher than the
Yugoslavian level. Such conditions might be a reflection of the restricted
range of consumer choices typical of centrally planned economies. All four
East European nations devote a considerably larger share of their total

TABLE 3.5

Consumption Patterns in the USSR and Four East European Communist Nations, 1975-76

	USSR	Hungary	Poland	Romania	Yugoslavia
Total Consumption	100	100	100	100	100
Food, Beverages, Tobacco	47	42	44	48	40
Clothing, Footware	17	11	13	15	9
Rent, Fuel	5	7	8	7	8
Household Expenditures	5	9	9	7	10
Transportation, Communications	6	7	6	7	9
Recreation	5	7	6	4	5
Education	6	5	6	5	7
Health Care	4	6	6	5	7
Other Expenditures	5	6	2	2	6

Sources: Underlying data for East European nations are in Kravis, Heston, and Summers, World Product and Income, pp. 219, 260, 276, 277, 284. Percentages for the USSR are in Schroeder and Edwards, Consumption in the USSR, pp. 206-207. As in Table 3.2, expenditures in restaurants and cafes are included in the "food, beverages, tobacco" category.

consumption outlays to housing and related expenditures than the Soviet Union. This is true of transportation and communications as well. Each of the five spends a similar proportion on education, but the proportion devoted to health care is smaller in the Soviet Union than in any of the others. In all five nations, government outlays account for more than 90 percent of all expenditures on these services, which are typically distributed without direct charge.

Data needed to assess consumption growth rates in Eastern Europe during the early decades of the postwar period are incomplete. Per capita growth rates were much more rapid in the USSR than in Poland, Hungary, and Czechoslovakia, but less rapid than in East Germany. Romania and Yugoslavia probably exceeded the Soviet rate, but one cannot be sure. Table 3.6 displays average annual per capita growth rates for seven East European nations and the Soviet Union from 1970-81. Per capita growth rates were higher in four East European nations than in the Soviet Union, the same in one nation, and lower in the others. After 1975, living standards improved at a much slower rate in the Soviet Union and all the communist nations

TABLE 3.6

Growth of Per Capita Private Consumption in the USSR and Seven East European Communist Nations, 1970-1981

	1970-81	1975-81
USSR	2.6	1.9
Bulgaria	2.2	1.3
Czechoslovakia	1.4	0.9
East Germany	3.0	2.1
Hungary	2.3	1.8
Poland	2.3	0.4
Romania	3.7	3.2
Yugoslavia	3.6	3.7

Sources: For the USSR, same as Table 3. East European growth rates, except for Yugoslavia's, were calculated from index numbers in Thad P. Alton and Associates, *Eastern Europe: Domestic Final Uses of Gross Product, 1965, 1970, and 1975-1982*, Research Project on National Income in East Central Europe, Occasional Paper, no. 77 (1983), pp. 7-12. Yugoslav growth rates were calculated from data published by the Federal Statistical Office of Yugoslavia, *Monthly Review of Yugoslav Economic Statistics.*

of Eastern Europe except Yugoslavia. Growth rates were below two percent per year in all communist nations from 1976-82 except in Romania and Yugoslavia. In 1982, Poland's per capita private consumption was below the level it attained in 1975. Broadly speaking, the Soviet Union and the communist nations of Eastern Europe have not been able to reduce the substantial disparities in living standards that prevail both among themselves and vis-à-vis the West. Yugoslavia seems to be the only exception.

As a contribution to understanding the complex and delicate politico-economic relationships that exist between the USSR and the six East European members of the Council of Mutual Economic Assistance (CMEA)—the so-called socialist common market—Table 3.7 provides official data on the per capita consumption of several important household goods. The data indicate that in many key areas East European consumers are appreciably better off than their Soviet counterparts. With regard to meat, which has become something of a political symbol, in 1981 per capita consumption was higher in at least five of the six East European CMEA nations than in the Soviet Union. Even with the addition of fish, which is eaten in much larger quantities in the Soviet Union than in Eastern Europe, Soviet consumers were still worse off than their East European counterparts. Moreover, no gains were made by the Soviet Union from 1975-82, whereas

TABLE 3.7
Some Physical Indicators of Living Standards in the USSR and Five East European Communist Nations in 1981

	USSR	Bulgaria	Hungary	GDR	Poland	Czechoslovakia
	Per Capita Consumption in Kilograms					
Meat	57	67	74[a]	91	72	87[b]
Fish	18	6		7	7	5
Dairy Products	305	236	172[c]		444	236
Eggs (units)	245	209	315	290	227	321
Sugar	44	36	36	41	33	37
Grain Products, Potatoes	243	189	176	236	283	147
Vegetables	98	131	159	95	118	67
	Household Stocks of Consumer Durables (per 1,000)					
Refrigerators	262	246	301	445	274	324
Washing Machines	205	225	305	341	258	432
Televisions	262	240	262	422	263	377
Radios, Phonographs	261	277		386	474	613
Automobiles	18[d]	94	103	156	73	148

Notes: [a] Includes about 2 kilograms of fish.
[b] Excluding lard.
[c] Excluding butter.
[d] Estimate.

Source: *Statisticheskii ezhegodnik stran-chlenov soveta ekonomicheskoi vzaimopomoshchi* (Moscow, 1982), pp. 48–50.

at least five East European nations improved their supplies of meat and fish. Although the evidence is uncertain, meat supplies likely rose in Romania as well. Since 1975, milk supplies have risen in Eastern Europe, but actually declined in the Soviet Union. Per capita Soviet supplies of eggs, sugar, and vegetables rose during this period, and Soviet consumers tended to be relatively better off than their East European counterparts in terms of total kilograms consumed per capita. But in 1981, the Soviet Union's per capita consumption of grain products and potatoes—241 kilograms—was higher than in any other East European nation for which we have data except Poland. As per capita consumption of these products amounted to 261 kilograms in 1975, it appears that the shift toward reducing the share of starchy foods in the Soviet diet has been quite slow.

Neither does the Soviet Union compare favorably to Eastern Europe with respect to stocks of household durables. The Soviet Union might be better off compared to Romania, but data for that country are not available. In 1981, the Soviet Union had fewer refrigerators, washing machines, and television sets per household than all the nations of Eastern Europe except Bulgaria. In the same year, roughly one-third of all Czechoslovak and East German families had cars. The figure was about one-quarter in Bulgaria and Hungary, and about one-fifth in Poland, but only about one-tenth in the Soviet Union. Supplies of consumer durables—symbols of modern (i.e., Western) consumption styles—have improved about as rapidly in the Soviet Union as in Eastern Europe.

Other Considerations and Near-Term Prospects

International comparisons of relative standards of living are inevitably imprecise, and the same can be said of the interpretation of their results. The above comparisons show that per capita consumption is much lower in the Soviet Union than in the West, but even these relatively low levels are probably overstated. Despite efforts to match goods and services of comparable quality in the basic set of U.S.-Soviet comparisons, data limitations forced matching choices that favor the Soviet Union. Moreover, Soviet consumer prices often deviate from equilibrium prices. This situation results in random shortages that bias international comparisons with market countries in the Soviet Union's favor. In addition, Soviet consumers are confronted with a narrow range of choice of goods and services as compared with their Western counterparts. Numerous items readily available in the West are hardly ever found in Soviet stores. Soviet press reports provide an abundance of evidence of the disappearance of low-grade items of one kind or another. This forces low-income consumers to purchase high-grade, high-priced items, or do without.

Finally, the "utility" of consumption in the Soviet Union is reduced by the notorious deficiencies of the Soviet retail distribution system. Soviet retail outlets tend to be few in number, small in size, poorly lighted, and poorly equipped by Western or even East European standards. In 1977, for example, the total number of retail stores of various types found in Moscow was only about a quarter or a third of the number found in New York, Chicago, or Los Angeles. In the same year, Moscow had only about half as many restaurants and one-third as many personal service establishments as these American cities. The discrepancy would be even greater if we included the small family-type outlets that are found in such abundance in the United States, but not at all in the Soviet Union.

Besides the shopping inconveniences resulting from too few retail outlets, Soviet consumers are forced to put up with the prevalent "three-stop" system of service—one to ascertain availability of a desired item, another to pay for it, and a third to pick it up. Although so called "self-service" outlets have been spreading rapidly, many would hardly seem deserving of the name. The result of these problems is that Soviet consumers must spend inordinate amounts of time either standing in line or going from store to store. One Soviet source assessed the annual total at 25 billion hours.[10]

On the other hand, the relative level of Soviet consumption might be understated because of the failure to take account of the Soviet Union's sizable "underground" or "second" economy. Although we cannot be certain, this is probably not the case. By all accounts, black markets, corruption, bribery, theft of public goods, and illegal production activities are prevalent in the Soviet Union. However, most of these activities merely raise prices and redistribute existing goods and incomes. What matters is the extent to which legal or semilegal private production increases supplies and is not counted in national estimates. Illegal economic activities, such as the production of drugs or *samogon* (moonshine), are excluded by definition. Activities that increase supplies or are not already counted in our estimates appear to play a minor role in the second economy of the Soviet Union. Moreover, Western nations also have "underground" economies. The second economy is not a factor biasing our comparisons of consumption in favor of the West. Indeed, the opposite might well be the case if we included the production of *samogon* in our calculations.

Two basic factors account for the Soviet Union's low levels of per capita consumption relative to the West. First, there still remains a large gap between worker productivity in the Soviet Union and the West. According to Abram Bergson, in 1976 worker output in the Soviet Union was only 38.6 percent of the U.S. level and 48 to 70 percent of the level of five major West European nations and Japan.[11] Soviet worker productivity improved between 1955 and 1976 relative to the United States and the United Kingdom, but in general the gap between the Soviet Union and the West has widened. Worker productivity remains low because the proportion of the population actually employed is uniquely high in the Soviet Union. In comparison to Eastern Europe, the Soviet Union's worker output appears to be roughly equal to the level of Hungary, Poland, and Yugoslavia, but above that of Romania.

Second, the Soviet Union devotes a considerably smaller share of its total national output to consumption than other nations. According to the International Comparisons Project, the nine Western nations considered in Table 3.1 devoted 62–73 percent of their respective gross domestic products to consumption, whereas the Soviet proportion was 54 percent in 1976. This relatively low share, which has changed little in real terms since 1965, reflects the Soviet government's well-known preference in favor of investment and defense over consumption. As a result of this allocation pattern, huge backlogs of neglect have accumulated in the consumer sector, notably in housing, retail, trade, services, and consumer goods industries.

Inasmuch as the above study has considered comparative living standards and consumption in the context of an assessment of the quality of life in the Soviet Union, it seems appropriate to mention some areas where the Soviet Union compares more favorably with the West. Education and health care are provided to everyone without direct charge, although as we have noted, not in equal quantities and qualities. State pension and disability benefits are now available to nearly everyone. The Soviet worker need not fear unemployment, and the Soviet workweek (generally 41 hours) is short in comparison with most Western nations except the United States. Finally, money incomes are probably distributed less unequally in the Soviet Union than in many Western nations, though not in comparison with the Scandinavian nations and the United Kingdom.[12] Depending on one's values, one might wish to take such considerations into account in assessing the quality of life in the Soviet Union.

In conclusion, it seems unlikely that the gap between Soviet and Western living standards will be reduced in this decade. Western assessments are virtually unanimous in forecasting slower Soviet economic growth in the near future, and therefore, even slower growth rates in per capita consumption. There have been sharp reductions in the growth of the Soviet labor force due to demographic factors, a reduced rate of capital formation as a consequence of slowing rates of investment, and there is little reason to believe that productivity can be boosted substantially. Such problems suggest an average per capita annual growth rate of under two percent for the rest of the 1980s. Unless the economies of the West falter badly, the Soviet Union cannot hope to close the consumption gap. Boosting productivity and radically upgrading the quality and variety of consumer goods and services and tailoring them to the population's preferences would require a major reform of the Soviet economic system. Few believe that such systemic alterations will be undertaken soon, and even if they are, the payoff will be slow in coming.

Notes

1. *Pravda*, May 5, 1960.
2. *Pravda*, October 19, 1961.
3. For the most recent assessment of these matters, see Gertrude E. Schroeder, "Soviet Living Standards: Achievements and Prospects," in U.S. Congress, Joint Economic Committee, *Soviet Economy in the 1980's: Problems and Prospects* (Washington, D.C., 1982), pt. 2, pp. 367–388.

4. Irving B. Kravis, Alan Heston, and Robert Summers, *World Product and Income: International Comparisons of Real Gross Product* (Baltimore: Johns Hopkins University Press, 1982).

5. Gertrude E. Schroeder and Imogene Edwards, *Consumption in the USSR: An International Comparison*, U.S. Congress, Joint Economic Committee (Washington, D.C., 1981).

6. Schroeder and Edwards, *Consumption in the USSR*, p. 8.

7. *Narodnoe khoziaistvo SSSR v 1980 godu*, p. 444.

8. For recent Western assessments of the state of Russian health care, see William Knaus, *Inside Russian Medicine* (New York: Everest House, 1982); and Christopher Davis, "The Economics of the Soviet Health Care System," and Murray Feshbach, "Issues in Soviet Health Problems," U.S. Congress, Joint Economic Committee, *Soviet Economy in the 1980's: Problems and Prospects* (Washington, D.C., 1982), pt. 2, pp. 203–264.

9. This and other matters related to comparative consumption in the USSR and the West are assessed in more detail in Schroeder and Edwards, *Consumption in the USSR*, pp. 18–31, and in Abram Bergson, *Productivity and the Social System: the USSR and the West* (Cambridge: Harvard University Press, 1978), pp. 170–192; also see Abram Bergson, "Soviet Consumption in Western Perspective," in *Economic Notes, 1972–1982* (Monte del Paschi Di Siena, Italy, 1983), pp. 199–218.

10. *Ekonomika i organizatsiia promyshlennogo proizvodstva*, 1981, no. 9, p. 48.

11. Abram Bergson, "Soviet Consumption in Western Perspective," p. 205.

12. For a recent review of the evidence on comparative income distribution, see Gertrude E. Schroeder, "Consumption," in Abram Bergson and Herbert S. Levine (eds.), *The Soviet Economy: Toward the Year 2000* (London: George Allen & Unwin, 1983), pp. 335–346.

Wolfgang Teckenberg

4. Consumer Goods and Services: Contemporary Problems and Their Impact on the Quality of Life in the Soviet Union

To evaluate the impact of different levels of income and consumption on the quality of life in the Soviet Union is a difficult task. In the Soviet Union, collectivist principles should favor social services and non-material welfare arrangements. Several authors have characterized the Soviet state's regulation of social services as based on allotment principles rather than on achievement criteria.[1] This applies to the Soviet system of social security where people are supplied with state provisions largely independent of their own investments and achievements. The provision of such services is restricted only by the condition that they must have been employed at some time in their lives. Soviet citizens are so accustomed to this arrangement that emigrants often claim it to be a major advantage of the Soviet system.[2]

The principles of the Soviet system of social security are not applicable to other public services, though one would expect them to be organized on collectivist principles. The availability of washing machines for individual use, or the alternative provision of public laundries, depends on the prior considerations of economic administrators in socialist nations. If systemic goals enhance collective behavior, such considerations should favor public goods over individualistic consumption.

The provision of public services might have socially integrative effects that Soviet citizens find more important than the official collectivist ideology. However, the Soviet policy of saving in the service (tertiary) sector has important consequences for the individual consumption preferences of the population. Short cuts in the service sector, except in education and health, are illustrated by aggregate-level data on spending and manpower planning.

31

Apart from economic and employment indicators that show a concentration of services in areas where they can be provided on a "rational" basis, a growing differentiation in the consumption preferences of various social strata has been reported.[3] This is partially a reflection of considerable differences in family income.

Soviet families try to maintain their étatist lifestyles by laying claim to specific goods and services and displaying a reluctance to purchase other items also distributed in the economy. Spending money on services rather than service-oriented consumer durables (such as washing machines) might indicate a vote for collectivist strategies of attaining social welfare. At the moment, however, Soviet families tend to opt for individual, household-oriented ways of life.

By realizing that the demands of the service sector are difficult to satisfy, the Soviet government could refrain from further investment and expansion in this sector. On the other hand, it could follow the old road of satisfying the needs of individual consumers by sustaining the "commodity fetishism" it normally criticizes in capitalist societies.

Although the Soviet Union's output of durable goods has increased in recent years despite slowing rates of economic growth, few efforts have been undertaken to improve the output of the service sector. Because public services are often unobtainable, or like transportation services, very cheap, the expenditure patterns of Soviet households differ greatly from those of their Western counterparts. As a result, Soviet economists have recently argued for an expansion of paid services in order to create favorable conditions for an expansion of the service sector.

Household services and retail trade displayed a very inefficient pattern of organization from 1975–82. Due to declining economic growth rates during the 1970s, the tertiary sector has been deliberately starved of resources. This is also true of the ratio of sociocultural expenditures to total government outlays, which fell from 46 percent in 1975 to 40 percent in 1982.[4] These figures include expenditures for education and health care. Contrary to collectivist principles, the provision of individual consumer goods seems to be on the increase.

Consumption Patterns

Although a large part of the Soviet population lives in relative poverty, the Soviet Union has a money surplus originating from the existence of a "shortage economy" in which consumption is restricted in favor of investment. Soviet authors claim that the proliferation of goods between 1970 and 1981 increased by a factor of 1.8 while total incomes more than doubled.[5] Savings grew even faster, by a factor of 3.6, but from the 8th Five-Year Plan (1966–70) to the 10th Five-Year Plan (1976–80), capital

TABLE 4.1
Durable Household Goods in the Soviet Union per 100 Households

Item	1975	1982
Refrigerators	77	101
Washing Machines	77	78
Television Sets	83	97
Sewing Machines	60	63
Vacuum Cleaners	24	42
Cameras	36	41
Telephones	24[a]	34[a]
Private Cars	7[b]	8[b]

Notes: [a] Calculations based on an average family size of 3.5.
[b] Estimates based on figures from endnote 8.

Source: *Narodnoe khoziaistvo v 1982 godu* (Moscow, 1983), pp. 324 and 413.

accumulation in the consumption sphere fell from 15.1 to 12.1 percent, and to 12 percent by 1981.

Soviet data concerning slower per capita consumption growth rates reflect slower rates of economic growth in general. However, the Soviet Union has made progress in the distribution of durable goods. Less impressive was its progress in the agricultural sphere in light of the goals of Brezhnev's 1982 food program. Soviet meat production, always the weakest link in Soviet agriculture, amounted to 57 kilograms per capita in 1982 and only 48 kilograms in 1970. Per capita meat production has not increased since 1975.[6]

The provision of consumer durables has increased in part because some are produced by heavy industrial enterprises. But because responsibility for such production is dispersed among up to 10 industrial ministries concerned with the same product,[7] difficulties in related repair services and the supply of spare parts are common. People spend more time having their equipment repaired than they would in well-run public service establishments. Table 4.1 shows the distribution of selected household durables in the Soviet Union.

The discrepancy between the Soviet Union and other industrialized nations is particularly visible with regard to private cars. The Soviet Union's extremely low density of motor vehicles, which is 18 times lower than in West Germany, is subject to considerable regional differences. It is highest in Estonia (61 cars per 1,000 inhabitants), Lithuania, and Latvia, and also quite high in Georgia and Armenia (32–35 per 1,000).[8] Such differences not only reflect the availability of private cars; they also reflect cultural standards and individual behavior preferences. One should further consider the basic proposition that when collective goods such as public transportation services are inexpensive and of reasonably high quality, individual goods such as private cars are less important. Compared to the availability of transportation in the Soviet Union, household services are in short supply. Soviet data show that a large share of families buy household equipment for home repair and cleaning.

Another important factor affecting overall consumption patterns in the Soviet Union is the quality of Soviet consumer goods. Western societies are already using second- or third-generation versions of the consumer durables identified in Table 4.1. For example, two-thirds of all West German sewing machines sold each year are electric. The same can hardly be said of Soviet machines.

Furthermore, there are important discrepancies between city-dwellers and rural inhabitants regarding the possession of consumer durables. In 1982, there were 101 refrigerators per 100 city families, whereas in rural areas there were only 69 per 100.[9] Nevertheless, rural inhabitants tended to have larger savings accounts than their urban counterparts. The average figure was 1,112 rubles per person in urban areas and 1,237 rubles in the countryside.

Expenditure Patterns of Soviet Households

Another way of evaluating Soviet living standards is by analyzing expenditures on goods and services. A high proportion of Soviet family expenditures is devoted to food and clothing. As is well known, comparisons between the Soviet Union and Western societies often neglect the fact that some expenses such as rent and housing maintenance are much smaller in the former than the latter. Furthermore, certain services are either unavailable or comparatively very cheap.

Soviet data from a large household budget survey conducted in the Ukrainian SSR show that 10 percent of all money income went to buying services in 1970. In 1975, the figure rose to 10.5 percent as can be seen in Table 4.2. With regard to retail transactions and purchased commodities, the Soviet Union fares less favorably than other industrialized nations. For example, the structure of retail trade in the Ukraine was dominated by food purchases in 1975. Food and beverages accounted for 38 and 11.1 percent of the total, and tobacco products accounted for 2 percent of all commodity transactions. Leisure spending on commodities such as books, radios, sports equipment, and motor bikes accounted for only 5.3 percent of the total.[10] It should be noted that many goods associated with cultural, holiday, and leisure activities are provided free and do not enter into retail

TABLE 4.2
Soviet Household Spending on Services in 1975

	Workers and Employees	Kolkhozniki
Total Expenditures on Services and Culture	100.0	100.0
Theater and Cinema	10.5	12.9
Kindergartens	7.5	2.4
Tourism and Recreation	6.1	4.7
Hygiene and Laundry	3.4	1.2
Personal Transportation	32.3	45.9
Rent, Housing, Communal Services	33.0	17.6
Other Expenditures	7.2	15.3

Source: A. I. Kocherga, Sfera obsluzhivaniia naseleniia (Moscow, 1979), p. 133.

TABLE 4.3
Individual and State Service Payments

Type of Service	Individual Payment	State Payment
	Percent	
Trade, Restaurant, Transporation, Household, Communication, Community	100	0
Housing	37	63
Health, Sports, Social Security	6	94
Education	5	95
Culture	26	74
Total	49	51

Source: V. F. Majer, Uroven' zhizni naseleniia SSSR (Moscow, 1977), p. 74.

trade statistics. The data in Table 4.3 show the percentage amounts of individual and state contributions allocated to certain services.[11]

Recently, Soviet sociologists have debated the advantages of paid services. They maintain that people would be willing to pay for services because most are even more scarce than consumer goods. They also believe that more money could be invested in the modernization of the service sector because the share of payable services in consumption expenditures is said to be four to six times smaller than in other industrialized nations.[12]

Shortcomings in the Service Sector

One way for the Soviets to cope with their money surplus would be to offer more services and initiate a policy of efficiency in this area. Evidently, they are far from doing so. Employment in consumer services, which rose about 58 percent between 1961 and 1970, increased by less than 30 percent from 1971 to 1980.[13]

As a consequence of the Soviet Union's continued policy of saving as regards investment in the tertiary sector, service industries and service trade are consigned to a low degree of mechanization and are lacking in infrastructure. For example, the Soviet Union lacks storage capacity for perishable goods,[14] and Soviet sources report a shortage of packing materials. Tons of milk are lost because of leaky containers, and complaints about shortages of spare parts in repair shops are common. Mechanics have difficulty servicing all of their orders, and as a result some retail shops have called for juridical measures against the producers of the goods to be repaired.[15]

In January 1982, a decree of the Central Committee ordered improvements in retail trade and commercial services. As shop assistants often hold back goods that are in high demand in order to sell them privately, one of the aims of the decree was to abolish corruption and black market transactions. Apart from disciplinary measures, no monetary solutions were offered. Retail sales have been targeted for growth although the number of employees involved in retail trade and food services, now estimated at 7.3 million workers or 6.5 percent of the workforce, is not likely to increase. This can be achieved only by improving organization and building larger retail stores. The quality of Soviet retail stores is still below the norm of other socialist nations. In 1976, the Soviet Union had 157 square meters of retail space per 1,000 inhabitants. The comparable figures for Czechoslovakia and East Germany were 210 and 290 square meters in 1971.

A 1983 decree highlighting problems in the household service sector noted that service shops annually repair about 65 million appliances (e.g., television sets and radios), 64 million shoes, and about one million houses and apartments. However, in money value terms, the largest share of this sector's business was devoted to sewing and mending of clothing.[16] Soviet citizens evidently prefer to buy textiles and have clothing made instead of buying standardized, mass-produced items. The decree further pointed to the low level of efficiency in consumer service shops. As a result, their inconvenient opening hours have been changed, but most people continue to avoid them because of their poor quality.

Access to Goods and Services

In characterizing the availability of goods and services in the Soviet Union, data on per capita retail trade in various Soviet republics can serve as a useful index. While the Soviet average was 964 rubles per capita in 1979, Estonia's was 1,418 and Latvia's was 1,383. Tadzhikistan's was 561, Azerbaijan's was 567, and Uzbekistan's was 604. Other republics had even lower per capita retail trade figures. This index is somewhat biased by the "terms of trade" that are typical for urban and rural areas. Urban regions show a different rank, and the discrepancies between them are smaller than those that prevail between rural and urban areas.[17]

Soviet sociologists have recently published per capita retail trade data for several cities.[18] Not surprisingly, Moscow held the top position. Its per capita retail trade was 1,722 rubles in 1975; Kishinev's was 1,316 in the same year; and Novosibirsk's was only 855 in 1973. Yet these figures ignore illegal transactions, which are probably more frequent in Southern republics than in Baltic republics, where commodities are more regularly distributed.

Another aspect of regional disparity in the Soviet Union concerns the availability of basic services in the Northern RSFSR, especially in newly-erected cities. Occasionally, complaints extend to new building sites, for instance to the new *microraions* around the Moscow area.[19] The creation of service facilities often lags behind the construction of new housing. This can be explained by the Soviet strategy of trying to minimize the costs of infrastructure and services. While complaints about deficiencies in communal infrastructure and the supply of durables are not among the six most widely-discussed topics found in letters to *Izvestiia*, they rank first in the mail of *Severnaia pravda*.[20]

Soviet endeavors to make services more efficient are based on economic criteria that indicate improvements are more costly in regions where earnings are high, for instance in the Northern parts of the Soviet Union. Therefore, economic rationality, which is supposed to foster production and high returns, necessitates that planners and managers try to cut down on services and live with consumer complaints as long as people stay in these areas. Another major consideration is the importance attached to "economies of scale" that favor large multifunctional service enterprises, which are not appropriate to small town conditions.

N. I. Moskaleva has noted that the nature of client-related service trade is to function better when based on small shops.[21] However, she also stresses the "economizing" aspects of large cultural and service organizations. Because service trade does not fit into the Soviet Union's large-scale organizational framework, where "think big" also means "think of your autonomy from unstable environments," those who engage in private transactions will always find a way to exploit poor coordination between mass-oriented organizations.

Given the Soviet preference for large-scale solutions, it seems that urbanization is the best way to improve the availability of goods and services, though not necessarily to the availability of food. This is because only in urbanized areas can resources be concentrated to a degree that makes large-scale organizational solutions feasible.

Soviet citizens often gain access to scarce goods by means of "connections," or *blat*. *Blat* usually involves friendship networks or incumbency in an influential organization or enterprise. It seems to be a prevailing Soviet principle that "little favors" are granted in exchange for loyalty. Such favors can include the opportunity to dine in the restaurant of the writers' union as described in Bulgakov's *Master and Margarita*, to see foreign films in the clubs of filmmakers, or to travel to a nice resort area. Allotment principles are clearly operative when enterprises distribute housing or food to motivate their employees and buy the loyalty of their workers.

Today, large Soviet enterprises function as "mini societies" that take up many of the distributive functions that communities normally provide in the West. For example, more than 50 percent of all available housing belongs to enterprises in the RSFSR. Thirty-seven percent of the 14 million seats in restaurants and other public eating places are run by firms or organizations.[22] In addition, workers are sometimes given scarce theater or ballet tickets. Recently, some services have been moved closer to production centers. The installation of 3,300 household service shops in firms of the RSFSR will allegedly save more than three million hours of work.[23] The decision to move services closer to production facilities might stem from the fact that they are not used to their full capacity in residential areas.

Consumer Preferences

The reluctance of Soviet citizens to use certain goods and services points to the subjective preferences and tastes of various population groups. Unsold consumer durables and underemployed service outlets are often described in the Soviet press. In the Baltic republics, it was reported that dry cleaners and shoe repair shops are used at only 60 or 70 percent of their capacity.[24] The same was found to be true in some recently-erected Moscow suburbs where people prefer to do their household work at home instead of giving it to available communal service outlets. In the suburbs of Moscow, 67 percent of all households have their own washing machines, and most people prefer to do their washing at home.[25] Working families particularly enjoy having their own equipment and do not like their washing to leave home.

Self-service laundries appeared in Moscow in 1973, and 19 percent of the population made use of them. By 1979, however, their popularity had declined, and only 10 percent frequented them. The share of those who shun communal laundries increased from 50 to 56 percent in 1979. The reasons for avoiding them were "poor quality" (95 percent), inconvenient locations or opening hours, and personal preferences.

Soviet citizens also exhibit an unwillingness to frequent public eating places. Most Soviet men and women prefer to eat at home, but traditional role perceptions are also in evidence. Sixty-nine percent of all men and 73 percent of all women affirmed the statement, "A good housewife always prepares her meals at home."[26]

Other communal institutions have lost their prior importance as well. In 1972, for example, 92 percent of the respondents of a survey conducted in Moscow said that they never used the so-called "bureau for good services," which offers various types of household assistance, and the figure rose to 95 percent in 1979. The authors of the survey hoped that rising levels of education would help create stronger collectivist attitudes. They admitted, however, that certain rules of conduct encourage private retreat and self-reliance.

By offering basic consumer durables for home use and by keeping the quality and public supply of services at low levels, Soviet planners have created a climate unfavorable to collectivist ideological goals. Many people now prefer to possess their own household durables, and after the acquisition of these commodities, the public supply of services is of little interest to them. This might be one reason why the Soviet leadership, after expanding the service sector in the 1960s, began to curb service-oriented expenditures in the 1970s.

Future Prospects

Even if the Gorbachev leadership achieves better economic results than its forerunners, increased growth is unlikely to alter the Soviet Union's priorities regarding the output of consumer goods and services. It seems likely that the Soviets will continue their policy of saving in the service sector, and no drastic changes in allocation patterns should be expected. Rather, it seems more likely that prices for marketed services will increase. For example, if principles of accountability are applied to housing and public transportation, the Soviet Union's family budget patterns would probably come closer to the spending patterns of Western households.

To assess Soviet preference structures by analyzing underlying aggregate demand would be quite complicated. Although Soviet economists claim that there is more demand for services than for goods, there is little evidence that this is true for large parts of the Soviet population. However, this is not meant to imply that the average Soviet citizen does not desire better health care. Indeed, the evidence suggests that those who could afford to do so would prefer to go to a doctor of their choice. Thus planning authorities must take account of a growing differentiation of consumer preferences. While workers can be appeased by the accelerated provision of consumer durables, the result tends to be a decreased interest in public services. The roots of this behavior seem to lie in traditional norms of conduct that are quite firmly established and probably not so different from the social behavior of workers in other societies at a similar stage of development. However, the materialistic and extrinsic orientation of Soviet workers does not fit in well with the regime's collectivist slogans. Ideological claims to the contrary, a certain retreatism from public life seems to be prevalent.

The intelligentsia, on the other hand, seems to be quite dissatisfied with its material position, though the average Soviet intellectual is privileged in comparison to the average worker in the Soviet Union, if not in other socialist societies. This dissatisfaction pertains mainly to poor quality and a lack of diversification of consumer goods, but the possession of certain "luxury" goods or rare books is a way of displaying specific lifestyles. Such behavior indicates "membership" in a certain status group or social circle.

As Soviet sociological surveys indicate, the problem is that standards of excellence vary more for services than for consumer durables. This is evident in the institutions of select social circles, for example, in the writers' club and the architects' house. Such institutions are closed to the general public, but are frequented by certain status groups. Max Weber's claim that estates can be discerned by "connubium" and "commensalis" seems to be an adequate description of the Soviet intelligentsia. In a society where trust is a relatively scarce commodity, individual retreatism into private lifestyles based on family and friendship ties can be seen as a counterbalance to the anonymity of the workplace in large enterprises and organizations. With their canteens, kindergartens, sports centers, and holiday offers, bureaucratic norms of organizations represent the collective type of organization.

Notes

1. K. V. Beyme, *Sozialismus oder Wohlfahrtsstaat?* (Munich, 1977).

2. S. White, "Continuity and Change in Soviet Political Culture," *Comparative Studies* 2, no. 3 (1978), pp. 381-395.

3. W. Teckenberg and H. Best, "Die Gesellschaften der UdSSR und der BRD," *Kolner Zeitschrift für Soziologie und Sozialpsychologie* 33, no. 1 (1981), pp. 202-205.

4. *Narodnoe khoziaistvo v 1982 godu* (Moscow, 1983), pp. 520 and 522.

5. E. Aleksandrova and E. Fedorovskaia, "Mekhanizm formirovaniia i vozvysheniia potrebnosti," *Voprosy ekonomiki*, 1984, no. 1, pp. 15-26.

6. *Narodnoe khoziaistvo v 1982 godu*, p. 411.

7. C. R. Nechemias, "Welfare in the Soviet Union: Health Care, Housing, and Personal Consumption," in G. B. Smith (ed.), *Public Administration in the Soviet Union* (New York, 1980), pp. 172-216.

8. M. E. Ruban et al., *Wandel der Arbeits- und Lebensbedingungen der Sowjetunion, 1955-1980* (Frankfurt, 1983), p. 232.

9. *Narodnoe khoziaistvo v 1982 godu*, p. 413.

10. A. I. Kocherga, *Sfera obsluzhivaniia naseleniia* (Moscow, 1979), p. 369.

11. V. F. Majer, *Uroven' zhizni naseleniia SSSR* (Moscow, 1977), p. 74.

12. V. M. Rutgaizer and A. V. Teliukov, "Kak vnedrit' novye vidy obsluzhivanii," *Sotsiologicheskie issledovaniia*, 1984, no. 2, pp. 79-88.

13. L. Sbytova, "Zaniatnost' i povyshenie effektivnosti truda v sfere uslug," *Voprosy ekonomiki*, 1983, no. 2, pp. 79-88.

14. M. N. Rutkevich, "O role torgovli v sotsial'nom razvitii sovetskogo obshchestva," in *Sotsiologicheskie issledovaniia*, 1983, no. 1, pp. 16-18.

15. *Sluzhba byta*, 1983, no. 4, p. 22.

16. *Narodnoe khoziaistvo v 1982 godu*, p. 452.

17. *Narodnoe khoziaistvo v 1979 godu* (Moscow, 1980), p. 455.

18. N. A. Aitov, *Sotsial'noe razvitie gorodov: Sushchnost' i perspektivy* (Moscow, 1979), p. 29.

19. Z. A. Iankova and I. Iu. Rodzinskaia, *Problemy bol'shogo goroda* (Moscow, 1982).

20. *Sotsiologicheskie issledovaniia*, 1982, no. 2, p. 93.

21. N. I. Moskaleva, "Osobennosti mekhanizma formirovaniia zatrat na uslugi i puti ikh snizheniia na predpriiatiiakh neproizvodstvennoi sfery," *Izvestiia Akademiia Nauk, seriia ekonomicheskaia*, 1983, no. 1, pp. 56-69.

22. V. G. Bychkov, *Obshchestvennoe pitanie* (Moscow, 1978).

23. *Sluzhba byta*, 1983, no. 4, p. 5.

24. *Sluzhba byta*, 1983, no. 5, p. 7.

25. Iankova and Rodzinskaia, *Problemy bol'shogo goroda*, p. 38.

26. Iankova and Rodzinskaia, *Problemy bol'shogo goroda*, p. 35.

5. Aspects of Poverty in the Soviet Union

Every nation in the world, including the richest, contains poor people. Even states that are small and opulent have a recognized "poverty" problem. No society, even the wealthiest, is immune from natural catastrophe or exploitative forces, and human beings who cannot, for one reason or another, ensure their own well-being seem to be found everywhere. It would be surprising not to find a large poverty sector in a large nation such as the Soviet Union, with a mixed population of over 270 million people and a questionable pattern of economic growth. A close look at the Soviet reality of the late 1970s confirms this expectation.

Poverty is always a relative and difficult-to-handle concept, but investigating poverty in the USSR is a particularly daunting task, lying more often than not beyond the bounds of indigenous, let alone foreign, scholarship. Even now, the term "poor" cannot be applied to any sector of Soviet society in economic or sociological literature. However, this stricture was overcome by using the euphemism "underprovision," or *maloobespechennost'*, instead of "poverty."

As outside observers, we must consider ourselves in some debt to the Khrushchev leadership for allowing minimal standards of well-being to be stipulated, for relaxing a ban on the publication of some scholarly findings, and for allowing the publication of idealized "minimum budgets." In the late 1950s, a number of institutes were instructed to assess and cost out the minimum consumption requirements of a contemporary urban family. Studies that had been done in the 1920s were reexamined. By 1959, several "minimum budgets" were prepared. The best-known variants of these studies,

---

The information in this chapter is provisional and is supplemented by the author's most recent book, *Poverty in the Soviet Union* (Cambridge: Cambridge University Press, 1986).

which were published by G. S. Sarkisyan and N. P. Kuznetsova in 1967, can still serve with some reservations as delineators of poverty in the Soviet Union.

The budgets as published covered the contemporary monthly needs of an urban worker's family, comprising a husband, a wife (both working), a 13 year-old boy, and an 8 year-old girl. Many people involved in poverty research are familiar with this study. The budget was costed in terms of official parental earnings, with due allowance for state subsidies and services, at 51 rubles and 40 kopecks per head per month.

The budget was both European and Soviet in orientation. Food purchases accounted for over half of all outgoing expenditures (56 percent), and clothing took up another 20 percent. On the other hand, expenditures on housing and communal services claimed only 5.4 percent of the total. This is partly because they are state-subsidized, and partly because they are in short supply. The tiny sums devoted to furniture and household goods betokened spartan accommodation. No outgoings were identified for medical or educational needs, as these are distributed by the state without direct charge to the individual. Neither was there any provision for savings. Furthermore, the budget contained unrealistically low figures for alcohol and tobacco consumption (2.7 percent). Public entertainment and holiday services were presumed to be almost free, though in fact they are not. Reflecting the exigencies of life in a collectivist society, a nominal sum was included for "membership fees."

The budget, as laid out, specified a minimal level of provision within the officially accepted framework of Soviet reality. However, it ignored the use of supplemental payments to obtain deficit goods and the use of collective farm markets, where prices are higher than usual. Certain expenditures, especially those devoted to alcohol, were evidently understated. Only with difficulty can one imagine how the average family's clothing needs could have been met with the monthly sums indicated.

Even so, the budget had some validity and has continued to serve as a silent marker in many sociological surveys. Moreover, several important social security benefits are still paid up to a 50–60 ruble per capita threshold today. The 51-ruble per capita poverty threshold immediately raised awkward questions about the extent of poverty when it was made public in 1967. A statistical family of two working adults and two children required earnings of some 206 rubles to reach the designated threshold, yet the average wage in 1965 was only about 97 rubles, or 194 rubles for two working adults. Therefore, it would appear in terms of simple arithmetic that the average family lived in a state of poverty. Indeed, a flurry of incidental survey results covering worker earnings and family income showed convincingly that large numbers of families failed to rise above the poverty level. As much as a quarter to a third of the urban working class must have been living below the poverty threshold, so defined. Moreover, as the proportion of the disadvantaged among the peasantry was certainly larger, the "poor" made up perhaps two-fifths of the entire Soviet population.

A "prospective," longer-term poverty budget, which Sarkisyan and Kuznetsova discussed at the same time, implied that it would serve the population's needs into the early or mid-1970s. As far as we know, it has not been subject to detailed revision. It was designed to reflect the improved opportunities that "expanding production would bring for broadening the circle of minimally essential needs, whose satisfaction requires a higher family income." This curious formulation suggested that an improved supply of goods and services would both prompt and satisfy higher expectations.

The new budget's per capita income requirement was 66.6 rubles based on the same prices used in the earlier budget, but in matters of proportion it closely resembled the first variant. Food requirements became a little more costly, but fell to 51 percent of all outgoings. Expenditures on clothes and housing likewise increased somewhat, but slightly diminished in percentage terms. Provisions for hair-dressing, public baths, and laundry services disappeared for unexplained reasons, but there was a small entry for "expenditures on other goods" and "savings." This still left the budget with a strong "poverty" configuration. Curiously, the biggest proportional increases were for holiday expenditures, transportation and communications, tobacco, and vodka. Presumably, the consumption of such items was thought to be unduly restricted; therefore, some increase could be permitted without negative consequences. This budget required two after-tax wages of 138 rubles—a national average reached only in 1974.

What changes have taken place since these budgets were introduced? The average wage, as registered in official statistical compilations, has continued to rise, reaching 172.5 rubles by 1981. Thus two working parents would take home about 310 rubles after taxes. The poverty budget must, however, be adjusted for inflation. Inflation admitted in Soviet price indices would in fact raise the 267-ruble threshold by four percent, to approximately 278 rubles,[1] but if American estimates are used, the figure would be significantly higher. Thus the "safety margin" would have been only about 32 rubles, or 8 rubles per head. This means that given the commonly observed distribution of wages in the Soviet Union, large numbers of workers and employees with statistically average families would have remained below the poverty threshold. Moreover, the peasant sector would seem to have had a higher incidence of poverty because rural incomes are about 10 percent lower than in urban areas.

A similar exercise for the United States yielded a "poverty" requirement of 178 dollars per week and an average double wage of 456 dollars for a family of four in 1979. This left a safety margin of 278 dollars, or nearly

70 dollars per week per head. Some 11.6 percent of all persons in the United States were nevertheless said to be "in poverty."[2]

Because of the absence of proper figures on Soviet wage and income distribution, the number of poor people in the Soviet Union can be assessed only in terms of probabilities—by considering which socio-occupational groups are most likely to fall below the threshold and the likely size of each group. These groups can be divided into earners and non-earners, but such an analysis is greatly complicated by the fact that detailed results of the 1979 Soviet census have not been made available.

Low-Paid Occupation Groups

In the Soviet Union, as elsewhere, the poorest workers and employees are most likely to be found in traditionally neglected economic areas, characterized not only by low basic wage rates, but also by smaller bonuses and supplements; in manual jobs with a low ranking in the wage-tariff system; and in unskilled jobs, which also rank low in the wage-tariff system. Only persons who are mature and have achieved at least a medium qualification in their chosen trade should be considered truly low-paid. Young people and students might well be poor for a given period of time, but they are sometimes prospectively well-paid, and their problems lie beyond the scope of this paper.

The various branches of the Soviet economy embrace at least 57 industries. Detailed data on Soviet labor is not usually published, but some general branch figures on wages are available, and these show an expected gradation. Personnel in extractive, energy-producing, and heavy industries are at the top of the league. By a quirk of fate, the glass and pottery industry has for two decades maintained an average wage close to the national industrial average. Low industrial averages continue to be paid in the 10 branches of light industry (textiles, footwear, and garment production) and the nine branches of food processing. Were figures available, we would expect to find seven to eight million persons employed in this below-average wage sector of the economy. See Table 5.1.

Personnel in trade, catering, and state farming are also low-paid. Most service sectors—education, public amenities, and health care—are likewise well below the national average, and "cultural" workers do worst of all, though each sector contains some relatively well-paid workers. In assessing the extent of Soviet poverty, one should note that the above sectors employ well over 30 million people—a figure approaching a third of the entire non-peasant labor force, including a high proportion of women. The publication of certain distributions of industrial workers according to their place in the tariff network has enabled us to construct rudimentary six- and eight-column distributions of industrial workers' take-home pay.[3] Al-

TABLE 5.1
Low-Paid Branches of the Economy, 1981

	Number Employed (millions)	Workers' Average Pay	Employees' Average Pay
		(Rubles per Month)	
Food Processing	2.7*	167.0	137.4
Light Industry	4.8*	155.2	133.0
State Agriculture	10.3	153.0	123.0
Trade and Catering	4.7	140.7	
Education	9.3	136.7	
Health Services	6.2	128.5	
Culture	1.3	112.8	
All Industry	30.7	190.2	148.2

Note: *Estimated.

Sources: Narodnoe khoziaistvo SSSR, 1922–1982, pp. 399 and 405; Vestnik statistiki, 1982, no. 8, p. 79; and L. S. Sbytova, Struktura zanyatosti i effektivnost' proizvodstva (Moscow, 1982), p. 59.

though industrial workers are among the best paid employees in Soviet society, the data indicate that about a third of them did not pass the poverty threshold, though a proportion probably were underqualified young people. In a word, Soviet official wage data by economic branch provide ample evidence of poverty if one continues to use Sarkisyan and Kuznetsova's figures as a measure.

Manual and unskilled jobs are to be found in all branches of the Soviet economy. In 1980, there were still some 40 million people employed in unmechanized jobs in "material production." See Tables 5.2 and 5.3 for a partial breakdown. Two especially low-paid categories are usually singled out. The first group consists of assistant workers (podsobnye rabochie), who are not directly involved in production, but perform unskilled supportive functions for those who are. They are sometimes classified as "laborers," "loaders," or "riggers." There were about two million of these workers employed in the industrial sectors of the economy at the time of the 1975 labor census, and their numbers have apparently increased since then.[4] It seems that they were almost exclusively men. According to figures published in 1977, their highest basic wage was 90 rubles a month, depending on their working conditions. People working alone on indoor jobs earned the least, and those in brigades handling exports were said to earn the most.

TABLE 5.2
Workers in Manual Jobs, 1980-81

	Percentage	Millions
All Branches of Material Production		over 40.0
Industry	about 40	11.8
Construction	over 50	4.7
Agriculture	over 66	7.1
Trade	over 66	3.2
Other Sectors		13.2

Sources: D. M. Palterovich, in Stroitel'stvo material'no-tekhnicheskoi bazy kommunizma, vol. 2 (Moscow, 1982), p. 48. All absolute figures are based on original data, given in approximate terms or fractions. Narodnoe khoziaistvo SSSR, 1922-1982, p. 402.

TABLE 5.3
Selected Low-Paid Occupations, 1980

Occupation	Basic Salary
Cleaners	75-80
Watchmen	75-80
Warehouse Personnel	80-85
Storemen	80-85
Dvorniki	75-80
Drivers	75-90
Clerks	75-80 (junior)
Secretaries	80-85 (senior)
Cashiers	80-85
Draftsmen	80-85

Source: A. N. Ershov and A. F. Yurchenko, "Spravochnik rukovoditelya predpriyatiia obshchestvennogo pitaniia" (Moscow, 1981), pp. 328 and 330.

The second group consists of so-called "junior service personnel," who do menial jobs unconnected with material production in all types of enterprises and organizations, and who cannot by definition aspire to the appellation of "worker." Junior service personnel include janitors, cleaning personnel, door-keepers, watchmen, heating attendants, and messengers.[5] Although these people are sometimes lumped together with higher grade white-collar staff for statistical purposes, they should not be confused with the latter. In 1981, the industrial sectors of the economy contained over half a million such personnel, and a recent article in *Vestnik statistiki* stated that the proportion of loaders, cloakroom attendants, sweepers, cleaners, and washers had not fallen in the period from 1970–79 and comprised 15.4 percent of the total number of workers.[6] Apparently, this is a combined figure for assistant workers and junior service personnel. The total number approaches five million.

A handbook published in 1981 listed basic wage rates for junior service personnel in trade, catering, and the state agricultural sector as ranging from 70–85 rubles.[7] It seems likely that the rates for similar jobs in industrial and productive sectors were a few rubles more. Some wage rates were subject to supplementation by incentive payments, but details are not revealed in statistical sources.

The economist L. Blyakhman, writing in *Sotsialisticheskii trud*, claimed that 21 percent of the Soviet labor force was made up of non-specialist employees in the early 1980s.[8] It would seem, however, that this figure referred only to personnel in branches of material production. Casual evidence of earnings in line with the basic rates quoted above is not difficult to come by. In addition, many specialist and semi-specialist jobs carry low salaries, most commonly in the lowest-paid branches of the economy. The opportunities for supplementary earnings are most restricted in such jobs.

Any industrialized state requires relatively large numbers of office workers to function. In 1970, the Soviet Union had approximately five million people so employed.[9] General labor data in *Norodnoe khoziaistvo* would suggest a significant increase over the course of the decade. Yet for various reasons, office work has always been disparaged in the Soviet Union. Office equipment is often primitive; stationery is a deficit commodity; and even photocopying has been inhibited by fears of illegal use. Only offices belonging to prestigious organizations such as the communist party, security organs, and central ministries appear to have been fully modernized.

Given this state of affairs, it is hardly surprising that secretarial and associated staff members are poorly paid. The great majority of such jobs are divided into only two grades—senior and junior. Soviet data published in 1981 indicate that the basic wage rates paid in non-productive organizations such as trade and catering varied from 75–85 rubles. Office staff in agricultural organizations, certain state committees, and construction did a little better, receiving from 75–95 rubles. It would seem that rates of this order were fairly standard in most branches of the economy.

Although our main concern is the delineation of poverty among workers and employees, the peasantry cannot be passed over without mention. Any discussion of the extent of poverty among the Soviet peasantry presents us with several all too familiar difficulties. The term itself is vague and is sometimes used to cover all members of a collective farm, from the chairman down to the simplest field worker. In 1981, the state collective farm sector had a registered labor force of 13.2 million. Farm income is subject to wide variations, and as far as we know, no separate "minimum budget" is available as a yardstick to judge peasant family needs. There is the additional problem of private or household plots, which still provide rural inhabitants with a quarter or more of their sustenance.

Despite these analytical problems, there can be no doubt that poverty is widespread among the Soviet peasantry. By 1981, according to an official statistical handbook, the average collective farmer's per capita income must have included costing for a private plot, and was said to be 89 percent of the amount that other Soviet workers received. This figure presumably embraced all *kolkhoz* (collective farm) personnel, from managerial personnel and specialists down to simple field workers. Soviet collective farms are highly stratified in terms of occupation and earnings. Manual field workers, who amount to half the total labor force, are at the bottom of the pyramid. A careful sociological analysis of the village population of the Novosibirsk *oblast* recently showed that completely unqualified manual laborers in state and collectivized agriculture averaged 100 rubles a month; laborers of similar standing outside the agricultural sector averaged only 90 rubles; and office and service staff averaged 105 rubles per month.[10] As is often emphasized, rural Novosibirsk is typical of Western Siberia, though the well-being of farm personnel probably varies with farm performance. Novosibirsk writers have pointed to increasing income differentiation in recent years as a result of growing upper wage rates.

One of the major disadvantages of collective farm work stems from the physical demands of the private plot itself. Studies conducted in Novosibirsk show that 82 percent of the respondents worked on plots, and nearly half of them devoted three or more hours to the task each day. Mechanization is of course minimal. Another disadvantage is that agricultural jobs usually lack the limitations on hours that characterize working conditions elsewhere. Data from the same source showed that in collective and state farms 40–45 percent of the labor force worked "9–11 or more" hours a day in the summer, and 25–30 percent worked as much in the winter. Free days are difficult to obtain, and labor turnover, particularly among machinery operators, is a major problem.[11]

Table 5.4 lists salaries paid by certain agricultural agencies, catering enterprises, cultural institutions, and the state school system. Similar professions are practiced throughout the economy, and many yield rates varying only by a few rubles. Thus a doctor working in a rest home belonging to the Ministry of Construction could not expect to earn much more if he switched to the same job in the rest home of a major industry.

TABLE 5.4
Low-Paid Specialist Positions

Positions	Sector	Basic Salary (rubles per month)
Engineers Veterinarians Agronomists	Agricultural Health and Social Security Institutions	95–140
Accountants Legal Advisers Translators Stocktakers	Catering Enterprises	95–130
General School Teachers Nursery and Special School Teachers		80–157 90–164
Librarians		100–115
Cultural Workers		90–110
Musicians		90–110
Doctors	RSFSR Collective Farm Health Service	110–170

Sources: Ershov and Yurchenko, "Spravochnik rukovoditel'ya predpriyatiia obshchestvennogo pitaniia" (Moscow, 1981), sect. 10; M. F. V'yaskov, E. A. Mil'ski, and A. A. Marushkin, "Oplata truda rabotnikov predpriyatii, organizatsii, i uchrezhdenii, obsluzhivayushchikh sel'skoe khozyaistvo," *vypusk* 2 (Moscow, 1981); and A. I. Shustov and V. I. Budarin, "Spravochnik direktora shkolv" (Moscow, 1971).

Apart from incentive payments, the main determinants of professional pay are years of service, relative seniority, and the size of the enterprise or organization where the specialist works. The point is not that young specialists start off on a "poverty wage" (lower earnings are characteristic of most worker's early years of employment), but that long years of service hardly hoist them above it. Table 5.5 demonstrates that middle grade posts—those that lie beneath the specialist level but are above service and manual grades—are also afforded modest remuneration.

Poverty in the Soviet Union is not merely an occupational characteristic. The overall sum paid to the Soviet Union's 50.2 million pensioners in 1981 (35.4 million rubles) translates into an average pension of only 58.8 rubles per month, while the formal minimum for the full pensions of workers and employees at that time was 45 rubles. The minimum for peasants was

TABLE 5.5
Low-Paid Middle-Class Posts Requiring Only Secondary Education

Position	Salary	Source
Technicians	80–100	Ershov, p. 357
	80–150	Vyaskov, p. 182
Medium Grade Veterinary		
Personnel	80–150	Vyaskov, p. 182
Laboratory Assistants	75–85	Ershov, p. 327
Teachers,		
Nursery Personnel	65–128	"Spravochik direcktora shkolv," p. 278
Medium Grade Library Workers	85–100	Vyaskov, p. 81
Medium Grade Club Workers,		
Musicians	80–100	Vyaskov, p. 78

set at 28 rubles in July 1978. The distribution of pensioners' incomes, which included personal pensions at the top end of the scale and partial pensions at the bottom, cannot be obtained directly from official statistics. Pensions, like any other form of income, must be considered in connection with family circumstances, reduced charges for certain amenities, and presumably limited needs. Nevertheless, the fact that the average is so close to the statutory minimum indicates a social problem.

The persons who received less than the average rate were primarily those who, for one reason or another, had not served the necessary number of years, those whose pensions had been fixed at low rates at an earlier time, and those on partial pensions. In recent years, a growing proportion of elderly people have continued to work after reaching retirement age—a trend strongly encouraged by the authorities.

Surprising though it might seem, a reasonably firm indication of at least one type of family need can be derived from official statistics if these are judiciously combined with U.S. estimates of the Soviet Union's child population. Since the end of 1974, families with a per capita income of less than 50 rubles have been entitled to monthly payments of 12 rubles for each child between the ages of one and eight. These benefits are paid for one year at a time at the full rate per child, and must be applied for anew each year. The published total figure for payments in any given year can be regarded as the sum of "child-months" paid in that year. This figure can be set against estimates of the number of children in the corresponding age group, multiplied by 12, to determine the total number of "child-months." The Soviet Union's proportion of subsidized children can be

TABLE 5.6
Child Support Payments

	1975	1976	1977	1978	1979	1980
Total Number of Possible Child Months (Millions)	400.7	405.7	412.0	423.6	431.3	439.1
Total Number of Child Months Paid (Millions)	43.4	75.4	73.1	70.1	67.6	65.3
Percentage of Children Covered	10.8	18.6	17.7	16.5	15.7	14.9

Sources: Narodnoe khoziaistvo SSSR v 1979, p. 557; and *Narodnoe khoziaistvo SSSR v 1980*, p. 527.

estimated by comparing the two nominal totals. Funds paid out in 1980 for child support were evidently sufficient to cover nearly 15 percent of all Soviet children as shown in Table 5.6. It seems likely that most of those entitled to the benefit, predominantly in large and single parent families, would have claimed it. To that extent, the above figures approximate reality. Of course, many children probably move into or out of poverty in any given year. Fifty rubles per capita is well below the prospective poverty threshold of 67 rubles, and if the latter had been used as a cutoff point, the poverty contingent would have been much greater. The degree to which the decline reflects a real reduction in family poverty or extraneous factors is a matter of conjecture.

It does not seem likely that many Soviet families were lifted out of the poverty bracket by the receipt of child care benefits. Twelve rubles is a modest sum compared to the costs of raising a child. Other state payments for children living at home in large families or with single parents varied from only four to a maximum of 15 rubles per head in very large households. Such payments were thus intended to alleviate financial difficulty rather than remove it.

Opportunities for Supplementary Earnings

If people do not earn enough to ensure themselves a reasonably satisfactory standard of living, their natural impulse is to earn more, even though full-time employment might place severe constraints on their time and surplus energy. How do the poor respond in such circumstances? Emigré survey data based on the responses of 200 families suggest that the monthly per capita income of the poor stands at about 59 rubles.[12]

Working overtime, which might appear to be the most obvious means of overcoming poverty, is not particularly widespread outside the agricultural sector, judging from official figures. Indeed, although the basic wage of the respondents averaged a modest 120 rubles a month for working men and 85 for women, only about 18 percent of them worked overtime, and then only for about 1.5 hours per week. In about half of these cases, overtime was not recognized as such by the management or involved voluntary duties for which no payment was forthcoming. Payments, when made, averaged about 20 rubles a month, which was not usually enough to affect family finances significantly. The main reasons given for working overtime were financial need, the requirements of the job itself, or the insistence of the management. About three quarters of the respondents said that the main reasons for not working overtime were the impossibility of finding any work to do, the pressures of one's existing job, and a lack of time. Less than two percent of the respondents were able to take on part-time second jobs.

Authorized work at home, usually devoted to garment-making or traditional crafts, is a possibility for a few people. In recent years, the authorities have encouraged more people to take on productive work, especially as the practice has long antecedents in Russian and Soviet history. Special enterprises that employ no other productive labor have been established in a number of republics. However, by 1980 the number of people involved in home production was still very restricted, apparently amounting only to 140,000 people on a permanent basis. According to one survey, pensioners and invalids accounted for 43 percent of the total; women with young children accounted for 35 percent; and students involved in full-time study accounted for another 18 percent.[13] The link between activities of this kind and the poverty of the practitioners is clear from figures published about their income. About 80 percent of the pensioners and housewives, and fully 100 percent of the students, had a per capita income of under 70 rubles a month, including part-time earnings. The significance of casual or short-term employment is difficult to assess, and only a few of the respondents declared that they were involved in such activities.

Work of an officially approved character is not, however, the only way of earning money in the USSR. There is no doubt that a considerable proportion of the Soviet Union's wage-earners supplement their income through their involvement in the so-called "second" economy.

The question of how the poorest people in the Soviet Union fare can be answered, albeit tentatively, by reference to the results of the above-mentioned émigré survey. Given the overwhelming predominance of Jewish families in the survey, the results might not be typical of the Soviet urban poor, but they are not without significance. Out of a total of 381 working husbands and wives, 151 (40 percent) admitted to various forms of "fiddling" at work, including bribe-taking, accepting various goods and services, and engaging in undeclared private money-earning activities outside the workplace, mainly in various repair jobs and private services.

However, the benefits of such extra activities were in most cases meager. The median income for each practitioner was about 25 rubles. For half of the sample, this raised family income by 14 percent or less. The top fifth of the sample raised their income by 30 percent or more. A few families obviously could not have managed without such extra earnings, but thus far we have not been able to correlate the intensity of such activities with any particular income or occupation group. As can be expected, low incomes are hard-felt by nearly everyone. Ninety-three percent of the families said they experienced financial difficulties toward the end of each month. The extent of borrowing between relatives, friends, and workmates is surprising. Seventy percent of the respondents said they did so regularly, the usual sum being about 15–30 rubles per month.

Food and Clothing

The necessity of maintaining an adequate diet is an important matter for families. The "family baskets" proposed by Sarkisyan and Kuznetsova were based on Soviet dietary norms and had a certain long-term validity. The assortment proposed for the mid-1960s was costed at just under 29 rubles per family member, or 56 percent of all family outgoings. A more ample "prospective" assortment was estimated at 34 rubles, or 51 percent of the total. It seems curious that the first of these variants contained a number of per capita requirements that greatly exceeded national consumption averages, though the two sets are not directly comparable. Thus Sarkisyan and Kuznetsova allowed for the consumption of substantially more meat, vegetables, fish, and vegetable oil than was common for the average man or woman on the street. It would appear that in the mid-1960s, attaining a level of "poverty" consumption was unrealistic for the average citizen, let alone the poor.

From the late 1960s until the end of the 1970s, the Soviet Union's national diet clearly improved. Most of the Sarkisyan and Kuznetsova norms for nutritious foods were surpassed and the consumption of carbohydrates fell. However, even when due regard is made for national idiosyncrasies, the improvement still left average Soviet consumption rates significantly lower than those of the United States. Soviet citizens still eat far less meat, fruit, and vegetable oil, and much more bread, potatoes, and milk than their American counterparts. In assessing how well the poor were eating at the end of the 1970s, émigré survey data suggest that the average "food basket" cost about 33–35 rubles, which was still 55 percent of the average family's income. The sample shows that about 9 percent of all meals were taken outside the home, principally by working adults and schoolchildren. Only one family in the sample had a garden plot.

The absolute sum that Soviet families spend on food has risen with family income, suggesting inadequacy at the lowest levels. Some 75 percent of the respondents stated that there were occasions every month when they were unable to buy essential food products, the average rate being 5–7 times. The reasons for this were given as the absence of goods (30 percent), a lack of goods and money (61 percent), or a lack of money alone (9 percent). These figures are approximate, and because of differences in family size they might not be closely aligned with Kuznetsova and Sarkisyan's norms. Nevertheless, the relative cost of the basket as a proportion of family income showed little change over estimates from the early 1960s. Given Soviet declarations that levels of national consumption have increased, one might have expected evidence of a fall.

As for the nature of the food consumed, the caloric needs of the poor were roughly met, but it was hard to find much in the way of surplus even by the most generous calculations. In general, the diet of the poor closely resembled the national average of a decade and a half earlier and was far behind the declared national average consumption rate for 1979. See Table 5.7. This betokened a meager level of sufficiency.

The above data raise questions concerning the relatively small quantities of bread, potatoes, and sugar that the sample consumed. The most likely explanations are under-reporting, insofar as the wide-spread consumption of these items has negative social overtones; a more selective and controlled diet on the part of the respondents; and a shortfall of 10 percent of the heaviest eaters in the sample—male heads of households.

Detailed sample returns have not yet been fully assembled, but there is no doubt that they will reveal rather specific patterns of purchase. Poor people bought very few vegetables over and above the most common—cabbage, beetroot, onions, and to some extent carrots. Sixty percent bought no fruit through the winter months, and 25 percent bought no salad ingredients. In any case, purchases of these products were in all cases minimal, and averaged less than a kilo per head on a monthly basis. An attempt to categorize meat purchases by quality revealed that average to poor cuts, meat loaf, and low grade salami comprised about 80 percent of the total. Indeed, half of the families said that they normally bought no quality meat at all. Conserved foods, imported citrus fruits, and bananas, cakes, and confectionary items seem to have been absent from the diet of about a third of the sample, and about a half in the case of coffee. Average amounts were again minimal.

TABLE 5.7
Annual Per Capita Food Consumption Patterns (in Kilograms)

Categories	Poverty Diet 1965	Official Per Capita 1965	Official Per Capita 1979	Provisional Poverty Sample Diet 1977–79
Meat, Meat Products, Animal Fat, Conserves	44	41	58	46
Milk, Milk Products	146	251	319	294
Eggs (units)	124	124	233	142
Fish, Fish Products	23	12.6	16.4	10
Sugar	30	34.2	42.8	13
Vegetable Oil	16	7	8.4	6
Potatoes	137	141	119	81
Vegetables	121	72	95	81
Fruits, Berries	28.6	28	38	33
Bread, Macaroni, Flour	145	156	139	101

Sources: Kuznestsova and Sarkisyan, pp. 55–62; Narodnoe khoziaistvo SSSR, 1965, p. 597; and Narodnoe khoziaistvo SSSR, 1979, p. 432.

Selective but significant use was made of collective farm markets by the respondents. Prices in these markets were 2.5 times higher than in state shops in the late 1970s. Thus it seems that such purchases were made reluctantly, as a result of shortages or poor quality. Although it was not feasible to determine exactly how much food the respondents obtained from collective markets, such purchases were important with regard to vegetables, fruit, and good quality meat, especially in the summer months when prices are lower. Only 15–40 percent of the respondents relied exclusively on the state shops for these comestibles. Collective farm market prices inevitably contributed to the high cost of the sample food basket. None of the respondents professed themselves to be "very" satisfied with their diet; 38 percent found it "satisfactory;" and another 11 percent had no particular complaint—perhaps reflecting more success in procurement, ignorance of what might be bought in conditions of plenty, or low expectations.

The costing of poor people's wardrobes is no easy matter. The attention that various families pay to clothing can vary greatly. Apart from personal proclivities, economic and cultural constraints, and the exigencies of climate, age, sex, and work-related requirements also differ among individuals. Soviet requirements are specific in that they must include garments that protect the wearer against severe frosts of many months' duration as well as garments that are comfortable in the short, hot summer. In more opulent families, long-standing tradition demands the purchase of expensive fur headgear, collars, and linings. Children always need such items. In terms of availability, official statistics indicate a steady improvement in the procurement of clothing. By the late 1970s, the supply of clothing, which had been grossly inadequate in the mid-1960s, was shown to have increased by about 2.5 times. This presumably indicates illegal price supplementation and easier second-hand purchasing. According to Soviet statistical handbooks, state prices fell by a percentage point or two. In addition, rising average wages eased the purchase of clothing for the average family.

The purchase of an item of dress, unlike food, is usually a capital outlay. Such purchases also occur relatively infrequently. Estimates of monthly outgoings on clothing can be obtained only by spreading the purchase price of garments over their life-span and allowing for less formal sources of supply. The poverty wardrobe stipulated by Sarkisyan and Kuznetsova is of little use as a yardstick in the case of clothing. It included, for unexplained reasons, a surprisingly lavish assortment of garments, together with bed clothes, various household linens, and soft furnishings. A husband for example, was assumed to have a winter coat, a light coat and mackintosh, two suits, work clothes, a "half coat," two pairs of trousers, seven pairs of socks, shirts, linen, and hats (shoes for some reason were omitted). Such a selection, translated into cloth length, was costed at about 43 rubles per person. This translates into the equivalent of eight and a half years of wear on every item. Low monthly outgoings on the order suggested could have been achieved only by greatly reducing the size of the wardrobe, extending periods of wear, or avoiding the purchase of new garments.

The great majority of male émigré respondents between the ages of 30 and 55 expressed only an average interest in their clothing needs. Nevertheless, 49 percent of them declared that clothing was an "acute problem," and another 46 percent said it was a "problem." As can be seen from Table 5.8, there appears to be a sufficiency of lighter garments, underwear, and hosiery, but marked deficiencies of heavier winter clothing and traditional fur headwear. Thus 27 percent of the respondents managed without a heavy winter coat, and 30 percent had no fur hat. Some 80–90 percent of the male respondents had a light overcoat or mackintosh, which must have been donned in lieu of heavier garments. Only three percent said their overcoats were "new" or "as new." Generally, less than 20 percent of all items were so categorized. Nine percent declared they had only one pair of shoes, and 40 percent had two pairs of outside shoes. Most garments

TABLE 5.8
Male Poverty Sample Wardrobe

Item	Median Number Owned Per Capita	Percentage of Sample Not Owning Item
Winter Coat	0.7	27
Short or Light Coat	1.2	21
Mackintosh	1.3	10
Fur Hat	0.7	30
Suit	1.9	1
Jacket	1.4	8
Trousers	2.6	0
Sweaters	1.8	5
Shoes	2.4	0

Source: Computerized results of poverty sample of 160 employed males. The median estimated value of the respondents' personal wardrobes, including worn items, was about 359 rubles. The approximate value of items listed as "as new" was about 1,000 rubles.

were bought in state shops, but between 10 and 20 percent of the more substantial items came from second-hand shops. The amount of clothing obtained by other means, for example, through home production, was negligible, or simply not admitted to by the respondents.

In considering the problem of housing for the poor, we must inevitably start with published Soviet data on per capita living space. These suggest that by 1981, urban housing stocks amounted to about nine square meters of "living" space, as opposed to "overall useful" space, per person—an increase of perhaps a third over the mid-1960s. The authorities report this advance as an indication of concern for the people's well-being, and indeed the amount of new construction was relatively high in absolute terms. However, the overall annual improvement averaged only 0.15 square meters of living space per person, and still left an overall occupancy rate of about two persons per room.

Obviously, with average occupancies at these levels, overcrowding must still be acute for some Soviet citizens. No conditions approaching those described in Antosenko's 1966 Novosibirsk investigation, which revealed average space endowments of about five square meters, have come to our notice, but émigré respondents apparently faced continuing difficulties. The median amount of living space was 7 square meters per capita, though 10 percent of the respondents had less than 5. Only a quarter had more than the "sanitary minimum" of 9 meters per person. The median family size was 3.9 persons, but no one had an accommodation of more than 3 rooms, and 28 percent lived in one room. Citizens were entitled to apply for rehousing if the amount of space they lived in was less than 4.5-6 meters per person, but some local authorities did not guarantee the sanitary norm upon resettlement.

Overcrowding often involves sharing. A recent article in *Voprosy ekonomiki* stated that as of 1980, some 20 percent of all urban families still lacked accommodation in a separate housing unit—a point recently confirmed in a statistical handbook—while the occupancy rate in Leningrad was authoritatively stated to be 1.9 persons per room in 1978.[14] Of the families in the émigré sample, 26 percent had space in a "multi-occupational" or "communal" flat, and another two percent actually lived in hostels.

Several Soviet observers have suggested that there is little correlation between per capita amounts of living space and one's socio-occupational group. In other words, the poor need not necessarily live in more crowded conditions than other people. Standing against the national average of the late 1970s, the émigré sample average of seven square meters suggests that there is some truth in this assertion.

When asked to give an opinion as to whether richer people in Soviet society had better-quality accommodations, 82 percent of the respondents considered this to be the case. The poor were thought to have less of the influence needed to ease their way through housing waiting lists. Poor people tend to have a lesser chance of living in accommodations erected by powerful organizations or enterprises and a greater chance of ending up in the lower-quality flats that characteristically belong to local soviets. They usually cannot buy ample amounts of living space in cooperative housing projects because such space is extremely expensive as compared to the nominal rents and other expenses that prevail in the state sector. Most of the families who in fact bought their flats were forced to do so by extreme overcrowding in other accommodations. The space they acquired was close to the minimum, and repayments of state loans exacerbated their financial difficulties.

The poverty budgets proposed by Sarkisyan and Kuznetsova assessed housing costs at a mere five percent of all family outgoings, but the poor in practice spend far more. While the average rent in the state sector was indeed very low—about nine rubles a month—family outgoings on rent, electricity, gas, telephone service, heating, cleaning, and repairs ran to about 20 rubles, or 9 percent of family income. Although this figure is low by Western standards if no state subsidies are paid, it is twice the proportion allowed for in the "ideal" minimum budget. It reflects low levels of provision as well as the fact that much repair work must be done by the tenants themselves.

Perhaps the people in the sample were more responsible in the fulfillment of their civic duties than the average Soviet citizen, but it should be reported that only four percent of the respondents admitted to falling into arrears. There were warnings, but no fines or evictions. As for the respondent's reaction to crowded conditions, it would seem that years of difficulty have engendered low expectations. About a third declared themselves very dissatisfied, and another third were rather dissatisfied. The rest believed that they had enough space for their personal comfort. As for structural conditions, most people declared them to be average or reasonable, and a fifth said they were bad or very bad. Although rat infestation was virtually unknown, a third of the respondents reported mice in their dwelling places, and half reported insects.

The degree to which the poorest people are—or feel themselves to be— "a group apart" is highly relevant in any assessment of poverty in the Soviet Union. "Apartness," in a prerogative sense, is something that many people would be unwilling to admit to, even when critically disposed toward a given regime. Emigré responses are in this sense questionable. As it was, less than two percent of the sample admitted to being "very poor," and only a quarter spoke of being "poor" at all. About 11 percent believed that they were not poor, while the remainder, nearly two thirds, had no clear opinion. Their per capita median income, as we have mentioned, was only 59 rubles. When asked whether they considered the "urban poor" to be a separate group in Soviet society, only a quarter of the sample replied in the affirmative. As far as personal mobility was concerned, only about 10 percent perceived any improvement in their general social position over the five years preceding the one under consideration; 73 percent said there was no change; and about 10 percent claimed a marked deterioration. The possibilities of poor people moving upward in any socioeconomic sense were generally thought to be limited.

An explanation for this reticence on the question of social cleavage emerged as opinions on the extent of poverty were solicited. About 90 percent of the respondents believed that poverty was widespread (most estimates varied from 25 percent to 80 percent of the population), while no less than 97 percent thought the average wage in Soviet society considerably lower than the official, published figure. The median estimate was in fact about 120 rubles as against a published figure of 160-163 rubles in 1978-79. This implied either a popular overestimation of the extent of poverty, unrealistic published data, or both.

The degree to which poor or predominantly poor people conglomerate in poor districts is another aspect of mobility about which Soviet scholarship reveals little. Fourteen percent of the sample replied that such differentiation was clear, while another 57 percent said that it was at least discernible. Only 16 percent affirmed that there was no housing differentiation. At the same time, there was much diversity of opinion on what characterized a "poor district." A moment's thought will show that, again, hesitation is reasonable. In the Soviet Union, tight control of urban development and limitations on private construction have tended to suppress rather than encourage locational social distinctions. Standardized housing at nominal rents, the provision of public amenities, and the absence of commercial interests mask rather than reflect social configurations. In this context, it is hardly surprising that the apartment block rather than the district or street tends to be the most socially homogenous unit. Thus while the overwhelming majority of the respondents believed that municipally-owned blocks of flats were likely to be occupied by a mixture of people from various social groups, relatively few believed this to be true of blocks belonging to specific ministries or building cooperatives.

Marxism-Leninism affirms that under capitalism the maintenance of a pool of unemployed and therefore poor people is essential to the working of the economy. Fear of poverty stimulates the proletariat to work harder. The same philosophy develops a curiously functionalist character in the Soviet context in proclaiming that all Soviet citizens are "justly" paid for their efforts. Nevertheless, an avowedly socialist state has long tolerated mass poverty. It would seem that poverty budgets elaborated over two decades ago by Soviet scholars are still apposite to a large proportion of Soviet families today. It might well be that the continuing existence of poverty in the Soviet Union serves as something of an incentive to make able-bodied members of society work a little harder.

Notes

1. *Narodnoe khoziaistvo SSSR, 1922–1982*, p. 476.
2. *Statistical Abstract*, pp. 377 and 415.
3. *Vestnik statistiki*, 1983, no. 6.
4. *Planovoe khoziaistvo*, 1979, no. 9, p. 46.
5. *Trudovoe pravo, entsiklopedicheskii slovar'* (Moscow, 1979), p. 230.
6. *Vestnik statistiki*, 1983, no. 6, p. 33.
7. A. N. Ershov and A. F. Yurchenko, *Spravochnik rukovoditelia predpryatia obshchestvennogo pitania* (Moscow, 1981), pp. 324 ff.
8. *Sotsialisticheski trud*, 1981, no. 1, p. 90.
9. *Perepis 6*, pp. 20 ff.
10. V. A. Artemov, *Problemy sotsial'no-ekonomicheskogo razvitia zapadnosibirskoi derevni* (Novosibirsk, 1981), p. 142.
11. T. I. Zaslavskaya and V. A. Kalmyk, *Sovremennaia sibirskaia derevnia*, vol. 1 (Novosibirsk, 1975), p. 92.

12. This survey was conducted by the author. Data for the survey were compiled in 1984.

13. A. G. Novitski and G. V. Mil', "Zanyatost' pensionerov" (Moscow, 1981), pp. 185 and 188.

14. *Voprosi ekonomiki*, 1981, no. 5, p. 12.

6. Medical Care in the Soviet Union: Promises and Realities

This chapter examines the "realities" of the Soviet health care system and its contribution to the quality of life in the Soviet Union. It posits that any medical system is the result of the universalistic forces of science and technology and the particular cultural and historical setting in which it exists. Thus an understanding of Soviet medicine is impossible without an understanding of the major features of Soviet society and Soviet life, including its system of social stratification and inequalities, which results in different medical "realities" depending on where specific individuals are located.

One cannot speak of the quality of life without speaking of health, for without health, whatever a society has to offer cannot be enjoyed. Indeed, this is what makes the principle of free and universally accessible medical service at the expense of society so attractive. There is no doubt that this principle is heartily endorsed by the people of the Soviet Union. It derives from the idea that health is such an indispensable aspect of the quality of life that, like education, its maintenance, enhancement, and repair should not be left to the vagaries of the market place, the individual's "ability to pay," or one's social origins or position. Medical care, which in earlier times was considered to be an item of personal consumption that one bought if one could afford it, or went without if one could not, is now considered a personal right.

Strange as it seems, Stalin might well deserve the credit for having presided over the development of Soviet socialized medicine. His successors have not altered the blueprint; they have only expanded the size of the enterprise. Mentioning Stalin and medicine in the same breath might at first seem surprising. The very idea of state-provided medical care flies against many assumptions regarding the nature of a totalitarian society. Medicine embodies a profound humanitarian concern and tradition that centers on helping the sick, the wounded, and the suffering. On the other hand, totalitarian societies rarely seem to be concerned with the individual's suffering, welfare, or well-being.

There are two interrelated yet distinct ways of examining the impact of morbidity and premature mortality. Morbidity is a generic term denoting illness, trauma, and disease—i.e., any impairment to the health of the individual. Premature or early mortality refers to deaths considered to have occurred before a "normal" or "natural" age. The first concerns the effects of morbidity and premature mortality on the individual in terms of the suffering, dependency, and anxieties they arouse as a result of their close association with death. The second has to do with their impact on social systems. The first can be called a "subjective" concern related to the quality of life; the second a "functional" or "societal" concern. The latter provides an important explanatory key for understanding the Soviet health care system.

The Soviet regime has not been particularly worried about the subjective impact of illness, but it has recognized that health is an important national resource, and illness and premature mortality are a critical threat to that resource. Obsessed with production and productivity since the first five-year plans, the Soviet leadership reasoned that the USSR could not industrialize or militarize with a population subject to high rates of debility, morbidity, and premature mortality. Not only does the principle of universal health care have a strong ideological appeal; it must also be seen as contributing to the functional strength of a given society, regardless of its political nature. This calculus is not much different from the idea of establishing a military medical corps to protect, maintain, repair and enhance the working and fighting capacity of its personnel. At the same time, there is every reason to expect that functionally motivated improvements in the Soviet medical system will simultaneously increase the quality of life in the Soviet Union. Indeed, "good health" is a fundamental ingredient of the "good life."

The Soviet medical care system is an excellent illustration of the gallicism *en principe*. In principle, it guarantees every citizen the full gamut of clinical and preventive services at the expense of the state. In reality, if one judges from Soviet sources and the rare testimony of outside observers, the system is but a pale reflection of what it claims to be. Unfortunately, there is no way of evaluating whether the gap between promise and reality is greater or smaller in medicine than in any other area of Soviet society.

The Principles of Soviet Socialized Medicine

On the most general level, the present Soviet constitution states that each Soviet citizen is entitled to qualified medical care in case of illness, at no cost to the individual.[1] The implementation of this general entitlement is via "Soviet socialized medicine," usually described as a socialist system of governmental or collective measures, having as their general purpose the prevention and treatment of illness, the provision of healthy working and living conditions, high levels of work capacity, and long life expectancy.[2] As such, the system has several well-defined formal characteristics that serve as bridges between generalized statements of intent and the actual organization and management of health care services. Public health and personal medical care are state responsibilities and a function of government; all public health care measures take place within a planned framework; the medical system is centralized and standardized; medical care and allied services are made available to the population at no direct cost at the time that services are provided; prevention stands at the core of the Soviet medical system; the system embodies a unity of theory and practice; and as the medical system belongs to the people, the people must help to support it, for example, through volunteer activities. Finally, due to the universal nature of the system, medical services are provided on a priority basis.

It should be noted that the Soviet medical system is not only the responsibility of society and of the state; it is also a functional tool in the hands of the polity in pursuit of its goals and programs. Such a system is incompatible with a private system unresponsive to governmental priorities. It is also incompatible with a strong and relatively autonomous medical profession, oriented both to the expressive welfare of the population and its own power, wealth, and privilege. Thus it is hardly surprising that there is no "medical profession" in the Soviet Union if this is taken to mean a relatively independent corporate group entitled to organize its members and take "political" stands in opposition to governmental policy. Whatever one's view of the American Medical Association or other similar associations in the West, there is no equivalent in the Soviet Union. Doctors are state functionaries, with all that this implies.

Equally important, the Soviet medical system is financed by the state treasury. Thus, in contrast to the United States, one can determine the percentage of the Soviet Union's gross national product (GNP) and the percentage of its national, republican, and lower administrative budgets that are allocated to medical care. The Soviets keep the salaries of their medical personnel at very low levels compared to other occupations in the Soviet Union, let alone physicians' incomes in the West. The Soviet medical system can be defined as labor rather than capital intensive in the sense that labor is cheap, and equipment and medical technology is expensive.

Soviet medicine is based on a prepaid (prospective) payment scheme that is considerably cheaper to operate than a reimbursement (retrospective) or insurance system in which services are rendered and bills are submitted. The latter system inflates costs in Western Europe and the United States. With some exceptions, Soviet citizens are not required to pay for services at the time that medical services are performed. Soviet propaganda continually stresses that the government provides medical care to its people almost as an act of generosity compared to the parsimony of capitalistic systems. The fact of the matter is that these services are paid for by Soviet citizens through taxes, unseen deductions, and levies. This is similar to how health care benefits are paid for by American employers. Both systems cause a reduction in discretionary incomes. Moreover, the evidence suggests that to some degree the idea of "free" medical care in the Soviet Union is a myth, not only because nothing is free, but because most Soviet citizens feel it necessary to give additional payments to physicians, nurses, and hospital attendants in order to receive better medical attention. Unfortunately, one cannot calculate what these "under the table" payments amount to or how much of the Soviet GNP they represent.

During the last few years, however, the percentage of the Soviet GNP officially allocated to the health care system has decreased by more than 20 percent. In 1950, 5.2 percent of all budgetary allocations went to health care. The proportion rose to 6.6 percent in 1960, then fell to 6.0 in 1970, 5.3 percent in 1975, 5.2 percent in 1978, and 5.0 in 1980.[3] Recent estimates of Soviet health care allocations both in ruble and dollar amounts are contained in Table 6.1.[4] The figures in parentheses refer to the percentage of the Soviet GNP allocated to health care. Whether calculated in rubles or dollars, these estimates indicate that health care expenditures decreased by more than 20 percent between 1955 and 1977, though absolute figures have more than doubled. According to Christopher Davis, per capita expenditures on medical care controlled by the Ministry of Health rose from about 29 rubles in 1965 to 57 rubles in 1980.[5] However, these figures are not corrected for inflation.

Recent reports during the last decade to the effect that infant mortality in the Soviet Union has increased by more than 25 percent have prompted some observers to tie this phenomenon to a degradation of the Soviet medical care system.[6] The relationship between medical care and infant mortality is not direct. Generally speaking, infant mortality is affected both by medical and nonmedical factors, the latter having a greater effect than the former. Nonmedical factors include considerations such as general economic well-being, housing conditions, and nutrition. It remains unclear whether the increase is "real," the result of better reporting, or both.

TABLE 6.1
Soviet GNP and Health Expenditures, 1955-1977

	1955	%	1965	%	1975	%	1976	%	1977	%
	1976 Rubles (billions)									
GNP	174	100	304	100	456	100	505	100	533	100
Health Care	5	2.9	8	2.6	11	2.3	11	2.2	11	2.1
	1976 Dollars (billions)									
GNP	464	100	793	100	1,202	100	1,253	100	1,294	100
Health Care	45	9.7	69	8.7	94	7.8	96	7.7	97	7.5

Source: Imogene Edwards, Margaret Hughes, and James Noren, "U.S. and U.S.S.R.: Comparisons of GNP," in *Soviet Economy in a Time of Change*, vol. 1, U.S. Congress, Joint Economic Committee (Washington, D.C., 1979), pp. 369-399.

The idea that Soviet medical services are provided on a priority basis might surprise those still under the impression that Soviet society is egalitarian. The Soviet Union lacks a single system of health care equally available to all citizens, such as the British National Health Service. Rather, the Soviet medical system is composed of several networks of different quality that deal with different populations and administrations.

The Reality of Soviet Socialized Medicine

Although the basic problems posed by morbidity and early mortality are a universal part of the human condition, our responses to these problems have been extremely varied, both throughout the ages and cross-culturally. However, science and of technology have tended to introduce an element of uniformity into our responses. Consequently, medical care can be seen as the result of at least two forces—particularistic elements, which are usually national or sociocultural in nature, and the universalistic elements of science and technology.

As a result of contemporary medical technology, one can argue that hospitals are increasingly likely to be organized and managed in a similar manner regardless of whether they are found in the Soviet Union, Sweden, France, or Nigeria. However, it seems that particularistic sociocultural factors shape the universalistic aspects of modern science and technology. If we fail to recognize the significance of these particularistic elements, we shall overlook an important explanatory framework. A balanced view of the Soviet medical system should therefore take account of both the universal aspects of contemporary Soviet medicine and the particularistic features of everyday Soviet life—the scarcity, the bureaucracy, the officiousness of state employees, the absurdities of formal rules, and the inequities that permeate it from top to bottom. A Soviet hospital is as much a distinctly Soviet entity as a medical one.

An important book by William A. Knaus, *Inside Russian Medicine*, provides us with a rare view of Soviet medicine usually not available to outsiders.[7] Admittedly, these views might seem overly critical, or based on limited contacts and experiences. They are the observations of a Western physician accustomed to working in a high-technology atmosphere under conditions that simply cannot be matched in the Soviet Union, except perhaps in facilities reserved for the Soviet elite. Yet most of his observations are corroborated by Soviet sources.

Stratification

Although the scientific universalism that underlies modern medicine should make it "indivisible," every society has more than one medical system. It seems ironic that a society whose original ideological appeal was equality—in the health field, its goal was the elimination of first and second class medicines—actually spawned a multi-class medical system. This was the case almost from the beginning, when those who governed received special attention and rations. Such practices were institutionalized as the result of Stalin's policy of eliminating egalitarianism as a "leftist" or "infantile" deviation in the early 1930s. Soviet society has given birth to an elaborate system of rankings and distinctions between those who are very important, important, and not so important.[8] The provision of medical care also follows such differentiations. Broadly speaking, the provision of medical services is divided into two unequal categories—territorial and closed networks. Territorial networks serve the general population and are accessible by virtue of residence. One's place of residence determines where one obtains one's primary medical care. Closed networks, on the other hand, are reserved for special groups.

Facilities reserved for the employees of industries with over a certain number of personnel are at the lowest level of the closed networks. Next are the special facilities of certain agencies or ministries, such as the armed forces, the Ministry of Internal Affairs, and the railroads. Another network is reserved for intellectual elites, such as members of the Academy of Sciences, the Union of Soviet Writers, and artists of the first rank. This is sometimes referred to as the "fourth administration" of the Ministry of Health Protection. With apologies to Alexander Solzhenitsyn, this network might also be called the "medical archipelago." Just as all Soviet cities have special detention facilities for prisoners, all maintain specialized clinics and hospitals where the elites can receive medical care protected from the scrutiny of the common man. These are either free-standing facilities or restricted sections of general hospitals.[9] They resemble, to some extent, the private wings of American hospitals or amenity beds in Great Britain, which are reserved for those who want more privacy, more luxury, and better, more attentive medical care. The major distinction, however, is that Soviet elites do not personally pay for these facilities, but receive quality medical care as a perquisite of rank, paid for by the state—in fact paid for with the taxes of ordinary citizens who must content themselves with run-of-the-mill hospitals and clinics.

Needless to say, these hospitals and clinics are better equipped than those found in ordinary health care networks. In the event that certain blood tests cannot be performed in the Soviet Union, samples are routinely flown to laboratories in Helsinki, and the results are flown back to Moscow, according to Knaus. Even within the Kremlin polyclinic, distinctions are made by rank. According to Knaus, "Deputy ministers and persons of lower rank are seen in regular private cubicles, but ministers have special examining rooms. . . . There are carpets on the floor, bookcases, a leather couch, and heavy red drapes over the windows. It is like a living room, not a clinic."[10] Equipment, drugs, and procedures not available in the Soviet Union are imported from abroad, either from Soviet satellites or from the West if necessary. In some instances, top specialists are invited to come to the Soviet Union to consult on important cases or perform operations.[11]

There are differences of opinion in the Soviet Union as to the quality of physicians who serve the members of the upper classes. Some view them as political appointees who are mediocre physicians. Others feel that they are top-ranking members of the medical profession. As a rule, elites prefer expert professionals to politically reliable hacks, and there is no reason that Soviet officials are different, particularly when their health and well-being are concerned.

But to what extent does medical stratification pose a "functional" problem to Soviet society? If we assume that health care has some impact on morbidity and mortality, then the fact that the great majority of the population receives second- or third-rate medical care might have some functional impact. Insofar as the state of Soviet health care in both subjective and functional terms adds to the quality of life in the Soviet Union, there is little doubt that life is more enjoyable if one is treated at a clinic that belongs to the "fourth administration" than in a neighborhood clinic or a medical dispensary in a village setting.

Bureaucracy

By no means is the Soviet medical care system immune to the bureaucratization of Soviet life. In fact, the bureaucratization of medicine and hospital care is a worldwide phenomenon—the result of the growing size of medical care facilities, increased specialization, the need for more coordination and integration, and third party payments. But there seems to be a special quality to the impact of bureaucratization on Soviet medicine that has resulted in the deprofessionalization of medical services, the unwillingness of health care workers to make personal decisions or shoulder personal responsibility, and a tendency to practice a medicine "by the numbers," which has made the accommodation of special situations, including emergencies, often difficult. Apparently, the Soviet medical system is routinized and proceeds according to officially established and rigid norms. Thus physicians and other personnel are expected to work a specific number of hours per day and to see a specific number of patients per hour. The number varies with one's specialty. This encourages a segmental sense of responsibility and a nine-to-five mentality. Soviet physicians will not hesitate to leave their work at the end of the day, even though patients might still be waiting to see them. They assume that someone else will take care of the sick, or that the patients will come back the next day.[12]

The existence of bureaucratic practices and attitudes in the Soviet medical care system is hardly a state secret. Time and again, Soviet newspapers such as Literaturnaia gazeta have reported complaints about the rigidities of health institutions.[13] Soviet hospitals will not admit new patients after a specific hour in mid-afternoon. In Irkutsk, for example, all emergency admissions are referred to a single designated city hospital after 3:00 p.m.[14] Every condition is tariffed according to a specific number of hospital days. A delivery is usually nine days; an appendectomy is 10 days; and a hysterectomy is two weeks. Even if the patient is well enough to be discharged earlier, this is not allowed.[15] Knaus reports that to order a radioisotope scan of the liver in Kishinev (a city in the Moldavian republic) requires five separate forms, the approval of six persons, and a 10-day wait.[16] Hospitals are assigned "death quotas," and investigations will follow if they exceed these quotas. As a result, hospitals will often refuse to admit terminally ill patients. Instead, their families are encouraged to take them home to die there.

Patients are often subjected to standardized procedures whether they need them or not. Very often, these bureaucratic routines degenerate into a meaningless ritual. For example, as the belief persists that infections are brought into hospitals from the outside, visitors are forbidden to retain their coats while in hospitals, and books and newspapers cannot ever be placed on a bed for fear of contamination. While these meaningless rules are ferociously enforced, sterility is poorly observed in operating rooms in disregard of the fact that most infections originate within hospitals. As a result, the incidence of postoperative infection is very high, affecting about one-third of all patients operated on. Most physicians who discussed the infection problem with Knaus preferred to compare the Soviet incidence of postoperative infection with the level found in developing countries such as Afghanistan, rather than with the United States or other developed nations.[17]

Bureaucratically determined procedures overload physicians in outpatient clinics, thereby reducing the time they can spend on patients who really need to see a doctor. Thus, according to an article in *Literaturnaia gazeta*, ". . . only one-third of the patients [at the polyclinic] had come for their initial appointment. The rest were there for follow-up. Only a few needed to see a doctor on that particular day; their appointments had all been made in accordance with the instruction. If it were not for this instruction . . . a polyclinic physician would have half as many patients . . . in some cases only one-third. Hence the doctor could give each of them 15 or even 20 minutes, instead of just 7 . . . we must place more faith in the physician and not force his actions into a Procrustean bed of instructions."[18]

There is nothing particularly lethal about Soviet bureaucratic routines in hotels, dining rooms, railroad stations, housing offices, retail stores, or government offices. Such are the annoyances of daily life in the Soviet Union. But the existence of the same phenomena in a system where one deals with human lives, with suffering, and with iatrogenic problems, suggests that deeply ingrained bureaucratic patterns can cause more than simple irritation.

Falsification

The use of falsification, "Potemkin villages," and "Dead Souls" in official data is an old tradition inherited from the Russian past that is alive and well in the Soviet medical system. This is why Soviet statistical data about health care must be taken with a grain of salt. Apparently, there are quotas for all types of operations, and these quotas are always met, at least on paper. If the number of operations actually performed falls below expectations, more cases are invented to fill the quota. The same applies to hospital occupancy rates. If these were to decrease, then budgets and supplies might be curtailed in the next fiscal year. As a result, high occupancy rates are routinely reported, whatever the actual situation might be.[19]

Hospital directors and managers play the same game as industrial managers. It is not unusual, nor seen as improper, for hospital administrators to request twice as many supplies as they need because they know they will be lucky to get half of what they ask for. Nor is it unusual for them to document this "need." According to Knaus, "such false reporting . . . has never been considered dishonest . . . the easiest way to stay out of trouble is to do exactly what is expected."[20] Here again, we are dealing with a phenomenon that is common in Soviet life and is publicly acknowledged as such. Several years ago, Dr. Boris Petrovskii, the former minister of health, said that hospitals in more than 60 cities had been built to be attached to emergency care stations. "However," he added, "in some cities they exist only formally."[21] By this, he meant that they exist only on paper.

The Soviet Union is proud of its system of preventive examinations, or *dispensarizatsia*. Here again, quotas are often met through the expediency of filling out forms without actually conducting examinations. The results of these ghost examinations are aggregated and published as another example of the preventive orientation of Soviet medicine. If sometimes the facts are too unpleasant or embarrassing, their publication is simply discontinued. For example, the absence of infant mortality statistics hardly means that there is no more infant mortality in the Soviet Union. On the contrary, it suggests that infant mortality levels have increased or remained relatively high. Indeed, Dr. Alexander Smirnov of the State Planning Commission reported in the course of a press conference held in Moscow in June 1981 that the infant mortality rate from 1978 to 1980 was approximately 28 per 1,000—i.e., not lower than the latest officially published figures for 1974 (27.9 per 1,000).[22]

According to Murray Feshbach, no information on life expectancy has been published for any year since 1971-72, and the same is true of age and sex specific death rates since 1973-74, cause of death data by age group since 1971-72, the number of doctors by specialty for any year since 1975, and age data from the 1979 census.[23] Given the bureaucratic nature of Soviet medical care, one can posit that the widespread misreporting of information and statistical data can only have a deleterious effect on the general provision of health services, and consequently on the quality of life in the Soviet Union.

Doctor-Patient and Nurse-Patient Relationships

The Soviets repeatedly claim that one of the greatest advantages of socialized medicine is that it has removed the "capitalistic cash nexus" between doctor and patient. According to Dr. D. I. Pisarev, "The Soviet physician is freed from any kind of financial arrangements with the patient . . . for the first time in the history of mankind the problem of the relationship between the physician and patient has been solved in the right way. The physician can do everything that is in his power to help the patient, since he has at his disposal everything that is necessary for free medical care for anyone . . . in capitalist countries private capital has made medicine an object of sale and purchase."[24]

Given the emotional significance of illness and the dependency needs it often triggers, nothing seems more appealing than the idea of a well-trained, scientifically-qualified physician who is devoted to the welfare of his or her patient to the exclusion of all other considerations, particularly pecuniary ones. However, the general impression that emerges from the reports of outside observers as well as Soviet sources is that Soviet physicians often display a lack of sensitivity to the feelings and emotions of their patients. This phenomenon has many roots, but anyone who has dealt with officials in the Soviet Union can well appreciate that this pattern is not unique to doctors. As mentioned above, Soviet doctors know they will be paid irrespective of their performance. Even in the case of the grossest infractions, personal responsibility is minimized.

Contrary to official theories, this encourages indifference, "formalism," and a nine-to-five mentality. Indeed, there is little incentive, except a personal one, to be gentle and considerate with patients, except when they are willing to present their doctors and nurses with supplementary payments or gifts. Furthermore, there is evidence that Soviet physicians receive very little orientation or training in medical psychology.

According to a *Literaturnaia gazeta* article written by Pavel Beilin, "Until recently, medical psychology and psychotherapy in fact were not taught. . . . Recently they started to teach these, but much too little. In all, 19 hours were allocated to medical psychology out of 7,800 hours. In other words, for knowledge of the body—7,781 hours, for knowledge of the soul [*dusha*]—19."[25] Hospital physicians tend to be brusque with their patients, and too many physicians regard patients as children who understand nothing about their health or their bodies.

These qualities tend to be exhibited more often in hospitals than in outpatient clinics, where patients and doctors may have a more sustained relationship. Hospital physicians rarely expect to see their patients more than a few times, as they are often rotated. Patients tend to be "processed" rather than treated as human beings who have fears, anxieties, and emotions. Reporting on a survey of 2,000 letters written by patients in Kiev, *Literaturnaia gazeta* noted that one of the major themes was the insensitivity of Soviet doctors who themselves feel frustrated, hampered by bureaucratic restrictions, a lack of supplies, and the absence of alternative treatment possibilities. One doctor was reported to have said to a patient, "You have a stomach ulcer and diabetes. You will not survive an operation. I simply do not know what to do with you."[26]

This attitude is also extended to the relatives of patients. They are often treated in the same way as those who inquire at police stations about a spouse or relative—with indifference and condescension, if not cruelty. Not surprisingly, Soviet hospitals are generally feared, as they were in the United States about a century ago. This is not only because patients fear rough and impersonal handling by indifferent staff members, but also because the Soviet Union's lack of supplies and equipment can make a hospital stay an episode dangerous to one's life and health, not to mention one's emotions.

Furthermore, the use of mental hospitals to incarcerate dissidents only emphasizes the similarities between Soviet hospitals and prisons.

Given the distance between hospital doctors and patients in the Soviet Union, the accepted view is that one does not question the judgement of a doctor. To do so would be *nekul'turno*—an act of arrogance. This attitude is often cultivated by doctors and nurses, for it makes their life and work easier.

Patients are referred to hospitals by clinic doctors. These doctors have no say or control over the care of hospitalized patients because of the institutional separation between outpatient polyclinics and inpatient hospitals. Generally speaking, the relationship between polyclinic physicians and patients is relatively close because they remain together for much longer periods of time than hospital doctors and their patients. Patients in territorial medical networks are assigned to doctors who serve them as general practitioners on the basis of residence.

One-third of all outpatient practitioners have held their jobs for less than a year, according to Paikin and Silina, and 3–10 percent of all such doctors have worked at the same place for more than 10 years.[27] However, as the conditions of everyday existence are similar for the average patient and the polyclinic doctor, social distances are lessened. Most Soviet doctors (*vrachi*), particularly the therapeutists (*terapevti*), practice a kind of relaxed, comforting, common sense, low technology type of medicine based on the assumption that most maladies will improve of themselves, that some conditions should be referred to specialists, and that the rest are beyond remedy. Thus, if time is available, a visit to a polyclinic doctor might approach a kind of social chit-chat. However, most of one's time is taken up by the necessity of filling out forms and other bureaucratic requirements. "I go through my appointments without looking up," admitted a woman physician who was required to see 36 patients every four hours.[28] While paying lip service to the patient, it seems that patient satisfaction is not considered important in evaluating medical services in the Soviet Union.

Relationships between patients and nurses appear to be even worse than those between hospital doctors and patients. Generally speaking, Soviet nurses are poorly educated and trained, do not have the prestige and power of physicians, and take out their frustrations on their patients. The most capable nurses aspire to move upward and become physicians themselves. In fact, many still partake of the attitude that nursing is not quite a respectable profession—a view that was prevalent in the West about a century ago. Due to the low quality of nursing in the Soviet Union and the relatively low incomes of health care personnel, patients often try to secure a more personal attitude from the doctors and nurses with money and gifts. To a certain extent, this negates the advantages of "free" medical care.

Soviet Hospitals

The Soviet Union has more hospital beds per capita than the United States and indeed most other nations. However, there tends to be very little in these hospitals in terms of equipment and medical technology. Housing conditions are such that it remains difficult to keep a sick person at home. This may be the reason that Soviet patients tend to stay hospitalized for relatively longer periods of time and tend to be hospitalized more frequently than their American counterparts. One might say that many Soviet hospitals are dormitories for individuals who do not feel well. Knaus reports that one-third of all Soviet hospitals do not have adequate laboratories for blood transfusion, and when they actually exist they are frequently closed, particularly at night and on weekends.

Many hospitals are located in old, dilapidated buildings that are adequate as dormitories, but are hardly typical of the kind of hospital that has become commonplace in the West. The Botkin Hospital in Moscow, which consists of prerevolutionary and more recent buildings, is fairly well-known because Westerners are sometimes hospitalized there. However, like many older Soviet hospitals, its toilet facilities are primitive. On the floor where an American citizen was hospitalized, there were three toilets for 76 men. These had no seats, and unless one brought along a morning copy of *Pravda*, no toilet paper. Compounding the problem, Soviet hospitals dispense enemas as readily as American hospitals give back rubs. Hospital toilets always seem to be in use, and they frequently overflow, covering bathroom floors with a sticky mixture of urine and feces.[29]

If this is the case for a Moscow hospital that admits foreigners, one can well imagine the situation in other hospitals, particularly outside the capital. Not surprisingly, most Soviet citizens feel that hospitals are to be kept away from, thus justifying the etymological roots of the Russian word for hospital, bol', which denotes pain and suffering. Hospital care is often primitive; operations are performed without required sterility precautions; and equipment and supplies are often in short supply or unavailable. Knaus even reports the amazing fact that the Soviet Union apparently does not manufacture wheelchairs. When patients cannot move on their own, they are placed on litters or stretchers. As the diet in Soviet hospitals is skimpy and monotonous, relatives and friends customarily bring or send food parcels to patients. It is not unknown for staff members to appropriate food destined for patients, as is sometimes the case in prisons.[30]

Western hospitals have been accused of being crisis-oriented, obsessed with technology, depersonalized, and expensive—and the accusation is sometimes well-justified. Such problems can lead to errors, the provision of unneeded services, and unnecessary surgery. But whereas American hospitals sometimes do too much for their patients, the reverse seems to be the case for Soviet hospitals. The Soviet hospital, while it partakes of many of the universal characteristics of hospitals around the world, is also a uniquely Soviet institution.

Biomedical Technology

If one finds Western health care depersonalized, inhuman, and alienating, the labor intensive nature of Soviet medicine might be seen as a positive feature of the system. Soviet patients see their doctors more often and are admitted to hospitals more frequently than their American counterparts. But in the final analysis, modern medicine is more than the mere "laying of hands." Modern medicine must have at its disposal the necessary equipment and supplies to practice medicine according to the state of the art, and the Soviet health care system is in principle dedicated to this proposition. Anyone familiar with Soviet production and distribution processes will find that the supply of medical equipment is plagued by the same general deficiencies. Given the fact that the health care system is not a high priority area, it suffers from the same shortages and erratic distribution problems as the rest of the consumer economy.

A review of Soviet materials on pharmaceutical products conducted several years ago revealed an extremely inefficient system riddled by bureaucracy, poor quality, and severe problems relating to production, shortages, distribution, retailing, and procedures to supply physicians with information about new medical items.[31] The American pharmaceutical system can be described as relatively expensive at the point of purchase, but efficient in supplying American patients and hospitals with precisely what is needed. In contrast, Soviet patients are often unable to obtain prescription or nonprescription items, sometimes only with difficulty, even though retail prices are relatively low. Time and again, complaints are voiced that pharmaceuticals are unavailable, and even the simplest items of medical care—bandages, absorbent cotton, aspirin, thermometers, and iodine—are difficult to procure. The supply of pharmaceuticals and medical equipment remains deficient and erratic to this day. The result is a black or "grey" market in drugs unavailable either from pharmacies or for use by hospital physicians. Hospitals tend not to have enough money to purchase needed equipment, and even when the money is available, equipment is often unavailable, of poor quality, or unusable.

Not only do these shortcomings affect clinical medicine; they also impede the practice of preventative medicine—the keystone of the Soviet medical system. For example, a lack of laboratory facilities to detect streptococcal infections has led to a high incidence of rheumatic disease and constitutes a definite health risk for thousands of Soviet children. Year after year, complaints are voiced in "investigative" articles and letters to newspapers confirming the shortcomings of the Soviet medical system. These usually reveal the incredibly inefficient manner in which medical supplies and pharmaceuticals are produced. Like peeling off the layers of an endless onion, those reporters who try to get at the root-cause of the problem always discover another link in the chain. Responsible officials, against whom public anger can be directed, are identified. Fines are imposed, but to no avail, particularly as they never come out of the pockets of the "guilty" parties. Needless to say, these problems are unlikely to be found in the health care network reserved for the elites.

The Quality of Care

The Soviet approach to health care is quantitative and labor intensive. With its plethora of physicians and hospital beds, Soviet medicine appears impressive when one looks at statistical tables proving the undeniable progress of the system since the revolution. In a truly dialectical sense, it seems possible that quantitative changes lead to qualitative ones. Yet a closer examination of clinical practices suggests that the quality of Soviet medical care is low when using West European and American practices as a measuring rod. In some instances, Soviet practices resemble what one witnesses in developing countries. The Soviet Union's level of infant mortality is certainly not what one might expect of a highly industrialized nation that pioneered a system of socialized medicine, and whose economy is the second largest in the world. With the exception of the elites for whom the best medical care is available or imported, the Soviet population receives mass, mediocre medical care, with little attention to detail, quality, or personal feelings and emotions.

This is not to say that Soviet medicine must continue to be a low quality operation. It could very well improve as Soviet officials and health care authorities increasingly realize how backward their system really is in comparison to what it could be. Any such improvements will require significantly larger budgetary allocations and important changes in the structure of the system and the motivation and attitudes of health care personnel. However, as the Soviet Union has experienced slower economic growth in recent years, a reordering of priorities and a significant increase in the quality of medical care is most unlikely at this historical juncture. Indeed, the reverse seems to be in the cards if rising death and infant mortality rates are any indication.

Conclusions

To a large extent, the Soviet medical system shares many of the features of the health care systems of other contemporary industrial societies. But the severe problems facing Soviet medicine are unlikely to be remedied as a result of financial exigencies tied in large part to the scale of Soviet defense expenditures. Given the investment priorities of the Soviet government, the fraction of the Soviet GNP devoted to health care is considerably smaller than the U.S. level, and recently it has decreased. At present, the Soviet Union spends about one-third as much as the United States on health care, though this is only a very rough estimate. Extra payments channelled into the second economy would lead to an upward revision of this estimate as the relatively low salaries of Soviet health care personnel are compensated for by illegal means.

It would be foolish to argue that there is no problem in Soviet medicine that cannot be solved with a few billion rubles. Even the United States cannot solve all of its medical problems by throwing money at them. The Soviet health care system would benefit from additional appropriations, but not necessarily to the degree we might expect. For example, one of the perennial complaints of the Health Ministry is that budgetary appropriations to build or repair hospitals are not used by health authorities, ostensibly because they cannot fund personnel and materials to do the job. And if the medical industry does not produce certain types of sutures, antibiotics, respirators, or even good artificial eyes, additional funding will not help unless such items are purchased abroad. Thus the problems of the Soviet medical system stem from the general problems of Soviet society, and the solution to the former are not possible without solutions to the latter.

The degree to which the reality of Soviet medical care contributes to the quality of life in the Soviet Union is affected by the fact that different populations are served by different medical systems. Members of the Kremlin elite served by the "fourth administration" are treated quite differently than cotton farmers in Kirghizia. It is therefore important to speak of the realities rather than the promises of Soviet medicine.

Notes

1. Article 42 of the Soviet constitution adopted in 1977 states that "Citizens of the USSR have the right to health protection. This right is ensured by free, qualified medical care provided by state health institutions; by extension of the network of therapeutic and health-building institutions; by the development and improvement of safety and hygiene in industry; by carrying out broad prophylactic measures; by measures to improve the environment; by special care for the health of youth, including prohibition of child labor, excluding work done by children as part of the school curriculum; and by developing research to prevent and reduce the incidence of disease and ensure citizens a long and active life."

2. Mark G. Field, *Soviet Socialized Medicine* (New York: Free Press, 1967), pp. 42–48.

3. Christopher Davis and Murray Feshbach, "Rising Infant Mortality in the USSR in the 1970's," U.S. Department of Commerce, Bureau of the Census (Washington, D.C., 1980), p. 30. Figures for 1965, 1970, 1975, and 1980 are from Christopher Davis, "Economic Problems of the Soviet Health System," Wharton Econometric Forecasting Associates, September 7, 1982, p. 5.

4. Imogene Edwards, Margaret Hughes, and James Noren, "U.S. and U.S.S.R.: Comparisons of GNP," in *Soviet Economy in a Time of Change*, vol. 1, U.S. Congress, Joint Economic Committee (Washington, D.C., 1979), pp. 369–399.

5. Davis, "Economic Problems of the Soviet Health System," p. 5.

6. Davis and Feshbach, "Rising Infant Mortality in the USSR in the 1970's," p. 30.

7. William A. Knaus, *Inside Russian Medicine* (New York: Everest, 1981), pp. 356–357.

8. See, for example, Walter D. Connor, *Socialism, Politics and Equality* (New York: Columbia University Press, 1979); Mervyn Matthews, *Class and Society in Soviet Russia* (New York: Walker, 1972); and Frank Parkin, *Class Inequality and Political Order* (New York: Praeger, 1971).

9. In Moscow, the Kremlin polyclinic is on Kalinin Prospekt; in Leningrad it is near the Neva river and the Winter Palace; and in Irkutsk it is a pink and white four-story building surrounded by large shade trees and protected by a high iron fence. See Knaus, *Inside Russian Medicine*, "Special Care for Special People," pp. 299ff.

10. Knaus, *Inside Russian Medicine*, p. 300.

11. Thus Dr. Michael DeBakey was asked to come to Moscow in 1972 and 1973, first to consult and then to operate on Mstislav Keldish, the president of the Soviet Academy of Sciences in 1972 and 1973. In 1979, Warren Zapol of the Massachusetts General Hospital was summoned to the Soviet Union to operate on the eldest daughter of Dr. Vladimir Burakowski, an internationally known cardiovascular surgeon and director of the Bakulev Institute of Cardiovascular Surgery. See Knaus, *Inside Russian Medicine*, pp. 303–312. This was widely reported in the Soviet press as an example of Soviet-American medical cooperation, but no reference was made to the identity of the patient.

12. Knaus, *Inside Russian Medicine*, pp. 104 and 125.

13. See, for example, the letter of G. Kozhukhantseva, "The Human Factor," *Literaturnaia gazeta*, December 14, 1977, in which she complains bitterly about the pain and suffering she had to endure to reach a clinic where a traumatologist was available after she was refused attention by a physician in a nearby clinic after she had fallen and hurt her back.

14. Knaus, *Inside Russian Medicine*, pp. 20–22.

15. Knaus, *Inside Russian Medicine*, p. 107.

16. Knaus, *Inside Russian Medicine*, p. 107.

17. Knaus, *Inside Russian Medicine*, p. 137.

18. "The Sector Physician," *Literaturnaia gazeta*, September 27, 1978, trans. in *Current Digest of the Soviet Press* 30, no. 40 (1978), p. 5.

19. Knaus, *Inside Russian Medicine*, pp. 20–22.

20. Knaus, *Inside Russian Medicine*, p. 108.

21. "High duty of physicians," *Izvestiia*, February 24, 1977.

22. Serge Schmemann, "Soviets Affirm Rise in Infant Mortality," *New York Times*, June 21, 1981.

23. Murray Feshbach, "Issues in Soviet Health Problems," Joint Economic Committee, Congress of the United States, *Soviet Economy in the 1980's: Problems and Prospects*, pt. 2 (Washington, D.C., 1982), p. 203.

24. D. I. Pisarev, *Etika i myshlenenie sovetskogo vracha* (Moscow, 1963), p. 87.

25. "The Human Factor," written as a commentary on the Kozhukhantseva letter referred to in note 13 above.

26. "Micro-district physician," *Meditsinakaia gazeta*, September 27, 1978, trans. in *Current Digest of the Soviet Press* 30, no. 40 (1978), p. 4.

27. "Micro-district Physician."

28. Knaus, *Inside Russian Medicine*, p. 345.

29. Knaus, *Inside Russian Medicine*, p. 123.

30. "In a number of medical institutions in Baku, Kirovabad, Agdam, Yevlakh and other cities and districts in the republics cases have come to light of . . . the misappropriation of food intended for persons undergoing inpatient treatment." The Azerbaijan Communist Party Central Committee, *Bakinskii rabochii*, June 16, 1979, p. 2, trans. in *Current Digest of the Soviet Press* 31, no. 31 (1979), p. 9.

31. Raymond A. Bauer and Mark G. Field, *The Soviet and the American Pharmaceutical System: Some Paradoxical Contrasts* (Cambridge: Arthur D. Little, 1962); Mark G. Field, *The Soviet Pharmaceutical System: Administration and Operations* (Cambridge: Arthur D. Little, 1966); and Mark G. Field, with Natasha Lissman, *The Soviet Pharmaceutical System Revisited: Developments, 1965–1972* (New York: Pzifer; Public Policy Research, 1972).

7. Aspects of Soviet Secondary Education: School Performance and Teacher Accountability

Starting from the assumption that the quality of education is a vital dimension of the quality of life, this chapter deals with the problem of assessing the performance of Soviet school and their teachers and students. This problem has gained prominence in the context of a policy directed toward the realization of universal or compulsory secondary education in the Soviet Union. Questions of schooling concern almost all families with school-age children, and problems arising from school achievement and assessment procedures are among the most tangible in the relationship between the family and the school as an institution that largely determines the career choices of individuals.

One of the major accomplishments of Soviet educational policy during the 1970s was the general introduction of "complete" secondary education—i.e., the extension of compulsory schooling from 8 to 10 years. This was achieved by the mid-1970s, when more than 95 percent of those leaving the eighth grade transferred to an educational establishment providing "complete" secondary education, which includes the entitlement to apply for admission to higher education institutions. Roughly 60 percent of those finishing the eighth grade are accommodated by the senior grades of the general secondary school system, which is still the main route to both higher education and employment.

A singular feature of Soviet education as seen from a comparative perspective is the fact that the time devoted to preparation for higher education is identical to the length of compulsory education. There is no intermediate cycle of schooling at the upper secondary level that is specially oriented toward preparation for higher education, as is the case in East

European communist nations, most notably the German Democratic Republic. Thus the Soviet 10-year school is assigned the dual function of preparing young people for higher education and work, although no more than every fifth graduate will eventually enter a higher education institution.

Universal secondary education was to be achieved not only within the existing structural framework of the school system, but also without major changes in the organization of teaching. Optional subjects and other differentiated approaches in learning arrangements were introduced reluctantly and have retained a marginal position. General education, as laid down in the school curricula, is to be mastered by all students, irrespective of their special interests or career plans. Reforms of school curricula in the 1960s and 1970s, as well as recent revisions of the curricula, have been aimed at modernizing the contents of teaching, omitting obsolete subject matter, and making the fundamentals of various disciplines more accessible to students. The changes brought about by the policy of universal secondary education has made the question of the quality of schooling particularly urgent for Soviet educational policymakers.

Evaluation of School Performance

In expanding student numbers, especially in the senior classes of general schools, care was taken to avoid any drop in educational standards. Moreover, secondary education for all young people was to be achieved without increased waste. Indeed, waste was to be reduced. It was up to teachers to see that students, irrespective of their individual abilities and learning capacities, completed each year successfully and graduated from school in due time without repeating a year or dropping out. Therefore, the evaluation of educational achievement became one of the issues that figured most prominently in public debates on educational matters in the 1970s. As was confirmed in the discussion on the guidelines for the 1984 school reform, this is still true today.

The traditional indicator for assessing school performance in the Soviet Union has been the percentage of students successfully completing each grade. As the promotion of students is based on the grades given by teachers for current school work, homework, and aggregated grades at the end of each term, the number of successful students together with their grades is another indicator of teacher performance. By marking their students' progress, Soviet teachers are at the same time assessing their own achievements.

This became a serious problem when educational authorities, in order to demonstrate that universal secondary education was accessible to students of all ability groups, began to exert additional pressure on schools to avoid grade repeating. Along with the modernization of teaching curricula, this was ideally to be achieved by raising the quality of teaching and applying

TABLE 7.1
Number of Students Repeating a Grade at Full-Time General Schools

	1970–71	1975–76	1981–82
Students in Grades 1–10 or 11	45,100,000	42,200,000	39,200,000
Repeaters	830,000	215,000	129,000
Percent	1.84	0.51	0.33

Sources: Vestnik statistiki, 1979, no. 6, p. 69; 1980, no. 7, p. 65; and 1983, no. 7, p. 66.

new teaching methods. In reality, however, many teachers prefer the easier method of adapting their grading practices to the expected results. The more reluctant ones are put under pressure by head teachers—who in turn have to satisfy their superiors in the school administration—to avoid negative markings, at least where it matters for the school's reputation. The Soviet obsession with the percentage of students obtaining positive grades came to be known as protsentomania—a catchword that embodies much of the discontent with the contemporary Soviet school that has accumulated in the population at large.

From a quantitative point of view, it seems that grade repeating is no longer of great importance, and indeed it seems to be of very limited value as a formal indicator for measuring school performance. Efforts to eradicate grade repeating and achieve the regular promotion of almost all pupils, which date back to the Khrushchev era, have met with considerable success, at least if regarded in statistical terms with no reference to the means used in this endeavor. See Table 7.1.

In 1970–71, the number of grade repeaters as a proportion of the total enrollment of the full-time general school (in grades 1–10 or 11) was no more than 1.84 percent, and had dropped to a mere 0.33 percent a decade later. For a school system the size of the Soviet Union's, this means that there were 830,000 grade repeaters in 1970–71 and 129,000 in 1980–81 who failed to achieve the objectives set for the respective grades. In the Soviet context, a number of this size might be of little significance. However, the social costs might be high because, according to Soviet research into the causes of juvenile delinquency, grade repeating in many cases is a first step to dropping out of school—a course that often ends up in a criminal career. The Soviet policy of avoiding waste at any cost therefore makes sense from the point of view of social policy.

There is little statistical material on the drop-out rate at the general school level, especially for its intermediate and senior cycles. This is not an item that figures in official data publications, but education officials and researchers have made passing mention of it time and again. According to one source, the drop-out rate has sunk to 0.8 percent of the total enrollment of grades 1–10 or 11. On the basis of 1980–81 data, this would amount to about 316,000 students.[1] This figure has been corroborated by Deputy Minister of Education Nozhko. Nozhko put the number of students who prematurely left grades 1–8 at 180,000, and has said that the trend is accelerating.[2] For grades 9–10 or 11, he cited a dropout rate of 2.6 percent, which amounts to about 138,000 students—a figure he seemed particularly concerned about. According to Nozhko, the percentage in some republics is still higher, reaching 5.7 percent in Moldavia—twice the all-Union average— and 4.2 percent in Estonia and Armenia.

Given the possibilities for manipulating grading practices, the "holding power" of the Soviet school system seems a more pertinent indicator of the system's performance than the percentage of grade repeaters.[3] But if grade repeating has lost its significance, *protsentomania* has not. On the contrary, its consequences make themselves felt in several ways for teachers, students, and their parents. Student achievement is assessed according to a scale of five grades. In its present numerical form, this scale was introduced in 1944. It ranges from 5 (excellent) down to 1 (very bad), with 3 indicating a performance just sufficient to pass. While grade 1 has never been widely used, "protsentomania" and the constant inflation of grades—this mostly applies to the upgrading of grade 2 to grade 3—have led to a situation where grade 2 has almost disappeared, virtually reducing the grading system to a scale of three grades. One consequence of this has been the artificial raising of students' grades.

The weak or average student profits from this situation in terms of satisfactory school reports and certificates, and also in terms of the encouragement offered by benign marking. Thus inflated grading might indeed contribute to the holding power of a school system designed to accommodate the entire range of its student's abilities. If, as empirical studies suggest, general school achievement influences the choice of educational paths, grade levelling has a direct bearing on the aspirations of students as regards higher education, and consequently on the number of applicants to higher education institutions.[4] As the expansion of higher education has not kept pace with the growing number of students enrolled in secondary schools, the competitive character of admission to higher education institutions has been increased. The main hurdle for secondary school graduates who wish to go to universities remains the entry examination.

Since the regulations for admission to higher education institutions were modified in 1972, school achievement—the numerical average of the grades students obtain in school-leaving certificates—has been taken into account in assessing entry examination results.[5] This, together with the increased selectivity of higher education, has given teachers an opportunity to exert more pressure on reluctant learners, which in turn has resulted in widespread criticism among parents concerning the stress that students have to suffer as a result of their being overburdened with schoolwork.

On the other hand, the practice of marking up grades has weakened their diagnostic and prognostic value—a fact that leads to severe disappointment if entrance examination results are not congruent with grades achieved in school-leaving certificates. Well-to-do parents make up for this by hiring private tutors to enhance their children's chances of gaining access to higher education institutions—another corollary of *protsentomania* that is heavily criticized in public discussions. Even the gold and silver medals awarded to students with exceptionally high grades in their school-leaving certificates are no longer a guarantee of success in entrance exams. On the contrary, they illustrate the degree to which school achievement can diverge from exam results. Thus in 1978, 5,307 medal holders applied for admission to teacher training colleges, and 1,694, or 31.9 percent, failed the exam in their chosen subject.[6]

Protsentomania finds its most fervent critics among teachers themselves. When General Secretary Brezhnev declared at the 26th Party Congress in 1981 that after the final establishment of universal secondary education, the main task in education would be to raise school standards and "to get rid of formalism in the assessment of results of teachers' and students' work," a discussion on school assessment evolved in the columns of *Uchitel'skaia gazeta* (Teachers' Gazette).[7] The ensuing debate was evidently fed by the frustration that *protsentomania* had created among many teachers and head teachers. They reported that in many cases, unveiled pressure was exerted on them to comply with demands to raise grades in complete contradiction to regulations laid down by the Ministry of Education.[8]

Teachers resent the percentage indicator for two reasons. On the one hand, they see the artificial raising of grades as contrary to their professional ethics, and on the other, they warn against the disastrous consequences of this practice on both the moral upbringing of students and their learning motivation. Some of them blamed universal secondary education for creating the "universal compulsory '3' for unsuccessful students,"[9] but for the most part the blame was laid at the doors of educational authorities and the school inspectorate.

According to a 1976 issue of *Uchitel'skaia gazeta*, "The problem of indicators for school performance is the sore point of the school."[10] This diagnosis is still valid in the 1980s, though education authorities have been seeking a cure for at least a decade. The main emphasis has been on attempts to replace the practice of using a single indicator to assess school performance—student success as reflected by grades—with a complex framework of indicators in which the main areas of a particular school's work are represented. When in 1976 the Ministry of Education published its Criteria for the Evaluation of the School's Work[11]—a document that had been preceded by a lengthy discussion of an earlier draft—its guidelines were in tune with the slogan, "quality and effectiveness," which had been coined for the economic and social policies initiated at the 25th Party Congress in 1976. Spurred by mounting public criticism of the prevailing tendency toward *protsentomania*, the ministry urged education authorities to adopt the criteria as a guideline for assessing school performance. The current version of the criteria, which were adapted to the rhetoric of the 26th Party Congress in 1982,[12] address four main areas—fulfillment of the law on compulsory education; standards of student upbringing and the state of ideological and political education; standards of teaching in academic subjects; and the standard of the work of the teaching staff.

Without going into further detail, the vagueness of some of the criteria as compared to the handiness of the percentage indicator is obvious. Neither the Ministry of Education nor the Academy of Pedagogical Science, which was charged with developing the criteria, have so far provided schools or educational authorities with the proper instruments for implementing the criteria on a day-to-day basis. Therefore, the ministry felt compelled to criticize the systems' neglect of the criteria and the continued use of traditional assessment indicators in a 1981 circular. The exertion of pressure on teachers was again declared inadmissible, thus repeating similarly worded demands that were raised for the first time in 1944.[13]

The Criteria for the Evaluation of the School's Work has not proven successful because of its extensiveness and lack of operability. Those in charge of their development admit mistakes in their implementation, but place the blame mainly on the intermediate levels of educational administration. However, to a certain degree, they seem to be at a loss as to how to overcome bureaucratic inertia and formalism.[14] Whether or not one can speak of the tacit connivance of the Ministry of Education in retaining the handy percentage indicator can only be surmised. After all, successful completion of general school education by all pupils is a fundamentally political issue, and teachers have been warned that any yearning for a return to an "avalanche of twos" would boomerang on themselves.[15] Thus the only solution is a steady improvement in the quality of teaching. In a recent round-table discussion on school assessment, the minister of education attempted to strike a balance by saying that there should be no return to mass grade repeating, but no abandonment of the use of bad grades, for "the school is not entitled to produce scrap."[16]

Other Methods of Assessing School Achievement

School performance is the instrument by which local and regional levels of school administration as well as school inspectorates—which are attached to both central and regional levels of administration—collect data on the quality of teaching. However, there are additional and more instructive methods by which education authorities are able to obtain information on school achievement. As mentioned above, the entrance examination scores of many applicants to higher education institutions often do not correspond to the grades that they received in their school-leaving certificates. Entrance examination results are one of the most important sources of information for Soviet educational administrators regarding the achievements of at least that section of school-leavers that intends to move on to higher education. Examinations are taken in Russian and additional subjects relevant to the specialization the applicant has chosen. The examination requirements in these subjects are based on the appropriate curricula of the general school system.

Although the examination results are analyzed by the Ministry for Higher and Secondary Specialized Education and made available to the Ministry of Education, no detailed data are published about the examinations. The few figures that have appeared in print seem to underline the position of those who have criticized the divergence between the grades that appear in school-leaving certificates and examination results. The average grade in history among applicants to the history departments of teacher training colleges in 1978 was 4.5. However, among the 383 candidates at the Faculty of History of Novosibirsk teacher training college, only 81 obtained a "5," 127 received a "4," and 91 managed no more than a "3." One can infer that the remaining 22 percent failed.[17] This tallies with mathematics entrance examination results for the Moscow Aviation Institute in 1979. The average grade for mathematics in the school-leaving certificates of the candidates was 4.11, but 30 percent received a "2" in the entrance exams and thus failed.[18]

Unsatisfactory mathematics examination results seem to have become a particular cause of concern to educational administrators. In 1979, the Minister for Higher and Specialized Secondary Education referred to these concerns in a generally-worded special circular on examination results. On the whole, however, the preparation of students for admission to higher education institutions was deemed "satisfactory"—a stereotyped verdict often found in earlier bulletins of this kind.[19] It is nevertheless noteworthy that these reports have revealed a considerable degree of differentiation among the examination results of various regions. It was emphasized that in the Caucasian and some of the Central Asian republics, up to 70 percent of the candidates failed their exams.

In analyzing the scant evidence on entrance examination results, it should be borne in mind that their value as an indicator of school achievement and the quality of work of the general school is tainted. Results are likely affected by the fact that candidates find themselves in a particularly stressful situation. Furthermore, the results, especially good ones, are influenced by the frequent practice of hiring private tutors for exam preparation.

Systematic evidence on the quality of teaching was collected by education authorities in connection with the implementation of new school curricula in the mid-1970s. In April 1975, a large-scale investigation of student performance in mathematics, physics, and chemistry was carried out for the first time. The study, conducted by the Academy of Pedagogical Sciences, involved about 20,000 students in each of these subjects and all grades of the general school—a total of more than 150,000 throughout the Soviet Union. The few results that have been released have confirmed significant variations in student performance between urban and rural schools, especially when the latter were located in non-Russian areas. But, again, no concrete data were revealed.[20]

More recently, studies have been undertaken in connection with the introduction of revised school curricula at the beginning of the 1980s. Their main goal has been to find out how students cope with new subject matter and whether theoretical materials—the principal generalizations and notions that form the backbone of each subject—are within the grasp of the student population. These studies indicated that for a majority of Soviet students learning takes place on the level of mere mechanical memorization of subject matter as set forth in text books. Only 15–20 percent of the students were capable of applying their knowledge creatively in non-standardized situations or under changed circumstances.[21] This suggests that day-to-day teaching methods are not in accordance with the goals of the revised curricula and that the concept of more autonomous, self-regulated learning, as put forward by educators and scientists in public debates on school reform, has not yet overcome considerable obstacles.

Accentuation of Teacher Accountability

Obviously, the caliber of the teaching force is of fundamental significance for the quality of schooling. The length and level of teacher training, the quality of teaching facilities, and the encouragement of in-service training play a vital role, but external factors, such as the student-teacher ratio and the extent of administrative control as opposed to teacher autonomy, also influence the quality of teaching. The traditional method of assessing individual teachers with reference to the overall percentage of successful students was deemed insufficient at a time when the introduction of universal secondary education and the modernization of school curricula required a higher quality and effectiveness of teaching. The Ministry of Education's 1972 decree heralding the final phase of the process of implementing universal secondary education proposed a new instrument for evaluating teachers and called for teacher "attestation"—a periodic review of the work, qualifications, and skills of Soviet teachers.[22] While the Criteria for the Evaluation of the Schools' Work focuses on the performance of the school as an organization, attestation is aimed at monitoring and influencing the achievements of individual teachers. Regular reviews of individual performance are common for other professional groups in the Soviet Union, such as research workers, university staff members, and engineers and other technical specialists.[23] The extension of this screening process to the entire teaching profession was clearly designed as a shake-up operation to make teachers more responsive, both to changes brought about by educational policies and to new developments in their respective fields of specialization.

The goals of attestation were laid down in a special decree of the Council of Ministers in 1974 and in subsequent regulations for attestation procedures. They include the dissemination of progressive teaching methods and the overall enhancement of the personal responsibility of every teacher to further the quality of education and the upbringing of students, thus advancing the quality of the work of the general school. Special emphasis has been placed on controlling the ideological attitudes and political activities of teachers.[24]

As laid down in the regulations, every teacher, with a few exceptions, has to undergo attestation once every five years. This is carried out by a special permanent commission consisting of experienced teachers, university staff members, and representatives of the Teachers' Union and the educational administration. In accordance with the general objectives of attestation, the indicators that are reviewed include classroom performance, the adequacy of professional qualifications and teaching skills, ideological standards, participation in in-service training, and the impeccability of the personal behavior and lifestyles of teachers in accordance with the norms of communist morals.

As the main emphasis of the attestation process is to stimulate "creative initiatives," the commissions, which are organized in a three-tier structure from the regional or city level to the all-Union level, are empowered to confer special honorary titles on those who excel in their achievements. On the other hand, those whose performance is deemed insufficient can be required to enroll in higher education correspondence courses as a condition for the continuation of their contracts, and they can be dismissed as well.

A trial run of the attestation process was carried out in 1975 in a limited number of regions. The first five-year round took place between 1976 and 1980. As a result, about two million teachers out of a total of 2.3 million underwent the review process by 1980.[25] Of these, 83 percent were declared fully efficient. About 380,000 were found worthy of special commendation, and honorary titles were conferred on 11,000. On the other hand, it was found that 17 percent did not entirely fulfil the demands of their jobs and were strongly recommended to compensate for their shortcomings, in particular by means of in-service training. Only about 1,000 teachers had to give up teaching because they were declared inefficient. Apparently, however, a certain number of less satisfactory teachers quit their jobs during the attestation process. The number for 1976 was approximately 1,500.[26] If this figure is extrapolated for the entire five-year cycle, the total number of teachers who presumably left their jobs as a consequence of attestation would amount to about 8,500, or about half a percent of those reviewed.

Interestingly, some Soviet republics show certain deviations from these nationwide results. Published evidence suggests that there are palpable differences between republics as regards the quality of the teaching force, at least according to the indicators chosen for the review process. In certain republics, a large number of teachers were declared conditionally efficient and urged to make up for their shortcomings—26.2 percent in Kazakhstan, 22.1 in Moldavia, and 21.6 in the Kirgiz SSR. Presumably, this is mainly due to the fact that there is a relatively low percentage of teachers with higher degrees in these republics.[27]

Attestation involves laborious organizational efforts, and it is still difficult to gauge its effects on the quality of the teaching force. Between 1975 and 1980, the number of teachers with higher education qualifications rose from 64.3 percent to 72.3 percent of the total,[28] and while this was mostly due to the influx of new graduates from teacher training colleges, attestation might have contributed to the trend. Due to the fact that educational administrators go to great lengths in trying to convince teachers of the objectivity and fairness of the review process, it can be inferred that attestation is regarded with reservations among teachers. In the first phase of the attestation process, a number of teachers were able to make their apprehensions public in letters to the press, and there is some evidence that conflicts arose from the handling of review procedures by head teachers and attestation commissions. A leading official in the Ministry of Education criticized the "liberalism" shown in the handling of teacher attestation in some of the Southern republics, but he also admitted to many instances of "formalism" and arbitrariness at odds with the stimulating function assigned to attestation.[29]

Perhaps it is not by chance that the authors of the guidelines for the 1984 school reform have sought to enhance the innovative capacities of teachers and promote their qualification standards, not by exerting additional control and pressure, but by developing teacher training. Improved teacher training is to become based on higher education, recruiting students, and improving the working and living conditions of teachers, including their remuneration.[30] This might be interpreted as a change of emphasis from bureaucratic to social policy, complete with the prospect of yet another honorary title awaiting distinguished teachers.

Notes

1. V. A. Miasnikov and N. A. Khromenkov, *Ot s'ezda k s'ezdu. Narodnoe obrazovanie: itogi i perspektivy* (Moscow: Pedagogika, 1981), p. 22.

2. K. Nozhko, "Planirovanie i ekonomiku narodgnogo obrazovaniia—na uroven' trebovanii XXVI s'ezda KPSS," *Narodnoe obrazovanie*, 1982, no. 7, pp. 8–9.

3. For terminology, see M. A. Brimer and L. Pauli, *Wastage in Education—A World Problem* (Paris and Geneva: UNESCO, 1971).

4. See, for example, Gendel's Syzran study as reported by R. B. Dobson and M. Swafford, "The Educational Attainment Process in the Soviet Union: A Case Study," *Comparative Education Review* 24, no. 2 (June 1980), pp. 252–269.

5. For problems and procedures of access to higher education, see a recent study by George Avis, "Access to higher education in the Soviet Union," in J. J. Tomiak (ed.), *Soviet Education in the 1980s* (London: Croom Helm 1983), pp. 199–239.

6. V. N. Iagodkin, *Pedagogicheskie kadry shkoly i sovershenstvovanie vospitaniia uchashchikhsia* (Moscow: Pedagogika, 1979), p. 66.

7. *Materialy XXVI s'ezda KPSS* (Moscow: Politizdat, 1981), p. 60.

8. See, for example, *Uchitel'skaia gazeta* March 10, March 24, and June 6, 1981; and G. Ryskin, "Pedagogicheskaia komediia. Zapiski sovetskogo uchitelia," *Grani* 34, no. 113 (1979), pp. 117–119.

9. *Uchitel'skaia gazeta*, July 18, 1981.

10. *Uchitel'skaia gazeta*, February 3, 1976.

11. *Spravochnik inspektora shkol*, ed. by F. I. Puzyrev (Moscow: Prosveshchenie, 1978), pp. 38–41.

12. *Biulleten' normativnykh aktov Ministerstva prosveshcheniia SSSR*, 1982, no. 8, pp. 43–45.

13. *Narodnoe obrazovanie v SSSR*, "Obshcheobrazovatel'naia shkola. Sbornik dokumentov, 1917–1973 gg.*" (Moscow: Pedgagogika, 1974), p. 179.

14. V. Nevskii and P. Khudominskii, "Kriterii otsenki i shkol'naia inspektsiia," *Uchitel'skaia gazeta*, February 14, 1980; and M. Portnov, "V ushcherb sushchestvu dela," *Uchitel'skaia gazeta*, March 23, 1982.

15. Iu. Babanskii, "Glavnoe v segodniashchei shkole," *Uchitel'skaia gazeta*, April 11, 1981.

16. "Glavnoe o glavnom," *Uchitel'skaia gazeta*, September 1, 1981.

17. "Nekotorye itogi vstupitel'nykh ekzamenov v vuzy po istorii," *Prepodavanie istorii v shkole*, 1979, no. 2, p. 41.

18. *Pravda*, August 31, 1979.

19. "Ov itogakh priema v vysshie uchebnye zavedeniia v 1979 godu i zadachakh po podgotovke k priemu v 1980 godu," *Biulleten' Ministerstva vysshego i srednego spetsial'nogo obrazovaniia SSSR*, 1980, no. 4, pp. 7–11; and "Ov itogakh priema v vysshie uchebnye zavedeniia v 1979 godu i zadachakh po podgotovke k priemu v 1977 godu," *Biulleten' Ministerstva vysshego i srednego spetsial'nogo obrazovaniia SSSR*, 1978, no. 2, pp. 8–10.

20. See M. P. Kashin, "Ob itogakh perekhoda sovetskoi shkoly na novoe soderzhanie obshchego obrazovaniia," *Sovietskaia pedagogika*, 1976, no. 3, pp. 24–32; "Ob itogakh

perekhoda sovetskoi shkoly na novoe soderzhanie obucheniia," *Narodnoe obrazovanie,* 1976, no. 6, pp. 100–127; and interview with Kashin in *Izvestiia,* April 22, 1976.

21. See, for example, E. A. Krasnovskii et al., "Usovershenstvovannye programmy obshcheobrazovatel'noi shkoly i povyshenie kachestva obucheniia," *Sovetskaia pedagogika,* 1983, no. 9, pp. 11–16.

22. *Narodnoe obrazovanie v SSSR,* p. 238.

23. F. G. Panachin, *Shkola i obshchestvennyi progress* (Moscow: Prosveshchenie, 1983), p. 167.

24. Decree of the Council of Ministers of April 16, 1974, in *Uchitel'skaia gazeta,* June 22, 1974; and regulations issued by the Minister of Education on June 12, 1974, in *Biulleten' normativnykh aktov ministerstv i vedomstv SSSR,* 1976, no. 9, pp. 41–43.

25. The following data are taken from Panachin, *Shkola,* p. 175; and G. Revenko, in *Uchitel'skaia gazeta* March 28, 1981.

26. F. G. Panachin, "Sovetskaia obshcheobrazovatel'naia shkola v 1977/78 uchebnom godu," *Sovietskaia pedagogika,* 1977, no. 9, p. 11.

27. "V Ministerstve prosveshcheniia SSR. Attestatsiia uchitelei obshcheobrazovatel'nykh shkol," *Narodnoe obrazovanie,* 1981, no. 10, pp. 93–94.

28. *Narodnoe khoziaistvo SSSR v 1982 godu* (Moscow: Statistika, 1983), p. 459.

29. G. Revenko, "Attestatsiia uchitelei i ee effektivnost'," *Narodnoe obrazovanie,* 1980, no. 2, p. 36; and *Uchitel'skaia gazeta,* March 28, 1981.

30. *Pravda,* January 4, 1984.

8. Housing Quality and Housing Classes in the Soviet Union

Of all Soviet urban problems, housing shortages remain one of the most intransigent. The tsarist legacy in housing was dismal. Under Stalin, conditions worsened. Stalin invested heavily in industry but failed to provide resources to house the millions who left the countryside to work in factories. Under Stalin, Soviet citizens invariably lived in communal squalor, and the crowding of many families into one apartment was universal. In 1950, it was estimated that each person had less than five square meters of living space—about seven by seven feet.

Shortly after Stalin's death, Soviet leaders decided to eliminate the housing shortage. Since 1957, the Soviet Union has built 2.2 million housing units per year—a remarkable achievement, even if the size and quality of the units are below Western standards.[1] The results of this effort are visible in almost every city and town. In most cities, new housing districts outnumber the old. By 1982, per capita living space in urban areas had increased to 9 square meters (about 9.7 by 9.7 feet) for the Soviet Union as a whole and to 11.3 for Moscow.[2]

Because housing conditions improved for a significant part of the population, the demands of those who were still waiting for their own apartments intensified. "The tremendous amount of apartment construction in the past 10 to 15 years has not been able to keep pace with the population's rising expectations . . . [and] this explains why waiting lists for new apartments are longer than ever," declared *Literaturnaia gazeta* in 1972.[3] But this is

---

This chapter is an abbreviated and revised version of "Who Gets What When and How? Housing in the Soviet Union," *Soviet Studies* 32, no. 2 (April 1980).

only a partial explanation. Housing has become increasingly stratified in the Soviet Union. The knowledge that a housing "rich" exists has aroused expectations and bred resentment among the housing "poor"— those millions who are still waiting to receive space in new apartment buildings. A survey conducted in Moscow revealed that the percentage of those who voiced dissatisfaction with their housing doubled between 1966 and 1969, chiefly among those who had observed close relatives and friends being assigned new apartments of their own while they remained behind.[4]

Measuring the Housing Shortage

Soviet citizens still suffer from the poorest housing conditions that exist in any industrialized nation, principally because so many families still live communally. In 1980, an estimated 20 percent of all urban dwellers still shared apartments, and an additional five percent—mostly single people— lived in factory dormitories.[5] The fact that conditions were worse in 1960, when 60 percent of all families lived communally, is of little comfort to the huge numbers of people still living in inadequate conditions.[6] The waiting period for a new apartment is indefinite. It may take from a decade to a lifetime unless one has connections.

The Soviet government seeks to persuade its citizens that their housing conditions are steadily improving. It regularly publicizes the fact that more than two million housing units with an area of more than 100 million square meters are built each year, and that 10 million people annually improve their housing situation by moving into these new housing units or by exchanging rooms or apartments.[7]

These statistical recitals serve the purpose of covering up the continuing critical shortage of housing units relative to the existing number of households. A "household" is defined as a married couple, a parental pair with children, a single parent with children, or a single individual living alone. A numerical comparison of housing units and households is crucial in measuring Soviet housing needs. Yet such information is not published in the Soviet Union. This statistical gap is not an oversight. The UN *Statistical Yearbook* provides such figures for all West and East European nations except the USSR.[8]

In practically all Western nations, the goal of matching housing units with households has been achieved. In the Soviet Union, the deficit of housing units relative to the number of households is very large and is the principal reason for the continuing housing crisis. According to un-published Soviet figures, in 1970 the deficit was 7.4 million units in urban areas alone. Other estimates show an even larger shortfall of 9.6 million units, or 128 households for every 100 units.[9] This deficit has not been overcome despite a vigorous construction program, partially because housing is no longer the Soviet government's primary consumer priority, as it was from the mid-1950s through the 1960s.

Because the numerical relationship between households and dwelling places is not available, the next best indicator is a comparison of yearly marriages and the number of housing units built. If more housing units are built than marriages registered, and if a given nation possesses an equal or superior number of dwellings relative to the number of households, then the basis for an adequate housing situation exists. This does not mean that a nation's housing problems are solved when this stage is reached. It does signify, however, that a basic goal has been achieved and that other pressing housing concerns can receive higher priority. These include paying for comfortable housing in a particular neighborhood or a house, the purchase of housing-related equipment, and the ability to commute to and from work. For example, Soviet citizens prefer housing made of bricks over buildings that are mass-produced from precast concrete panels. In the Soviet Union, comfortable housing applies to cooperatives, private homes, summer houses, and to the use of bribes to acquire state housing.

In a deficit housing situation, the ratio of marriages formed to housing units produced greatly affects housing conditions nationwide. From 1973–82, 6,175,226 more marriages were formed than housing units built. This huge imbalance was also reflected in 29 major cities and republic capitals. Of these, only Kiev and Minsk registered more dwellings than marriages registered in 1982 (3,643 and 863, respectively). Moscow's "deficit" was 43,947 units, and Leningrad's was 26,000 units.[10] This is the reason why newlyweds have little chance of moving into their own apartment and are destined to live with in-laws perhaps for decades.

However, the urban housing deficit is really much larger than these figures suggest. With a zero vacancy rate in Soviet urban areas, the desire for each household to live in an apartment is strictly, if not always successfully, monitored by the authorities. To discourage new households from forming, singles who wish to split off from an extended family—for example, grown children, grandparents, and aunts or uncles—are frequently denied places on waiting lists. Many who live beyond city limits and commute to work, not by choice, but of necessity, are also denied places. Many of these are the "urban poor" of Soviet society, not due to unemployment, but because of a lack of urban amenities. Large population centers are closed off to them to prevent cities such as Moscow, Leningrad, and Kiev from being overrun by rural and provincial migrants. Permission to move to large cities is rarely granted. Beyond the city limits, with the last high rise apartment buildings still in sight, a harsher life style prevails, greatly lacking in creature comforts. Sprawling suburbs as Americans know them, with comfortable homes and bustling shopping centers, do not exist in the Soviet Union.

The Propiska System

Large cities, especially republic capitals and Moscow, are magnets to those living in the provinces, but moving to them is extremely difficult. To live in a city, a residence permit (*propiska*) is required, but to be eligible for a residence permit, one must have housing, for which one needs a *propiska*. Because of severe overcrowding, many large urban centers are closed to would-be immigrants. Some, however, are more closed than others. Moscow is the most closed of all, but an official list identifying closed cities has not been published. The chance of finding a crack in the door that will admit a select few depends on the attractiveness of the city under consideration, the presence of military installations and defense-related industries, the relative weight of the agency sponsoring an individual, and the individual's profession, needs, and trustworthiness, as based on references (*kharakteristiki*). Every step in the process, from acquiring a *propiska* to receiving comfortable housing, is measurable in years of anguish, aggravation, discouragement, and resignation.

The likelihood of receiving permission to move to Moscow, Leningrad, or Kiev without official sponsorship or without an apartment to exchange from another city is next to nil. Even with these prerequisites, many obstacles have to be overcome. Of course, the more prestigious an individual's position, the greater the need for one's skills, or the higher one's rank in the party hierarchy, the better one's chances. Semi- and unskilled laborers, if desperately needed by a factory, might be admitted if dormitory beds are available.

If unsponsored, an individual has to battle the bureaucracy alone, and few attempt this discouraging procedure. First, a residence must be acquired. This is because a *propiska* is for a specific street address that is affixed to a person's internal passport. Getting on the waiting list without an apartment is out of the question because only residents are taken. Finding a room or part of one as a subtenant is the only way around this obstacle. Once this task is accomplished, the individual then goes to the local housing office and asks for the *pasportist*—the official in charge of residence permits, who takes the application to the district militia station where the processing takes place. In practically all cases, permission to reside in Moscow will be denied unless strong sponsorship prevails or a bribe succeeds.

Residence permits are of two kinds—temporary and permanent. A temporary *propiska* is issued for the duration of one's work assignment in a city, for example, a tour of duty for an officer of the armed forces or an engineering assignment for a specific time period. It need not be a professional position. Workers from the provinces are also imported to fill menial jobs. For example, in recent years it has become exceedingly difficult to get a Muscovite to be a *dvornik*—a person who cleans hallways and the immediate exterior of buildings and also serves as an agent for the local militia. Such persons are usually given ground-floor apartments. If dismissed, or if they leave their jobs, they are evicted and lose their *propiski*.

The chances of receiving a permanent residence permit improve if two families of approximately the same size living in different cities agree to exchange apartments of approximately the same size. Such an exchange is more likely to be approved between Moscow and Leningrad than between Moscow and Gorky, unless strong support from a Moscow organization is forthcoming.[11]

Who Gets On the Waiting List?

Those who have a *propiska* but wish to improve their housing situation by moving into an apartment of their own are officially dependent on the housing authorities. In the Soviet Union, the rationing of urban housing is primarily by allocation, whereas in the United States it is primarily by price. With more than 70 percent of all urban housing units owned by the state, it is primarily bureaucrats who decide when, where, and how well one will be housed. But even under these conditions, a market in state housing also exists.

The attempt to improve one's housing situation can be a full-time occupation. If one's sanitary norm of nine square meters of living space has been satisfied, getting on the waiting list is virtually impossible without connections. Depending on the locality, it is usually necessary to have less than seven square meters per capita to get on the list. There are two kinds of lists for which individuals may seek registration—those belonging to enterprises and organizations, and those belonging to municipalities. It is now permitted to get on both. Waiting lists of enterprises and organizations are much preferred because their allocations are usually carried out in less than half the time taken by municipalities.

In new towns, of which there are over one thousand in the Soviet Union, housing is primarily financed and controlled by large enterprises of one or several industries that "run" the city. In such "company towns," housing is nominally distributed by a trade union committee and formally approved by the executive committee of the local soviet. In fact, however, a *troika* consisting of the director, party committee, and trade union committee of the enterprise decide on the allocation process in concert.[12]

In older towns, in capitals of republics, and in large cities such as Leningrad, municipalities sometimes own over half of all housing stock.[13] The municipal waiting list is organized by the districts into which a city is divided. Following general guidelines, a housing commission of the district soviet determines who will be accepted onto the waiting list as well as the priority in which applicants will be considered. The commission makes its recommendation to the executive committee of the district soviet, which invariably gives its approval. Those turned down by the commission can appeal to the district executive committee, but unless a petitioner has a spokesman from his organization pleading his case he has little chance of overriding the housing commission's decision. Petitioners are generally from privileged groups of Soviet society—party activists, engineers, scientists, artists, academics, foremen, and athletes who seek to be taken out of turn to avoid a 10-year wait.[14] Housing owned by enterprises and organizations is distributed in a manner similar to how it is distributed in company towns.[15]

In 1973, a partial list of the types of people whose applications would be considered for a place on Leningrad's municipal waiting list, provided that they were permanently registered and had lived in the city for many years, included those with less than 4.5 square meters of living space (currently, threshold is probably 7 square meters); those living in housing units declared unfit for habitation; those living in dormitories; those who have worked for a district housing department for some time; and those who are registered in Leningrad *oblast* but have worked for many years in a Leningrad city enterprise.[16]

To be legally taken out of turn is a privilege reserved for the recipients of high awards such as the Hero of Socialist Labor or the Order of Glory; officers and enlisted men of the armed forces and the troops of the Committee of State Security (KGB); blue- and white-collar workers employed by the army and navy; World War II invalids and the families of those who died in the war; those suffering from tuberculosis; and those sharing a room with strangers.[17]

Certain categories of people have the right to additional living space in excess of the nine square meter norm because of their occupation. Most of these categories have existed since the early 1930s when they had little application because living space during that period was at a premium for everyone and averaged less than five square meters per person. The establishment of these special categories was part of Stalin's campaign against egalitarianism. Housing, wages, and other perquisites of the system were to be awarded for ability rather than need in order to provide incentives for the capable and the diligent, and to help Stalin in his drive to industrialize the Soviet Union at breakneck speed.[18]

Those entitled to an additional room (about 10 square meters) are termed "responsible workers"—a deliberately vague category that includes Heroes of the Soviet Union and of Socialist Labor; officers of the armed forces with the rank of colonel or higher; and inventors and industrial efficiency experts. Particularly favored by law, presumably because many work at home, are writers, composers, sculptors, architects, and scholars who have the equivalent of a Ph.D. degree. They can have 20 square meters above the norm.[19] This right to additional space has made apartment living much more comfortable for many in privileged categories who have been able to take advantage of this prerogative.

Figures on how many succeed in getting placed on official waiting lists have not been published. But according to A. V. Bazaluk, the former head of the Moscow Department of Registration and Allocation of Living Space, 180,000 Moscow families, or 590,000 persons, were on the list in November 1974. This accounted for 7.8 percent of the capital's population. Sixty percent of these persons averaged less than five square meters of living space. The others lived in dilapidated quarters or lacked basic conveniences such as central heating or hot water. Of the total, 70 percent were on preferred lists. They might be accommodated in a matter of a few years; the other 30 percent might have to wait a decade or longer if they are registered in their district.[20]

Many urban residents in large cities do not live at their place of registration. The *propiska* system, like many other controls in Soviet society, is in the good Russian tradition "beatable," and housing bureaucrats frequently deal with phantom figures. Like any scarce commodity, housing is hoarded. For example, two apartments, or parts of them, might be swapped for a larger apartment as a standby in case of divorce, rental, or most importantly for the benefit of one's children. A married man living in a cooperative apartment might remain registered in his mother's apartment so that, although it is municipally owned, it will legally become his to occupy after her demise.

The Housing Market

Those who wish to bypass the tyranny of the allocation process can try their luck in the housing market. The Soviet Union's housing market picks up where the allocation process leaves off and depends largely on one's ability to pay. Private rentals, cooperatives, apartment exchanges, and private houses are all part of an active housing market. The cost of a transaction, except in the case of cooperatives where the price is set by the government, is based on the going market rate, which is invariably much higher than the officially permitted price, and therefore illegal.

If an individual or couple has a residence permit but is not actually the lessee of an apartment or a room, there is no housing to exchange. Hence, their options are few. They can try to rent a room or an apartment. This is difficult and expensive because of black-market processes, and merely a temporary solution. They can also try to join a housing cooperative, but several obstacles must be overcome in order to do so. Married couples seeking improved living conditions have to prove their need for better housing. Unless they average less than seven square meters of living space, the district housing commission will not approve the application.

Before 1977, the downpayment for a two-room unit including a kitchen was 5,000 rubles, or 45 percent of the 11,111 ruble cost, the rest to be paid off at low interest rates over a period of 15 years. Since then, the down-payment has been increased to 6,500 rubles—a sum that takes an industrial worker averaging 175 rubles a month 37 months to earn. White-collar parents frequently "build" cooperatives for their children as this is the only way newlyweds can hope to move into an apartment of their own.[21] Even at 6,500 rubles, cooperative units are at a premium and are very hard to obtain in Leningrad and other cities where fewer are built than in Moscow. Most cooperatives are built in newly-created districts far from city centers. This makes shopping virtually impossible because many stores are not completed until several years after the residents move into the area. For the rare cooperative built near a metro station, a bribe of 1,000 rubles might be necessary to satisfy the chairman of the cooperative and the housing inspector who processes the applications because the demand will far exceed the supply.

The Exchange System

To engage in a housing exchange, a person must have a room or an apartment registered in his or her name. It can be state-owned or part of a cooperative. One finds out about housing exchanges through notices beginning with the phrase "I am exchanging" plastered all over kiosks, bus stops, lamp posts, fences, and building walls.[22] They are also found in the *Bulletin for Housing Exchanges*, published in most large cities. The Moscow bulletin is published every Thursday with a supplementary issue appearing about once a month on Saturdays. It averages 63 pages and lists more than 1,000 notices. The Leningrad bulletin appears bimonthly and carries about 630 notices.[23] The Moscow bulletin prints only 25,000 copies, and like many Soviet publications it is capriciously distributed. Only certain news stands carry it and copies are not available in libraries, nor in Housing Exchange Bureaus.[24]

Soviets citizens describe their housing conditions very specifically, using categories quite different from our own. In the best of all possible worlds, the ideal housing unit is a self-contained apartment with one more room than the number of persons living in it. Its location should be in the center of town in a brick or stone building with high ceilings and it should have modern conveniences, such as gas, hot water, and central heating; the toilet should be separate from the bathroom; and it should have a balcony and a telephone. One should be able to enter the rooms from the hallway, not by having to go through one room to reach the other. The apartment should be located on an upper floor, but not the top floor as the roof might leak; nor should it be on the ground floor, which is usually too noisy and subject to burglary; and the building should be close to a metro station and have an elevator and an incinerator.

Every large city has a Bureau of Housing Exchanges, which is an agency of the Department of Registration and Allocation of Housing Space. It has an office in every city district that accepts advertisements for housing in the local *Bulletin for Housing Exchanges*. For a fee of three rubles per entry, it also maintains a card file of those persons who wish to exchange their present housing, and it keeps a separate list for those who wish to make an intercity exchange. Unfortunately, exchange bureaus do not assist clients in finding living quarters. This failing has been criticized by a number of specialists. Although the number of persons wishing to make exchanges has increased 12-fold in 10 years, critics deplore the fact that "the person who wishes to exchange his apartment for one more suitable is left to his own devices. He may haunt the exchange bureau's threshold for months, even years, poring over notices and contacting interested parties."[25] Suggestions that exchange bureaus could best help individuals by using computer technology to organize complex exchange chains involving many families or create a national data bank to assist in arranging intercity exchanges have thus far fallen on deaf ears.[26]

Because exchange bureaus provide little help to individuals, a lively open-air "stock-market" trading in rooms and apartments operates in all weather just outside the central exchange bureau's office. In Moscow, such a market is located just off Prospekt Mira in one of the oldest sections of the city. Hedrick Smith of the *New York Times* observed one blustery October Sunday that:

> . . . hundreds of people, hands thrust in their pockets and scarves wound tightly against the cold carry placards around their necks or hand-scrawled signs pinned to their sturdy cloth coats. Occasionally, they paused to converse quietly in twos and threes and then walk on.
>
> But these are not Soviet strikers, they are walking want ads: Muscovites advertising apartments for exchange, eager to improve their living quarters. A modish young couple offers an attractive "split"—the exchange of a four room apartment, large by Soviet standards, for two smaller ones. . . . An elderly woman tries to coax a man in a dark fedora to take single rooms in two different communal apartments in return for his separate one room apartment with kitchen, bath and phone.
>
> At the far end of the lane, students and officers swarm around a few landlords offering a room, a bed, or a small apartment for rent. Some students turn up their noses at a two room unit in an old building with gas heat but no indoor plumbing. But a middle-aged woman and a married couple, less fussy, compete for it. In minutes, their apartment is gone for 50 rubles monthly, paid a year in advance.[27]

Not all housing exchanges are approved by the authorities, principally because they suspect that money is being exchanged for unfair gain. Frequently they are right, but such an attitude is counterproductive because, according to one critic, putting obstacles in the way of "simple exchanges only leads to black markets and brokers."[28]

One noteworthy example of the complicated and time-consuming negotiations needed to organize a housing exchange involved Andrei D. Sakharov, the well-known nuclear scientist and dissident, before he was exiled to Gorky in 1980. The Sakharovs wanted to move with their daughter, son-in-law, two small grandchildren and Mrs. Sakharov's mother into a four-room apartment communally occupied by three other households. In all, the exchange chain involved 17 persons and five apartments and took a year to arrange. "As Dr. Sakharov told it, everyone welcomed the prospective move. Two of the women sharing the kitchen and bathroom of the communal apartment had been quarrelling constantly. A widower wanted to give up his room for a separate one-room unit so that his mother-in-law could move in to help care for his three-year old child. The rest saw a chance to improve their own living conditions." The plan, first approved by the housing commission of the district soviet, was vetoed six days later by the district soviet executive committee, ostensibly on the grounds that one of the women, already exceeding the legal norm by six square meters, would gain another three-quarters of a square meter if the move were permitted.[29] While the real reasons for annulling this exchange might have been political, Sakharov's ability to bring his difficulties to the attention of Western journalists nevertheless documents a highly complex housing exchange, the likes of which are frequent in the Soviet Union.

The Sublease of Rooms and Apartments

Every Wednesday, *Vecherniaia Moskva*, Moscow's evening paper, publishes a separate advertising supplement of four pages, one of which lists personal advertisements for housing exchanges, the sale and purchase of houses and *dachas* (summer homes), and the sublease of rooms and apartments. With adult children away at school or work, or perhaps married and living elsewhere, a couple might have an extra room to let. Those located in the center of town are in the greatest demand and can fetch 50 rubles per month or more. Subleased apartments are of course more expensive. Certain Soviet citizens—for example, diplomats, journalists, members of the armed forces, bureaucrats, academics, and engineers—who are sent on work assignments to different cities or out of the country and take their families with them can make a good deal of money by subleasing their apartments during their absence. Those letting rooms and apartments benefit from a highly favorable sellers' market. They can specify who their applicants should be, and tend to favor students, postgraduate students, army personnel, and couples in their advertisements.[30] Once the parties agree on a price, the prospective subtenant files an application with the local housing office. If he or she has a residence permit, permission is usually granted even though the authorities know that the real rent charged will be many times higher than the legally permitted fee of a few rubles. They overlook this practice, fully realizing that the black market in apartment letting is a necessary safety valve that takes care of a portion of the overflow of persons desperately in need of lodging. To try to suppress such deals would place housing officials under even greater pressure to distribute rooms and apartments that they do not have.

The Lucrative Second-Home Market

A second-home market in letting also flourishes in the Soviet Union. Each summer, more than 25 percent of all Muscovites and Leningraders rent a *dacha* and another 35 percent have access to one. For the elites as well as the less privileged, a *dacha* serves a strong Russian need to communicate with nature, to sunbathe in a country backyard "lush with weeds."[31] Dachas come in all sizes, from stately villas with servants for the political leadership to an overpriced room rented from a *kolkhoznik* (collective farm worker).

Except for high party and government functionaries who live in state-owned *dachas* and members of the managerial, scientific, educational and cultural elite who frequently own their *dachas*, the *dacha* hunt begins as early as February. The *dacha* market is strictly a sellers' market, and prices go up every year. "Before we thought that 500 or 600 rubles for the summer was expensive. But now it is common to go up to 1,000," a *dacha*-hunting wife told a *New York Times* reporter.[32] This is the going price for a comfortable *dacha* with modern conveniences. To rent a room in a *dacha* with electricity, running water, no gas, and an outhouse shared with other tenants can cost 20 rubles per month. Legally, the rent on which the landlord pays taxes is one ruble and 32 kopeks per square meter, but this limit only exists on paper because, as *Sovetskaia kul'tura* has admitted, "everyone knows that the actual rents are based on demand and that both the landlords and the tenants keep the real figure secret."[33] Leningrad architects have estimated that city dwellers who seek fresh air pay *dacha*-owners in the Leningrad *oblast* 25–30 million rubles a year. "This is not surprising, considering that, in terms of numbers accommodated, dachas account for approximately 80 percent of all suburban holiday facilities," according to *Literaturnaia gazeta*.[34]

Letting single rooms to summer holiday seekers is common practice almost everywhere. Because of insufficient space, Soviet hotels cater primarily to foreigners and domestic clients who are on official business trips. In the Baltic republics, to stay in a private home costs four rubles a day, and usually three or four persons share a room. The rates in Sochi, the Soviet Union's biggest resort, are cheaper at about two rubles per person. Sochi had about three million visitors in 1975. Of these, nearly two million found private accommodations. The estimated income from such home-letting was 700 million rubles.[35]

Buying a *dacha* is even more difficult than renting one. The market is fierce because so few are for sale. The cheapest is a *khibarka*, a little shack with a small plot that costs about 5,000 rubles, if one can be found. The price for a comfortable country home with four or more rooms and modern conveniences will range from 15,000 to 50,000 rubles, but they are scarce. When one buys a house, one also buys a plot, although the sale of land is not legally permitted because in theory it belongs to the state. The problem is finding a plot of land to build on. In Estonia, plots are available only through cooperatives, and there is usually a long waiting list. One way around this problem is to buy a phantom cottage for several thousand rubles. According to *Pravda*, "Once a person buys a house—often one that has collapsed or does not exist—he gains the use of the land and can build his own house or dacha.[36] This form of land speculation under the guise of selling houses has become common practice in many districts of Estonia."[37]

The hopes of prospective dacha owners in the RSFSR might well have to rest on the purchase of abandoned farmhouses in small villages. *Literaturnaia gazeta* pointed out in 1973 that "The large scale migration from the countryside to the city has left many abandoned but fully habitable houses in rural areas." The reluctance of rural soviets to give their approval to such sales has been the chief obstacle to such purchases. Some feel that this would be squandering state farmland.[38] But the main reason for their reluctance is based on Article 73 of the Land Code, which implies that land can only be transferred between permanent residents of a rural community.[39] This controversial code is obviously open to interpretation. "If you can come to an understanding with the local soviet to help them in some way or simply bribe them, you can get a *dacha* cheap, from 800 to 4,000 rubles," according to one *dacha* expert.[40]

Marriages and Divorces of Convenience

A quick route out of the provinces to Moscow, Leningrad, or Kiev involves finding a marriageable resident with a *propiska*. To help individuals whose efforts have failed to produce results, "marriage brokers" sometimes materialize. Leonid Kazakevich, a Baku resident, got into the business when he married Marina to obtain his Moscow residence permit, which cost him a car. To recover expenses and make further profit, he married Lyuba,

Natasha, and Margarita in succession so that they could legally live at his address. Then he began to arrange marriages for others. He made thousands of rubles before he was finally apprehended.[41]

Another example of hoarding is the fictitious divorce that takes place so that couples can get more spacious accommodations than they otherwise would have obtained had they stayed legally married. Leonid and his family of three were living in one room when they were put on the waiting list. By the time they were assigned a three-room apartment, the husband adamantly refused to give up his room on the basis of the fact that he had divorced his wife. Afterward, it was found that all four still lived together and that they had exchanged their new housing as well as the "divorced" husband's room for more spacious quarters.[42]

Jumping the Queue

To reduce one's waiting time from 10 years to two or less, a person must find a way to be taken from the waiting list out of turn. For such a "miracle" to take place, *blat* (influence), a bribe, or both are needed. Not surprisingly, these are among the most frequently cited violations found in the Soviet housing system. In the Soviet Union—a "society of connections"— whom you know often dictates how well you are housed, what food you eat, what clothing you wear, and what theater tickets you can get. This is not simply a question of money, although money helps and might be essential at some point to "buy" an official. One's connections are more important because there are many commodities in the Soviet Union that money cannot buy and can only be obtained as a favor that in turn must be repaid either immediately or at some later date. The Soviet "society of connections" is composed of interlacing networks of friends and acquaintances, who by virtue of their position have access to scarce resources that they trade for others. A good apartment is one of the scarcest commodities in the Soviet Union, and to get one quickly an individual must be well connected. As *Pravda* explained in 1973, "Too often the decisive factor is not the waiting list, but a sudden telephone call . . . [after which] they give the apartments to the families of soccer players and the whole queue is pushed back."[43] It helps immensely if one's father has influence, as was the case when the director of a large factory in Magnitogorsk obtained a flat for his son illegally.[44]

Just as the Soviet housing market has led to a score of extralegal practices, so has the *propiska* system, the housing allocation process, and the network of restrictions placed on private-home ownership. Understandably, housing bureaucrats are the focal point of bribery because housing demand far exceeds supply and government officials monopolize the supply of housing. Obtaining housing *na levo*, under the table, or as a result of one's influence is a well-established practice that lubricates a rusty bureaucratic machine and inequitably rewards those with influence and money. Officials are frequently on the take. Trying to sniff out which ones will accept money is tricky, and to initiate such an act without some kind of signal is dangerous because conviction brings a sentence of eight years. However, openly asking for money is another matter. A senior housing inspector in Rostov charged 1,000 rubles for an apartment that he "delivered" in six months time.[45] Another extorted 500 rubles from a worker with the threat that he would lose place on his factory's waiting list, even though he was first in line for a new apartment. The amount of money changing hands can be considerable. One factory director and his associates pocketed 48,000 rubles in four years.[46] A middle-aged lady in Astrakhan was rumored to have contact with an important member of the city's executive committee. She asked 800 to 2,500 rubles per apartment. "In four years some forty desperate apartment seekers, including professional people and Party members, paid her a total of 50,000 rubles in bribes before it was discovered that she had no contacts at all," according to Sotsialisticheskaia industriia.[47]

Flagrant and systematic abuses in the housing allocation process are exposed when a general campaign against corruption is launched in a republic. One such campaign began in Georgia—a republic well-known for its high-living and illegal business mentality—with the appointment of Eduard A. Shevarnadze as First Secretary of the Georgian communist party in the autumn of 1972. He denounced Georgia's housing practices, and triggered off an avalanche of investigative reporting. In one case, only six apartments were given to workers and employees of the Tbilisi trade association, which had built a block of 46 apartments. More than 100 families in urgent need of improved housing, including 11 wounded veterans of World War II, were ignored.[48] A construction cooperative in Tbilisi had initially intended to build three housing units of 160 apartments, but those in charge succeeded in erecting 16 high-rise buildings with 1,281 apartments. Many of these dwellings were assigned with the district soviet's illegal approval to families who did not even live in Tbilisi and were adequately housed by Soviet standards.[49] High officials of the Georgian Ministry of Trade were discovered living in high style. The deputy minister illegally combined two apartments with a total living space of 105.6 square meters, and his associate unlawfully acquired an apartment of 156.7 square meters and passed his previous apartment on to his daughter.[50]

The Armenians rival the Georgians in illegally acquired housing. Local party and government officials brazenly accept bribes as they speculate with state-owned apartments.[51] For example, more than half of the units of an 11-story house constructed by the Yerevan champagne factory for its employees and workers in the center of the capital were reportedly given to people who did not work at the plant.[52] The lure of living in the center of Yerevan also proved too much for the directors of a semiconductor factory in the new satellite town of Abovyan. They decided to build new housing for their workers in the center of Armenia's capital, which was 16 kilometers away from the factory. The location of the building as well as the design of the apartments, illegally built according to individual specifications, was in complete disregard of regulations. Furthermore, all 48 units were assigned to the management of the factory.[53]

Private Homes for the Influential

Local party and government officials, factory managers, state bank directors, and others sometimes use their connections to build well-equipped, oversized homes on illegally assigned plots using stolen building materials and illegally loaned construction machinery. These are usually far in excess of the permitted 60 square meters of living space. Soviet officials sometimes own several private homes, although only one is allowed to each household while maintaining a state-owned apartment in a city. Such practices are reported throughout the Soviet Union.

Officials of the Executive Committee of Kaunas, the second largest city in Lithuania, have illegally assigned land to officials and other influential people who built homes according to individual plans drawn up by private architects. The houses were not approved by the design institute as required, and illegally obtained building materials were used for their construction.[54] In Zaleshchiki, a small and very attractive resort town on the Dnestr River in the Ukraine, "two- and three-story homes are popping up like mushrooms in the rain." Ukrainian officials have approved the construction of oversized homes averaging 100 square meters of living space. The plots for these homes were obtained illegally from *kolkhozi*, and building materials in critically short supply provided by the inter-*kolkhoz* construction trust were used.[55]

More than 50,000 homes were built illegally in Georgia in 1974. In the small Georgian community of Tskhvarichamia, 990 "imposing" mansions were built with the aid of modern equipment, materials, and manpower that for the most part was charged to the state. Influence in the right place and enough ready cash made this possible. Among others, mansions were built for the first secretary of a district committee in Tbilisi and the deputy director of the Tbilisi restaurant trust.[56]

An investigation by the Armenian Central Committee exposed the unlawful use of many expensive villas in Kirovkan, Abovyan, Sevan, Dilizhan, and other localities that were built and maintained at the state's expense. They were falsely registered as rest homes belonging to various ministries. Implicated in the scheme were local ministers of agriculture, road construction, and industrial construction, the head of the State Committee on

Forestry, a section chief of the Ministry of Communications, and the director of the "22d Party Congress" *sovkhoz*.[57] Typical of the violations were those committed by G. S. Katchatryan, a bank manager who already owned a house in the city and decided to build a large two-story private residence in the countryside using illegally acquired construction materials. Another case involved A. B. Mirozyan, the director of the Impul's plant in Dilizhan. Although already registered for two apartments, one in Yerevan and another in Dilizhan, Mirozyan built another private house in Dilizhan, though the construction of single-family homes had been banned there since 1962.[58]

While provincial and small republic officials are periodically criticized and some even removed for corruption, the top elite—Politburo members, national ministers, high-ranking military officers, and KGB officials who live well by Soviet or any other standards, but practice their consumption inconspicuously away from the public eye—is seldom publicly reprimanded for its sybaritic life style, for this would put the top leadership in a bad light.

Housing Differentiation and Housing Classes

Housing is an intrinsic part of the reward system that operates in Soviet society. The three most sought-after consumer acquisitions are an apartment, a car, and a comfortable *dacha*. A state-owned apartment is the only one of the three that is "free;" a car costs 8,000 rubles, and a comfortable *dacha* runs to five figures, but only a few are available on the market. Rent prices do not dampen consumer demand for housing because they are kept artificially low. Nearly everyone can afford to pay his or her rent, as it accounts for only three percent of the average family's monthly earnings. Because rents are so heavily subsidized, they fail to cover even a portion of construction costs, and cover less than two-thirds of all maintenance costs, not including capital repairs. Thus, in contrast to the arrangement that prevails in capitalist nations, the Soviet citizenry's "ability to pay" has little influence on the quality of housing it enjoys.

Urban housing in the Soviet Union is a state monopoly. In 1981, the state owned 75.6 percent of all housing in cities and towns, including cooperatives.[59] Government agencies distribute all state housing and must approve cooperative and private housing transactions, but do not do so equitably on the basis of need, and never have. After the Bolshevik revolution, the homes and apartments of the nobility and bourgeoisie were divided among workers and peasants, but some received more than others and some did not receive anything at all. Nadezhda Mandelstam recalls in the second volume of her memoirs, *Hope Abandoned*, that in the early 1920s writers who were in favor received privileged housing, even if only a room, which at that time was as treasured as today's apartment. Those who were not in favor, such as the futurist poet, V. Khlebnikov, were given nothing.[60]

Urban housing in the Soviet Union is frequently unrecognizable by neighborhood or building as containing middle class, worker, or poor occupants. This is because differentiation can take place within a building that has communal and individual family-occupied units—a phenomenon that is common in older and middle-aged housing districts. Even within communal units, there is further differentiation between those that have more space than others. In the same building, a typical communal apartment of four rooms might house a retired couple, a factory worker, his divorced wife and daughter—who still live in the same apartment because they cannot find any other accommodation—a widow, and a young couple that works during the day and studies at night. Another communal apartment of similar size might accommodate only two families, and a third may contain a single privileged household.

In newly constructed developments sponsored by individual organizations, differentiation by building and neighborhood is increasing. Departments of ministries, the armed forces, the KGB, the Academy of Sciences, institutions of higher education, factories, and other organizations construct apartments for their employees and workers. An example of this is the cluster of cooperative buildings erected by the Writers' Union on Red Army Street near Dynamo Station in Moscow. Not only do those in higher paid and more prestigious positions receive better housing, but because they are well connected they can use their influence to provide close relatives with apartments even though the latter do not work for the organization that built the housing. Another example of housing differentiation is cooperative housing that is largely occupied by the intelligentsia and their children. Setting a much higher premium on space and privacy, they are willing to pay huge sums to get better housing more quickly than workers.

Housing Classes

Housing in the Soviet Union was and continues to be differentiated among the least, less, more and most favored.[61] The poorest urban housing class, the "least favored," are the millions who cluster beyond the borders of large cities. They are also the most segregated. Many semiskilled and unskilled workers commute to work, but not by choice. Large population centers are closed to them to prevent Moscow, Leningrad, Kiev, and other cities from being overrun by migrants.

In the city, the housing poor are the "less-favored." They live communally or in dormitories. Possessing a legal right to live in the city, they can at least hope that in the distant future they will receive an apartment. In the meantime, they can take advantage of the amenities that Soviet urban life offers as compared to rural living.

Much better off are those households living in self-contained apartments in newly-erected housing districts. They are the "more-favored," even though they are located far from city centers. Commuting to work can take an hour by crowded bus or metro, and shopping is difficult. Therefore, food often has to be bought and carried home from shopping centers closer to the inner city.

The "most favored" are those families living in apartments in or near a city center. These are mainly the political, military, state security, economic, scientific, cultural, educational, and worker elites. They are also the most heavily subsidized because they pay the same low rent per square meter as those living communally. Thus the most advantaged become the beneficiaries of redistributed social wealth—even more so because they can pass it on to their children.

Of course, there is further differentiation within each housing class. The table of contents of the Moscow *Bulletin of Housing Exchanges* provides the best quick illustration of this phenomenon with its 16 major and minor categories for which housing demand exists. It should be mentioned that a small percentage within each of the first two housing classes is not upwardly mobile by preference. Some of the elderly who have lived communally all their lives might not wish to move from the inner city away from their friends or from convenient shopping places. Similarly, a number of those living outside cities might prefer a rural lifestyle that permits them to tend a vegetable garden in the summer.

The Soviet Union's acute housing shortage is very much of the government's making. Citizen initiatives to improve their housing situation are consistently stifled. On the one hand, the government continues to invest heavily in industry, attracting workers and management personnel to urban areas, and on the other, it deliberately underinvests in housing construction and other consumer services. Upward movement from one housing class to the next, though not impossible, is difficult and may take a good part of one's life.

Notes

1. *Narodnoe khoziaistvo SSSR v 1965 godu* (Moscow: Statistika, 1966), p. 7; *Narodnoe khoziaistvo SSSR v 1978 godu*, pp. 7 and 26; *Naselenie SSSR* (Moscow Statistika, 1975), p. 150; *Vestnik statistiki*, 1979, no. 11, p. 70; *Vestnik statistiki*, 1980, no. 12, pp. 67–68; *Vestnik statistiki*, 1981, no. 12, pp. 63–69; *Vestnik statistiki*, 1982, no. 11, pp. 73–74; and *Vestnik statistiki*, 1983, no. 11, pp. 56–57.

2. *Vestnik statistiki*, 1983, no. 11, pp. 56– 58. Housing in the USSR is primarily measured by the number of square meters of "living space" (*zhilaya ploshchad*) that

an individual occupies, not by the number of persons per room, which is a common yardstick in the West. The measurement includes bedrooms and the households' living room, but not the kitchen, bathroom, toilet, corridors, or storage space. Living and non-living areas make up the aggregate amount of "useful space" (*obshchaia ploshchad*) in a dwelling. Living space is approximately two-thirds of the total. By law, Soviet authorities measure housing accommodations in terms of living space.

3. *Literaturnaia gazeta*, July 12, 1972.

4. A. Belova and I. E. Darski, *Statistika mnenii v izuchenii rozhdaemosti* (Moscow: Statistika, 1972), p. 123.

5. *Pravda*, December 2, 1980.

6. N. Bobrovnikov, "Razvitie zhilishchnogo stoitel'stva v tekushchei pyatiletke", *Voprosy ekonomiki*, 1972, no. 5, p. 24.

7. See the report by N. K. Baibakov, chairman of the USSR State Planning Committee, in *Pravda*, November 24, 1982.

8. *UN Statistical Yearbook, 1974* (New York: United Nations, 1975), pp. 804–811.

9. Henry W. Morton, "Housing Problems and Policies of Eastern Europe and the Soviet Union," *Studies in Comparative Communism* 12, no. 4 (Winter 1979), pp. 302–303.

10. *Vestnik statistiki*, 1983, no. 11, pp. 56– 58.

11. I wish to thank Professor Yuri Luryi for explaining how the *propiska* system works.

12. See William Taubman, *Governing Soviet Cities* (New York: Praeger, 1974), pp. 116–131.

13. Taubman, *Governing Soviet Cities*, p. 97.

14. See Alfred John DiMaio, Jr., *Soviet Urban Housing* (New York: Praeger, 1974), pp. 116–131; and Henry W. Morton, "The Leningrad District of Moscow—An Inside Look," *Soviet Studies* 20, no. 2 (October 1968), pp. 206–218.

15. By virtue of precedent, enterprises and organizations with claims to a portion of municipal housing stocks assigned to a member of a particular organization—for example, the Writers' Union—will claim the right to continue placing one of its members in the unit when it is vacated. If housing is built by a factory or institution, then the municipality will claim 10 percent of the units for city employees. This claim does not apply to cooperative housing. This might be one of the reasons why cooperative housing takes longer to build.

16. Yu. K. Tolstoi, *Sovetskoe zhilishchnoe zakonodalet'stvo* (Leningrad: Leningrad University, 1974), p. 10.

17. Tolstoi, *Sovetskoe zhilishchnoe zakonodalet'stvo*, pp. 11–12.

18. See Stalin's speech on cadres in *Voprosy Leninizma*, 11th ed. (Moscow: Gospolizdat, 1953), p. 367.

19. Tolstoi, *Sovetskoe zhilishchnoe zakonodalet'stvo*, p. 91.

20. Interview, November 5, 1974. Bazaluk was subsequently jailed for accepting bribes.

21. According to a survey conducted in Kiev, only 5 to 6 percent of all newlyweds moved into their own apartments. *Komsomolskaia pravda*, September, 15, 1975, trans. in *Current Digest of the Soviet Press* 28, no. 10 (April 7, 1976), p. 22.

22. *Izvestiia*, July 6, 1973, trans. in *Current Digest of the Soviet Press* 25, no. 27 (August 1, 1973), p. 23.

23. Leningrad's bulletin is called *Spravochni po obmenu zhiloi ploshchadi.*

24. *Izvestiia*, July 6, 1973, trans. in *Current Digest of the Soviet Press* 25, no. 27 (August 1, 1973), p. 23.

25. *Literaturnaia gazeta*, March 16, 1977.

26. See *Izvestiia*, July 6, 1973, trans. in *Current Digest of the Soviet Press* 25, no. 27 (August 1, 1973), p. 23; *Izvestiia*, March 19, 1974, trans. in *Current Digest of the Soviet Press* 26, no. 11 (April 10, 1974), p. 26; and *Izvestiia*, October 6, 1974, trans. in *Current Digest of the Soviet Press* 26, no. 40 (October 30, 1974), p. 30.

27. *New York Times*, November 11, 1974.

28. *Izvestiia*, March 19, 1974, trans. in *Current Digest of the Soviet Press* 26, no. 11 (April 10, 1974), p. 26.

29. *New York Times*, March 4, 1977.

30. See *Vecherniaia Moskva*, Weekly Advertising Supplement, November 6, 1974.

31. *Literaturnaia gazeta*, July 2, 1975, trans. in *Current Digest of the Soviet Press* 28, no. 16 (May 5, 1976), p. 24; and *New York Times*, August 17, 1977.

32. *New York Times*, August 17, 1977.

33. *Sovetskaia kul'tura*, March 30, 1973.

34. *Literaturnaia gazeta*, July 2, 1975.

35. *Literaturnaia gazeta*, July 2, 1975.

36. *Pravda*, July 13, 1976, trans. in *Current Digest of the Soviet Press* 28, no. 28 (August 11, 1976), p. 22.

37. An Estonian purchased a cottage on a picturesque site for 2,500 rubles in 1972. The following day the seller arrived with the proper documents stamped by the rural soviet and smilingly presented him with a stone in lieu of the house. *Pravda*, August 10, 1972, trans. in *Current Digest of the Soviet Press* 24, no. 32 (September 6, 1972), pp. 32–33.

38. *Literaturnaia gazeta*, January 1, 1973, trans. in *Current Digest of the Soviet Press* 25, no. 19 (July 6, 1973), p. 18.

39. *Literaturnaia gazeta*, August 15, 1973, trans. in *Current Digest of the Soviet Press* 25, no. 40 (October 3, 1973), p. 22.

40. *New York Times*, August 17, 1977.

41. *Izvestiia* December 12, 1970, trans. in *Current Digest of the Soviet Press* 22, no. 51 (January 19, 1971), pp. 30–31; and *Pravda*, December 26, 1974, cited in *Soviet Analyst* 4, no. 3 (January 30, 1975), pp. 7–8.

42. See Peter H. Juviler, "To Whom the State Has Joined: Family Ties in Soviet Law," New York, October 29–31, 1976, p. 26; and V. Zimarin, "Rastorzhenie braka," *Sotsialisticheskaia zakonnost'*, 1975, no. 3, p. 61.

43. *Pravda*, February 16, 1973.

44. *Sovetskaia Rossiia*, May 16, 1975, in ABSEES. *Soviet and East European Abstracts Series* 5, no. 4 (October 1975), p. 69.

45. *Trud*, August 12, 1975, cited in *Soviet Analyst* 4, no. 17 (September 21, 1975), p. 8; see also *Trud*, February 1, 1973.

46. *Pravda*, May 19, 1973, trans. in *Current Digest of the Soviet Press* 25, no. 20 (June 20, 1973), p. 20.

47. *Soviet Analyst* 2, no. 14 (July 5, 1973), p. 7, citing *Sotsialisticheskaia industriia*, June 7, 1973.

48. *Zarva vostoka*, October 2, 1973, in *Joint Publications Research Service, Political and Sociological Affairs*, December 12, 1973, p. 70.

49. *Pravda* March 19, 1974.

50. *Zarya vostoka*, October 28, 1973, cited in *Radio Free Europe Research*, no. 1935, December 6, 1973, p. 6.

51. See the speech by First Secretary Karen S. Demirchyan, *Kommunist* (Yerevan), February 2, 1975, trans. in *Current Digest of the Soviet Press* 27, no. 10 (April 2, 1975), pp. 3–4. He complained that "violations of the procedure for distributing housing, which have become widespread in the past few years, arouse great and justified indignation among the working people. The state of affairs is especially bad in the city of Yerevan. In many of the capital's organizations and institutions housing is distributed without the active participation of party and trade union organizations. Matters have reached a point at which certain dishonest elements, who have built themselves nests in local Soviet agencies, are engaging in speculation with state flats and brazenly taking bribes."

52. *Pravda*, August 21, 1973, cited in *Soviet Analyst* 2, no. 18 (September 6, 1973), pp. 7–8.

53. *Trud*, July 13, 1974, cited in *Soviet Analyst* 3, no. 16 (August 1, 1974), pp. 7–8.

54. *Kimjaunimo tiesa*, December 12, 1974, in *American Bibliography of Slavic and East European Studies* 6, no. 2 (April 1975).

55. *Pravda*, May 25, 1975, trans. in *Current Digest of the Soviet Press* 27, no. 21 (June 18, 1975), p. 18.

56. *Pravda*, October 19, 1973.

57. *Kommunist* (Yerevan), March 28, 1974, in *Joint Publications Research Service, Political and Sociological Affairs*, May 14, 1975, pp. 9–10.

58. *Trud*, August 2, 1973, in *Joint Publications Research Service, Political and Sociological Affairs*, December 12, 1973, p. 73.

59. *Narodnoe khoziaistvo SSSR, 1922-1982*, pp. 431–432; and *Narodnoe khoziaistvo SSSR v 1975 godu*, p. 567.

60. Nadezhda Mandelstam, *Hope Abandoned* (New York: Atheneum, 1974), p. 90.

61. I am greatly indebted to Ivan Szelenyi for this section. I have adapted his seminal analysis of Hungarian housing classes, which he developed with Gyorgy Konrad, for the USSR. See his "Housing Systems and Social Structure," *The Sociological Review Monographs* 17 (February 1972), pp. 269–297.

Anna-Jutta Pietsch

9. Self-Fulfillment Through Work: Working Conditions in Soviet Factories

"Workers only come to themselves when not at work; at work they feel estranged. Work is not the satisfaction of a need, but a means to satisfy . . . needs external to work. The estrangement is embodied in a single fact that, as soon as all physical coercion or coercion of any other sort disappears, workers flee from their work as if it were the plague."[1] These drastic words are Marx's description of work in a capitalist system. The idea of overcoming the alienation of labor is an integral part of every communist party program. The Soviet Union has undertaken two broad attempts on quite different levels to attain this goal.

The first was linked to the liquidation of private property. The hope was that the alienation of labor would disappear along with private ownership of the means of production, as Marx predicted. This appeared to be occurring judging from the revolutionary behavior of workers shortly after the revolution, when they joined to form workers' councils and factory committees. Lenin enthusiastically welcomed the activities of these spontaneously built councils, but in March 1918 he suddenly began to consider the Russians to be "poor workers." The reason for his change of mind was the limited success of workers' councils in developing new forms of production that would take account of the needs of workers to satisfy their working conditions, and at the same time guarantee the level of production required for providing the Soviet population with the necessities of life.[2]

The willingness of a large number of Soviet workers to participate in the modernization of their country lasted for quite some time, as indicated by their high level of participation in Stalin's work campaigns during the first five- year plans.[3] However, Soviet factories were organized in a hierarchical

117

fashion, and shortcomings in the organization of labor often nullified their efforts. The organization of American factories as developed by Taylor and Ford was seen as a model—a necessary step on the ladder of progress.[4] On the one hand, a strong division of labor enabled the building of modern industries with unskilled workers, and on the other, managers became more independent of the motivations of individual workers as a result of increased mechanization and the setting of "norms" (production standards). This form of organization, which remains practically unchanged to this day, presumes that workers have no particular interest in their work except for the wages they receive. Soviet workers that came from rural areas, where there is little "industrial socialization," adapted to these processes only with difficulty. The same universal phenomenon occurred in many nations at the beginning of industrial age—for example, in the United States in the 19th century. Today, it is common in most of the Third World.

Stalin reacted to these integrational and motivational problems with a series of draconic laws that Werner Hoffman, a well-known German researcher, has termed the "third serfdom."[5] Stalin's labor legislation can be considered a tacit admission that more coercion is needed in the Soviet Union than in most capitalist nations to prevent workers from fleeing their jobs. The elimination of private ownership of the means of production did not lead to the elimination of the alienation of labor, even though this postulate still holds a firm place in Soviet ideology.[6]

The second attempt to eliminate restrictive working conditions was made in the post-Stalin period. Instead of trying to change the structure of society, it was expected that technological developments would bring about an end to the alienation of labor. Discussions about the effects of the scientific-technical revolution began to take place in the Soviet Union in the mid-1950s.[7] The first congress on the subject took place in Moscow in 1961. From then on, the concept of a scientific-technical revolution spread rapidly. A qualitative change in technological development was predicted in the West as well as the East.

It was hoped that full automation would remove workers from the immediate production process. Automation would liberate workers from subordinate, monotonous, and heavy physical activities not subject to his control. Automation would set them free to develop their talents, especially for scientific activities. Science would become the first productive power. It was thought that a new level of industrial development would begin in the immediate future and would be especially beneficial to socialist nations, for it was assumed that only they had the necessary preconditions for the full utilization of the positive effects of such processes. However, these hopes had no empirical foundation. At the time, empirical sociology was barely beginning to establish itself in the Soviet Union. In recent times, doubts have developed concerning the effects of the scientific-technical revolution on the Soviet Union. Such doubts emerged much later than in East Germany, where fully automated production was once seen as a technological panacea.[8]

Changes in the Attitudes of Soviet Workers Toward Work

Empirical sociological research has contributed to a more realistic assessment of Soviet working conditions.[9] Large-scale surveys of the attitudes of industrial workers were conducted in Leningrad, Gorky, Kiev, Siberia, and the Baltic republics during the 1960s. These investigations sought to analyze the reasons for high rates of labor turnover (about 20 percent of all industrial workers change jobs each year) and lay foundations for social planning.[10] They were repeated in Leningrad in 1962 and 1976, in Gorky in 1964-1978, and in Litauen in 1974 and 1981.

At the same time, Soviet sociologists began to study the relationship between worker and working places. This new sociological concept, as explained by V. A. Jadov, addresses the technical and social aspects of work in the context of life-styles and living conditions.[11] Sociological investigations became more effective and generated more realistic viewpoints. Jadov summarized these views by saying, "The economic and social resources of our society will neither now nor in the near future permit pursuit of a profession for the pleasure of its creativity."[12] In other words, the hope that technological developments would eliminate restrictive working conditions in the foreseeable future has vanished. There was progress in the introduction of complex mechanized and automated equipment, but it lagged far behind expectations, especially in auxiliary areas such as loading, storing, and intrafactory transportation, all of which are characterized by heavy physical labor.[13] For many years, there have been complaints that these areas have been practically ignored in terms of technological development.

The expectation that technical progress would raise qualifications and create better conditions has not been fulfilled. Based on data from repeat surveys in Gorky, Riabushkin determined that the number of working places employing unskilled workers was one and a half times higher than the number of workers.[14] Skilled workers aside, there are twice as many workers as workplaces in Gorky. This is surely not the case only in Gorky, for the educational level of the labor force rose sharply from 1970-79 as can be seen in Table 9.1.

The number of blue collar workers with university, technical, high school, or general secondary education more than doubled during the 1970s.[15] In 1972—the last year for which statistics on jobs in industry and construction by degree of mechanization were available—a large portion of the Soviet working force was employed in unskilled manual work. Thirty-six percent of all workers were employed in industry, and 52.2 percent were involved

120   Anna-Jutta Pietsch

TABLE 9.1
Educational Levels of Soviet Labor Force, 1970 and 1979

Level of Education	1970	1979
	Percentage	
Total Employees:		
University, Unfinished University, or Technical High School Education	18.3	26.7
General Secondary Education (10 years)	15.9	27.6
Unfinished Secondary Education (fewer than 10 years)	31.1	26.2
Blue Collar Workers:		
University, Unfinished University or Technical High School Education	3.1	7.7
General Secondary Education	14.5	31.5
Unfinished Secondary Education	36.7	34.0
White Collar Workers:		
University, Unfinished University, or Technical High School Education	60.2	72.0
General Secondary Education	19.1	18.6
Unfinished Secondary Education	16.0	7.7

Source: Vestnik statistiki, 1981, no. 5, p. 64.

in construction.[16] Frequent complaints about the large proportion of workers doing this type of labor seem to indicate that the Soviet Union's progress in this area has not been very rapid.

It seems possible that the problem of overqualification, which is visible in the data cited above, will be alleviated only by a change in the organization of labor. In 1981, the brigade form of organization, which is widespread in the Soviet Union, became obligatory.[17] Among the various types of brigades, the complex brigade is able to free workers from highly specialized unskilled jobs. Plans have been made to promote the formation of complex brigades in which workers with various skills are united to assemble a certain product or parts of a product. Workers divide up their tasks and are not confined to a particular function in such brigades. Oftentimes, they learn other professions while working in a complex brigade. They take over some of the functions of lower management—for example, supply procurement, intrafactory transportation, and some bookkeeping tasks. It was hoped that this form of organization would raise worker productivity, reduce the monotony of work, and increase the satisfaction of Soviet workers.

However, the brigade system leaves much to be desired. While production has increased and worker discipline has improved, attempts to raise product quality have not developed according to plan.[18] Calculations of the contribution of individual workers have aroused concern. In principle, workers are paid according to their contribution to the final product. Therefore, individual earnings are calculated using coefficients determined by the workers themselves. Attempts to overcome such conflicts have resulted in the implementation of a complicated bonus system.[19]

Not only have the technological aspects of production lagged behind the expectations of the 1960s; the same applies to the attitudes of Soviet workers toward their work. The most important determinants of worker satisfaction are "the content of work," wages, and working conditions.[20]

This has been interpreted as a sign of the development of a new socialist attitude toward work. But there are methodological problems with investigations of worker satisfaction. Respondents probably tend to lower their standards when they might seem unrealistic to interviewers (an example of resignative dissatisfaction), or give socially desirable answers instead of their own opinions.[21] The latter factor probably plays an important role given the ideological context in which the first surveys of worker attitudes took place.[22] According to Jadov, there was ample criticism of consumerism by the media during the 1960s. Owning nice clothes and the desire to own a home were stigmatized as "grimaces of the past," or indicative of petty bourgeois values.

Soviet sociologists observe that workers have arrived at a new system of values characterized by an "instrumentalization of the relationship to work."[23] Consumer attitudes have increased, and societal engagement has given way to a retreat into the private sphere. Jadov and other Soviet sociologists believe that the causes of this change stem from better standards of living, better education, and a modification in the social composition and age structure of the Soviet working class.[24] Better standards of living and better education have led workers to demand better working conditions. Younger workers sometimes react to unsatisfactory working conditions by refusing to work. Absenteeism and tardiness are also common, and the number of such offenses is increasing. While in 1962, only 9 percent of the work force refused to carry out commissioned work, in 1976 the proportion was 11 percent. The number of reprimanded workers rose from 10 to 20 percent during the same period.[25] At the same time, labor turnover rose sharply among unskilled workers largely because of their changed social composition.[26] In earlier times, most unskilled laborers came from rural areas. More recently, the proportion of young workers from families with technical or college training has increased. They tend to stay at their jobs for an average of about one and a half years before they change professions, become specialized workers, or attend universities. In 1962, 40 percent of the unskilled workers in Gorky stayed at the same factory for 3–4 years; in 1972 the figure was only 7 percent.

Workers over 40 are more self-disciplined and try to keep the production process going in spite of poor organization. In contrast, young workers react to poor organization with ample criticism and little self-discipline. They blame engineers and production managers who are responsible for keeping the production process running smoothly. Disciplinary measures are relatively ineffective because they fail to address the real cause of the offense—the poor and often irrational organization of the production process.

It appears that perceived necessity is the decisive factor behind young workers' attitudes toward their work. For example, Jadov cites a decrease in disciplinary offenses at the end of each quarter, when the plan has to be "saved." Afterward, self-discipline again decreases because workers no longer see the necessity of observing labor discipline.[27] V. S. Magun has shown that productive workers react especially negatively to organizational shortcomings because such deficiencies reduce their earnings.[28] Eighty percent of all Soviet workers receive wages for "piece work," and intrashift downtime often leads to a loss of earnings.[29]

The less constructive attitudes of younger workers in comparison with their older colleagues are the result of the different levels of socialization that each group has received.[30] The hardships of the postwar economy have left a lasting influence on the attitudes of older workers. It was up to each individual to help improve matters. On the other hand, the conditions under which younger workers grew up were quite different. "For many years the belief that a pleasant, creative and especially interesting job awaited every boy and girl as soon as they had grown up and finished studying was quite widespread," according to Jadov.[31] As to labor conditions, the slogan "scientific work organization" determined their outlook. But factory work is toilsome and often poorly organized. As a result, young workers become disillusioned when they are confronted with this reality. To a certain extent, this is considered a consequence of better education. Norms of behavior taught in school are not in agreement with the norms of daily conduct. Soviet sociologists believe that this has negative effects on worker motivation. Not only do workers react negatively to poor labor organization; they have become increasingly sensitive to sanitary conditions, undesirable hours, poorly maintained equipment, safety risks, and unsatisfactory production norms.[32]

In 1962, 62.6 percent of the Leningrad work force overfulfilled the norm, 10.7 percent substantially. The equivalent figures for 1976 are 43 percent and 4.4 percent. In the same year, 79 percent of these workers thought that they could produce from 10–30 percent more if they fully concentrated on their work and were financially rewarded for their efforts. Only 30 percent thought that they were working up to their full potential. Two-thirds of those questioned were unsatisfied with this state of affairs. Workers were interested in more effective production, under the condition that they would benefit from the improvement.[33] In addition, some Soviet sociologists speak of a growing demand for factory democratization—i.e., broader and more effective worker participation in factory administration and the organization of work.[34]

Jadov and other sociologists abstain from criticizing the attitudes of Soviet workers. They believe that Soviet society is passing through a normal phase of development in which a manifest lack of conscientiousness, responsibility, and exactness is a consequence of the historical and cultural past of the Soviet Union. They find that initiative, innovation and a break with antiquated values are characteristic of socialist industrialization. Soviet workers were never subject to the economic knout of the capitalist factory, which they see to be the origin of American objectivism and German precision.

Inasmuch as such characteristics are seen to be important for the intensification of production,[35] some feel that workers should be trained to have a responsible attitude toward their work and their duties, even if these involve unimaginative and monotonous tasks or hard physical labor.[36] However, the above-mentioned surveys show that workers display a readiness to work more intensively if a regular pace of work is guaranteed and individual contributions to production will be financially rewarded. Although the results of these surveys are not representative of the entire Soviet Union, they are not atypical in reflecting the self-consciousness of Soviet workers. Soviet press reports corroborate these results. They were one of the motives behind Andropov's discipline campaigns.

The pragmatism that the results of these opinion polls were met with is very instructive. Quoting Andropov as saying that "We have to display our findings exactly and dispassionately,"[37] at least the above-mentioned Soviet sociologists have accepted the fact that socialist workers see their work as nothing more than a means to satisfy needs extraneous to their work—that is, they have the same attitude toward work that Marx ascribed to workers in a capitalist system. Jadov even uses the same terminology as Marx in saying that a large number of workers see their work "as a means for reaching goals outside of the production-process."[38] The workers themselves have accepted this fact, but the conditions under which they work remain the target of their criticisms.

The attitudes of Soviet workers have parallels to those of Polish workers before 1980.[39] As in the Soviet Union, increased consumption in Poland during the Gierek period was accompanied by retreat into the private sphere and strong criticism of the disorganization of production. Especially younger workers had little tolerance for organizational shortcomings because they often felt more competent than their managers. Bahro's concept of the revolutionary impetus of surplus consciousness resulting from overqualification is relevant to the Polish case, M. Tatur has shown.[40]

This is not meant to imply that a similar radicalization of worker demands for better working conditions and higher wages will occur in the Soviet Union. The process that led to the formation of Solidarity was influenced by many factors that do not exist in the Soviet Union. Nonetheless, V. Zaslavsky has pointed out that demands for economic reform are increasingly being voiced by skilled Soviet workers[41]—a fact recently confirmed by a Novosibirsk newspaper.[42] Unfortunately, the political importance of the dissatisfaction of this group is impossible to assess.

Systemic Causes of Shortcomings
in the Organization of Soviet Labor

The most frequent complaint of Soviet workers concerning shortcomings in the organization of labor is the so-called unrhythmical use of their working time. Down-time can be ascribed to an absence of materials, machinery failures, regular maintenance, and managerial shortcomings. As A. McAuley and A. Helgeson have shown, intrashift down-time is substantial. According to their calculations, which are based on Soviet surveys, intrashift down-time accounts for 10.8 percent of all existing working time. As Table 9.2 indicates, this represents 50 percent of all working time lost.

In contrast, working time lost as a result of absenteeism and worker turnover amounts to only 2.3 percent of all available working time. Young workers seem to believe that intrashift down-time is not solely caused by managerial shortcomings, though managers can of course aggravate the problem if they are responsible for inadequate coordination. Intrashift down-time seems to be an inherent feature of centrally planned economies linked to problems caused by endemic shortages.

Janos Kornai analyzed this phenomenon in great detail in *Economics of Shortage*, where he argued that planned economies suffer from stochastic shortages in all economic sectors.[43] According to Kornai, socialist firms have no hard budget constraint. This peculiarity generates what he calls investment hunger. If capitalist firms exceed their budget, they run the risk of bankruptcy, but socialist firms can always expand their budgets. If they experience financial difficulties, they ask for subsidies, tax exemptions, or higher prices for their goods. If the budget constraint of socialist firms is "soft," demand can be expanded until it hits the resource constraint. Once this happens, additional demand pressures cannot be covered. This gives rise to bottlenecks that can result in intrashift down-time if they occur in the production sphere. In addition, if production shortages are prevalent, complementary

TABLE 9.2
Average Time Utilization per Industrial Worker, 1960–1974

	1960	1965	1970	1974	1974*
Total Calendar Days	366	365	365	365	
Rest Days,					
Public Holidays	59.3	60.0	93.2	96.5	
Paid Holidays	17.4	17.5	17.2	18.4	
Days Worked	289.3	287.6	254.6	250.1	
Total Loss of Labor Time	60.6	56.6	55.5	51.1	20.4
Sickness	13.3	12.0	14.7	13.5	5.4
Maternity	3.3	3.2			
Leave of Absence	5.1	5.1	5.0	4.6	1.8
Absenteeism	0.7	0.8	0.8	0.6	0.24
Intra-Shift Down Time	33.0	30.3	29.3	26.9	10.8
Turnover	5.2	5.2	5.7	5.3	2.1

Note: *Loss of labor time as a percentage of days worked.

Source: A. McAuley and A. Helgeson, *Soviet Labour Supply and Manpower Utilization,
1960–2000*, p. 5a, unpublished manuscript, cited by permission of authors.

goods cannot be used. In order to avoid this, socialist firms attempt to
hoard goods in short supply, which in turn increases the incidence of
shortages.

Most socialist firms do not simply wait until shortages are overcome.
Normally, they adjust themselves to shortages by substituting missing materials
or parts with either more expensive substitutes or inferior ones. The former
tactic leads to higher costs, while the latter lowers the quality of production.
The resulting spillover effects can lead to mechanical breakdowns in other
parts of the economy. This aggravates problems that stem from the rate of
liquidation of capital stocks.[44]

Socialist firms substitute parts, spare parts, and other semifinished goods
by producing them in factory-owned "backyard workshops." More Soviet
workers are involved in backyard production than in firms that specialize
in such items. While specialized enterprises employ approximately 70,000
persons, as many as 450,000 workers are involved in backyard production.[45]
Some claim that specialized enterprises producing tools and equipment for
the machine construction industry are responsible for 40 percent of the
sector's total output. The remainder is produced in workshops attached to

individual enterprises. Backyard production is extraordinarily labor intensive and is characterized by obsolete working conditions.

Shortages also result in the tendency to concentrate scarce resources in areas where short-term needs often override long-term considerations. This tendency is rather widespread. It helps to explain why the subsidiary areas of factories are neglected when it comes to technological improvement. It also helps to explain why preference is given to the construction of new factories instead of modernizing older ones, thus perpetuating unsatisfactory working conditions. In the short term, it would seem that investment in production is more beneficial to managers than investment in technological advancement. However, investment in subsidiary areas might "release" workers who could be employed with better results in production facilities.

As a result of chronic shortages, Soviet workers are confronted with difficulties unknown to their colleagues in the West. Unfortunately, it remains impossible to compare Soviet and Western labor conditions on a statistical basis because there are no official data on working conditions, protective measures, or "environmental" factors in the Soviet economy. Although the selective payment of bonuses might be thought of as an indicator of poor working conditions, they are often paid as hidden wage supplements designed to prevent workers from leaving their jobs, or to recruit workers from other firms.[46] The same can be said of holidays granted to workers subject to harsh working conditions. In 1977, for example, nearly half of all Lithuanian workers received holiday bonuses of 6 to 12 days. On the other hand, the Soviet system does not guarantee that workers laboring under harsh working conditions will actually receive the bonuses and holidays they are entitled to. This seems especially true of women involved in unskilled labor. Table 9.3 shows that there are great discrepancies between official and subjective, individual assessments of what constitutes poor working conditions.

The differences between subjective and objective assessments of working conditions have to do with the obsolete classification of jobs. Factors exacerbating psychophysiological problems received increasing attention in Soviet writings on working conditions during the 1970s. As a result, new standards of work have been elaborated,[47] but the classification of jobs has not been affected.

The Position of Workers in the Soviet Labor Market

It should be noted that the foregoing is only the dark side of the picture. Soviet workers enjoy certain advantages over their Western counterparts, most notably their stronger position in labor markets. This is because widening practices have led to labor shortages, which in turn have strengthened the bargaining power of Soviet workers.

TABLE 9.3
Working Conditions in the Production Association "S" in 1974

Firms	Official Assessment of Working Conditions	Worker Assessment of Working Conditions		
	Normal	Normal	Difficult	Detrimental
1	72.8	53.8	11.0	27.0
2	71.3	44.2	8.0	47.5
3	78.9	65.2	9.8	23.0
4	84.3	51.7	5.0	43.3
5	68.4	47.0	10.5	41.4

Source: M. Huber, Betriebliche Sozialplanung und Partizipation in der UdSSR (Frankfurt, 1983), p. 126.

Until 1970, it was possible to draw additional labor from the ranks of unemployed women. The number of employed women climbed steadily until 1970, when it leveled off at 81.97 percent. By 1979, the figure had risen only slightly, to about 83.14 percent.[48] Likewise, the number of employed retirees cannot be increased, and declining birth rates have aggravated the situation. As a result, with the exception of Central Asia, the Soviet Union now suffers from acute labor shortages. However, this does not apply to factory workers. The logic of the system forces Soviet factories to hoard workers just as they hoard other factors of production. Labor reserves in factories are estimated at about 10 percent of the total number of workers employed.[49]

Soviet factories need large worker reserves to compensate for irregularities in the work cycle, to be able to release workers during the harvest season, to react flexibly to changes in the plan, and to make up for production shortages. The need for worker reserves is determined by the constant occurrence of peak situations. Thus, under normal or subnormal production circumstances, factories often have a superfluous reserve of workers. Disregarding the need to maintain such a reserve contributed to the failure of the Shchekino experiment. After 10 years, the Shchekino factory was no longer able to fulfill its plan targets because too many workers had been laid off.[50]

Tight labor markets also serve to further protect workers from being laid off. Rather well-protected by Soviet labor laws against dismissals, workers can be laid off for only two reasons—serious offenses such as repeated drunkenness, or "rationalization" measures. In the latter case, the factory has to offer the worker an equivalent position, if not at the same enterprise,

TABLE 9.4
Fulfillment of Scientific Norms in Industry

Ministry	Percent for Whom Norms Might Be Set	Percent for Whom Norms Have Been Set	Percent Fulfilling Norm
Gas Industry	90	70	53
Non-Ferrous Metallurgy	65	61	49
Machine-Tool Production	80	70	41
Road Construction Machinery	80	74	39
Paper Industry	70	59	37
Light Industry	75	65	56

Source: McAuley and Helgeson, Soviet Labour Supply and Manpower Utilization, 1960-2000, p. 27.

then at another factory. Yet even these possibilities are seldom taken advantage of by factory managers. Irresponsible workers are often tolerated when they cannot be easily replaced. Furthermore, investment allocations that result in certain workers being made obsolete are often coupled with new construction in order to keep valuable laborers in the work force.[51]

Although the interests of Soviet workers are hardly represented by official trade unions, labor shortages improve the bargaining position of Soviet workers. In essence, workers can increase their wages and influence norms simply by threatening to change where they work. Managers also contribute to a permanent "wage drift" in their efforts to tempt workers away from other factories. As they depend on the motivation of their workers, managers try to give space to worker demands when possible. Managers have a certain amount of leeway in classifying workers into various tariff groups, and they advocate higher wages for those in possession of specially needed skills. As mentioned above, bonuses can be used for this purpose as well. Furthermore, wages can be increased by changing production norms. For many years, factories were able to set their own production norms. This explains why the central authorities are attempting to set scientifically-determined production norms—a process that now takes place in special institutes to prevent it from becoming a subject of debate between employers and employees. One can see the fruits of such measures in the results of the aforementioned surveys. The frequency of the overfulfillment of norms has decreased, but the process of introducing scientific norms is far from complete. Many factories have special regulations, but as can be seen in Table 9.4, there is no guarantee that they are applied even in factories where scientific norms have been set.

The bargaining position that Soviet workers have come to possess and defend has given them more power than was originally intended by the authorities.[52] Soviet workers have substantially more room for the expression of their interests than many Western analysts assume. As a consequence of unintended but inherent labor shortages, conflicts between workers, managers, and the planning bureaucracy have not been eliminated even though democratic forms of labor representation have been suppressed.[53] These conflicts take the form of tough, covert struggles continually occurring in Soviet factories. Although one of the original aims of Soviet society was to guarantee workers' self-fulfillment through work, its realization has not come nearer, as even Soviet sociologists now confirm.

Notes

1. K. Marx and F. Engels, *Werke*, Dietz Verlag (Berlin 1968), p. 51

2. R. Lorenz, *Anfange der bolschewistischen Industriepolitik* (Cologne, 1965).

3. A. Karpov, *Wissenschaftliche Arbeitsorganisation in der Sowjetunion. Zur Entwicklung des "menschlichen Faktors"* (Munich, 1979).

4. M. Tatur, *Talyorismus in der Sowjetunion* (Frankfurt, 1983), p. 72.

5. W. Hoffman, *Die Arbeitsverfassung der Sowjetunion* (Berlin, 1956).

6. See J. Habermas' critique of Marx's theory with respect to the impact of private ownership of the means of production on the alienation of labor. J. Habermas, *Theorie des kommunikativen Handelns*, vol. 2 (Frankfurt, 1981), p. 500.

7. R. Richta, *Richta Report. Politische Ökonomie des 20 Jahrhunderts* (Prague, 1968).

8. A. J. Pietsch, "Interactions between the Educational and Employment Systems in the German Democratic Party and the Soviet Union," *Organization Studies*, 1983, no. 4, p. 304.

9. W. Teckenberg, *Gegenwartsgesellschaften: UdSSR* (Stuttgart, 1983), p. 360.

10. M. Huber, *Betriebliche Sozialplanung und Partizipation in der UdSSR* (Frankfurt, 1983); and Tatur, *Talyorismus in der Sowjetunion*, p. 33.

11. V. A. Jadov, "Otnoshenie k trudu: Konceptual'naia model' i tendencii," *Sotsiologicheski issledovaniia*, 1980, no. 4, p. 21.

12. V. A. Jadov, "Otnoshenie k trudu," p. 60.

13. G. V. Osipov et al., "Rabochii klass i inzhenerno-tekhnicheskaia intelligentsiia v SSSR: Pokazateli sotsial'nogo razvitiia," *Sovetskaia sotsiologiia*, 1982, no. 2, p. 15.

14. T. V. Riabushkin, "Pokazateli sotsial'nogo razvitia rabochego klassa," *Sotsiologicheskie issledovaniia*, 1980, no. 4, p. 21.

15. General secondary education lasts 10 years in the Soviet Union. Passing a final examination at the end of this period enables one to apply for university entrance. Special secondary schools administer medium level professional education, which takes 2 years for pupils who finished general secondary school, and 4 years for pupils who did not.

16. E. V. Klopov et al. (eds.), *Sotsial'noe rabochego klassa SSSR* (Moscow, 1977), p. 238.

17. M. Drach and Ch. Revuz, *La brigade sous contract dans l'industrie soviétique et la réforme de juillet 1979* (Paris, 1981).

18. Jadov, "Otnoshenie k trudu," p. 58.

19. M. Lewin, "Jugend und Arbeit, Interview mit W. A. Jadov, A. N. Alexejew und W. J. Schtscherbatow," *Sowjetwissenschaft—Gesellschaftswissenschaftliche Beiträge*, 1984, no. 1, p. 35.

20. V. A. Jadov and A. G. Zdravomyslov, "Otnoshenie k trudu molodych rabochikh," in G. V. Osipov and Ia. Shehepan'ski (eds.), *Sotsial'nye problemy truda i proizvodstva* (Moscow, Warsaw, 1969), p. 121.

21. E. Gloeckner, "Arbeitsmotivation und Arbeitszufriedenheit," in M. S. Ruban et al. (eds.), *Wandel der Arbeits- und Lebensbedingungen in der Sowjetunion, 1955–1980* (Frankfurt/M., 1983), p. 597.

22. Jadov, "Otnoshenie k trudu," p. 55.

23. Lewin, "Jugend und Arbeit," p. 30.

24. A. A. Kissel', "Ob izmeneniiakh v sfere motivacii truda," *Sotsial'nye faktory povysheniia effektivnosti truda* (Leningrad, 1981), pp. 116–125.

25. V. B. Golofast and T. Z. Portasenko, "Sotsial'no- professional'naia mobil'nost rabochikh Leningrada (1962–1976 gg.)," *Sistema obrazovaniia i sotsial'nye peremeshcheniia* (Moscow, 1981), p. 10–113.

26. Jadov, "Otnoshenie k trudu," p. 57.

27. Lewin, "Jugend und Arbeit," p. 34.

28. V. S. Magun, "Dva tipa sootnosheniia produktivnosti truda i udovletvorennosti rabotoi," *Sotsiologicheskie issledovaniia*, 1983, no. 4, p. 69.

29. Tatur, *Talyorismus in der Sowjetunion*, p. 80.

30. Jadov, "Otnoshenie k trudu," p. 57.

31. Lewin, "Jugend und Arbeit," p. 35.

32. Jadov, "Otnoshenie k trudu," p. 58.

33. Jadov, "Otnoshenie k trudu," p. 58.

34. Lewin, "Jugend und Arbeit," p. 36.

35. Lewin, "Jugend und Arbeit," p. 30.

36. Lewin, "Jugend und Arbeit," p. 30.

37. Lewin, "Jugend und Arbeit," p. 30.

38. Lewin, "Jugend und Arbeit," p. 31.

39. J. Staniszkis, "Ein Jahr nach dem August 1980. Die Autonomie einer Revolution," in R. Fenchel and A. J. Pietsch, *Polen 1980–82, Gesellschaftgegen den Staat* (Hannover, 1982), p. 88.

40. M. Tatur, *Arbeitssituation und Arbeiterschaft in Polen, 1970–1980* (Frankfurt, 1983), p. 88.

41. V. Zaslavsky, *Geschlossene Gesellschaft* (Berlin, 1982).

42. Die Studie von Novosibirsk, *Osteuropa*, 1984, no. 1, pp. A1–A25. Presumably written by T. I. Zaslavskaia; Russian text in *Materiali samizdata, vypusk* no. 35/83, August 8, 1983.

43. J. Kornai, *Economics of Shortage* (Amsterdam, 1980).

44. Tatur, *Talyorismus in der Sowjetunion*, p. 45.

45. A. McAuley and A. Helgeson, *Soviet Labour Supply and Manpower Utilization, 1960–2000*, p. 34, unpublished manuscript, cited by permission of authors.

46. Huber, *Betriebliche Sozialplanung und Partizipation in der UdSSR*, p. 105.

47. Tatur, *Talyorismus in der Sowjetunion*, p. 109.

48. Calculated from the annual statistical yearbook, *Narodnoe khoziaistvo*, and the 1970 and 1979 censuses.

49. *Trud*, July 17, 1979.

50. *Pravda*, March 28, 1977, and March 29, 1977.

51. See also Zaslavsky, *Geschlossener Gesellschaft*, p. 50.

52. Cf. A. J. Pietsch and H. Vogel, "Displacement by Technological Progress in the USSR," in J. Adam (ed.), *Employment Policies in the Soviet Union and Eastern Europe* (London, 1982), p. 145.

53. See also Ch. F. Sabel and D. Stark, "Planning, Politics and Shop Floor Power: Hidden Forms of Bargaining in Social-Imposed State-Socialist Societies," *Politics and Society*, 1983, no. 1, p. 439.

10. The Vanishing *Babushka*: A Roleless Role for Older Soviet Women?

Like her North American counterpart, today's older Soviet woman differs radically from her forebearers.[1] As a group, Soviet women aged 55 and over, who numbered about 30 million in 1982, are better educated, have raised fewer children, have longer experience in the labor force, and have a greater life expectancy than those of any previous generation.[2] Their level of political involvement, as exemplified by communist party membership and participation in the activities of local government bodies, has risen steadily over the past few decades, and their professional credentials cover a wide range of specialties.[3]

Mounting evidence suggests that female old-age pensioners in the Soviet Union have not entirely managed to avoid the burdens of aging that fall upon the shoulders of older women in other industrialized societies. A recent commentary on the status of the aged in the United States might apply equally well to the Soviet Union. "Some people grow old gracefully, few gratefully, [for] the average mortal balks at paying the dues of age for the boon years of youth."[4] More importantly, Matilda White Riley, who has eloquently described the position of older American women, has noted that Soviet women of pension age "have more to offer to society than

This chapter was previously published as "The Vanishing Babushka: A Roleless Role for Older Soviet Women" in *Current Perspectives on Aging and the Life Cycle*, Zena Smith Blau, ed. (Greenwich, CT: JAI Press Inc, 1985) and is reprinted with permission. The research on which this essay is based was supported by the National Institute of Aging as part of a larger project, "Retirement and Aging in Cross-Cultural Perspective." The views expressed in this chapter do not necessarily reflect those of the United States government.

society is ready to receive, and more to offer themselves than they believe possible."

What Riley observes in the United States might hold true for the Soviet Union as well. Women of retirement age are doubly disadvantaged "because they are old and because they are old women."[5] As in the United States, older Soviet women outnumber older Soviet men. Increasingly, these women live alone, and frequently they exist on largely inadequate state pensions. One-fifth of all older Soviet women live in cities, and one-fourth live in the countryside. The forces of social change, particularly the nuclearization of the family, threaten to deprive these women of their traditionally sanctioned role as babushki, or grandmother-nannies. These same forces may strip this role of much of its social and economic meaning, even for those older women who assume it.

From a theoretical perspective, this chapter represents a "case study" of a larger sociological issue. Is the "roleless role" of older Soviet women the product of socio-demographic factors that show no respect for national or ideological boundaries, or a function of industrial structures? From a public policy perspective, the following represents an analysis of some of the reasons why government policies regarding the aged fail to speak to the problems of older females, both East and West.

The Demographic Picture

In the aggregate, older Soviet women shoulder a disproportionate share of the burdens or benefits of aging owing to the "feminization" of the Soviet pension-age population—males 60 and over, and women 55 and over. Unfortunately, age-specific results from the 1979 Soviet census have not been published. Indeed, they might never see the light of day because of the gloomy picture they paint regarding declining life expectancy. However, in 1980, Soviet gerontologists, with presumed access to what is still treated as "secret data," authoritatively stated that women in the over-60 age group outnumber their male counterparts by a factor of more than two to one. Other recent Soviet sources suggest an even larger demographic dispro-portion, on the order of 7–8 females over 60 for every 2–3 males in the same age group.[6]

These imbalances in the Soviet pension-age population have been dwin-dling, but slowly. In 1959, there were 284 females of retirement age for every 100 males over 60, and U.S. calculations suggest a decrease to 263 Soviet females per 100 males by 1980. The size of the female majority, which was 19.5 million in 1964, is scheduled to drop to 4.7 million by the end of the century. Still, a balanced sex ratio probably will not appear before the year 2010.[7]

In the rural areas of the Russian Soviet Federated Socialist Republic (RSFSR), the nation's political, economic, and ethnic heartland, the distribution of older women is skewed in other ways as well. First, the "iron laws" of Soviet demographic processes—the outmigration of rural males, the outmigration of rural females of childbearing age, and a low rural birthrate—have produced a situation in which pension-age citizens rose from one-fifth of the rural Russian population in 1966 to one-fourth by 1978. On a national basis, however, pension age persons comprised only 15.3–15.5 percent of the Soviet Union's combined urban and rural population in 1980. By 1975, the Soviet Union had become a predominantly urban society (56.3 percent of the population lived in cities), but the proportion of elderly people living in rural areas exceeded the proportion living in urban centers by 11.4 percent.[8] Meanwhile, the number of rural females over 60 grew by 15.3 percent from 1959 to 1970, even as the share of males in these age brackets increased at less than half this rate.[9]

Such evidence suggests that older, rural females in the Soviet Union might be increasingly thrown back on their own resources. By 1979, for example, over two-fifths of all rural women over 60 living in Estonia were widowed and living alone.[10] In Latvia, the proportion was about one-third, and in the Russian republic, the Ukraine, Belorussia, Lithuania, and Moldavia, older widowed single females accounted for at least one quarter of the total number of rural women of all ages. The national average of older widows in 1979 stood at about 24 percent of all Soviet women.

The roots of the problem run deep. Soviet males over 60 are twice as likely to remarry as females, and at least a third of all males who remarry choose a mate aged 50 or less.[11] Whereas widowed females account for less than half the total number of males and females aged 40 or younger who are single or widowed in the rural population, the female segment increases in size in each successive age group. Older widowed women comprise over nine-tenths of those individuals aged 60 and over who are single or widowed and live in villages.[12] In urban areas, this problem is widespread, but perhaps less chronic. In 1975, 23 percent of all Soviet urban women over 60 lived alone, as did a larger proportion in republics such as Estonia, where the figure was 35.9 percent.[13] Interviews conducted in 1981 revealed that in cities such as Moscow, old-age pensioners form one-fifth of the total population.[14] Within this group, the largest single component consists of elderly females, either single or widowed.

Part of the problem, as Soviet gerontologists and demographers are quick to point out, can be attributed to male population losses in World War II. But the passage of time alone will not correct the demographic imbalance. For example, the growing number of divorces in the over-40 age group— what one Soviet demographer terms the *otsrochennyi*, or "postponed," divorce—promises to create additional numbers of single, older women, even as the demographic impact of World War II fades into history.[15]

Demographic changes therefore set the stage for the altered roles that older women perform in Soviet society. Certain roles, such as those of the "spouse" and the "independent homemaker," seem to be increasingly foreclosed, and the traditional *babushka* role is also being curtailed. This is paradoxical because state-run child care facilities cannot accommodate half of all eligible children in the cities, and as few as one-fourth in the countryside.[16] However, many rural women cannot take over the role of child-minder and housekeeper simply because their families have left the area. Likewise, many elderly Soviet females living in cities no longer live with their families, thus making the *babushka* role even more tenuous. Work roles for female old-age pensioners have yet to take up the slack.

Roles for Soviet Pension-Age Women

The Soviet social system has been built around Marx's contention that the social identity of the individual is based on work. Soviet pensions are justified both as remuneration for past labors and as compensation for those who theoretically are no longer able to work. As in the United States, the history of the Soviet retirement system suggests that the system emerged and has been periodically transformed mostly as a matter of short-term concerns regarding labor policy rather than substantive ideological shifts.

In the mid-1960s, Soviet policies that favored retirement since 1956 were reversed. A variety of incentives designed to entice old-age pensioners to remain in the labor force were enacted. Whatever the success of these policies, continued employment has not been an option that a majority of older Soviet women have eagerly embraced.[17]

Current Soviet estimates concerning the pension-age population's capacity for work hold that four-fifths of all old- age pensioners are still capable of full- or part-time work for the first year after they reach retirement age. Soviet medical studies suggest that working old-age pensioners are two times less likely to display signs of organic aging than nonworking pensioners.[18] In macroeconomic terms, such findings are probably encouraging to Soviet policymakers. In theory, able-bodied working pensioners can increase the size of the Soviet Union's labor reserve to partially offset the looming manpower shortage among younger age groups. By 1971, working pensioners comprised 6.8 percent of the RSFSR's work force, and 8.2 percent and 9.0 percent of all those employed in large urban centers such as Moscow and Leningrad.[19] However, it seems unlikely that old-age pensioners could actually increase the size of the Soviet work force. From 1959–70, old-age pensioners displayed an increased preference for nonwork roles, and from 1971-82 retirement continued to be the preferred role of old-age pensioners.

Among older women, the number of working pensioners declined from 3.0 million to 2.2 million between the 1959 and 1970 censuses, representing a decrease of 27 percent. The number of male working pensioners declined more dramatically, from 2.6 million to 1.2 million, probably owing to the relatively higher pension benefits they enjoyed. As a proportion of the entire working age female population, female working pensioners dropped from 4.6 percent in 1959 to 3.3 percent in 1970. The number of male working pensioners as a share of all working males declined from 4.7 percent to 1.9 percent. For both sexes, the preference for nonwork roles increases with age. While four-fifths of all those in the 55-59 age bracket continue to work, the proportion fell to 32 percent for those aged 60-64, and to 17.5 percent for those aged 65-69.[20]

The leveling off of retirement rates among older Soviet males and females after 1970 was accompanied by a gradual rise in the number of working pensioners to roughly one-third of all pension-age citizens by 1982. Yet today's older Soviet female still displays only a lukewarm interest in the idea of remaining at work. A study carried out in Moscow in 1973-74 showed that even though Soviet women become eligible to receive pensions at 55, whereas Soviet men become eligible at 60, these "young-old" females are less likely to work even a year beyond retirement age than their older male counterparts. Among individuals who receive old-age pensions for four years or more, the proportion of females still working is over one-third less than the figure for males, as can be seen in Table 10.1.

A study carried out in Taganrog, the Soviet Union's version of Middletown, found that male working pensioners remain employed for an average of 6-7 years, whereas females continue to work for an average of 3-5 years.[21] Another survey covering the entire RSFSR, carried out in 1973-74 and 1976-77, found that the average female working pensioner is employed for four years and two months, versus five years and five months for her male counterpart. Breakdowns by branch of the economy and profession indicated that continued employment rates are highest among female junior service personnel working in industry and male white-collar personnel involved in what the Soviets call "the local economy"—for example, repair services, maintenance work, housing construction and repair, sanitation, and public service establishments such as cafeterias and theaters.[22]

These data show that the marked preference of older Soviet women living in the RSFSR is to choose retirement over continued employment. Among those surveyed, 32.4 percent of all males and 28.4 percent of all females of pension age expressed a desire to return to the labor force. Among those individuals of pre-pension age, 71 percent of the males who were interviewed planned to continue working, whereas the figure for

TABLE 10.1
Female-Male Differences in Employment Propensity by Length of Retirement Eligibility

| Period of Eligibility | Males | | Females | | Percentage Difference |
	Working Pensioners	Non-working Pensioners	Working Pensioners	Non-working Pensioners	
3–4 years	65.2	34.8	41.2	58.8	24.0
2–3 years	61.0	39.0	49.0	51.0	12.0
1–2 years	77.3	22.7	61.3	38.7	16.0
0–1 years	100.0		92.5	7.5	7.5

Note: Figures are based on data for 464 males and 631 females. Coefficients of the difference between dichotomized male-female breakdowns in 2-year groups (0–2 and 2–4 years) are: Q = −.52 for males, and Q = −.50 for females.

Source: V. D. Shapiro, "Faktory zaniatosti pensionerov v obshchestvennom proizvodstve," unpublished candidate dissertation, vol. 2 (Moscow, Institute of Sociology, 1979), tables 15 and 16.

females was only 65 percent. Further breakdowns by age-specific categories revealed a lower propensity to "reengage" in work among recently retired females aged 55–59 as opposed to older males aged 60–64 who had just become pension eligible. The respective proportions were 33.3 and 35.3 percent for each group. An even lower proportion of females aged 60–64 expressed a desire to reenter the work force (21.4 percent).[23] For the most part, these data apply to urban Soviet females of pension age. The picture for older rural female old-age pensioners is similar, at least with respect to formally sanctioned work roles in such areas as collective agriculture. The data, which are for rural, pre-pension age males as well as females, indicated that 36 percent of the latter planned to cease work as soon as possible, but only 22 percent of all Russian males anticipated a similar decision. Moreover, for every type of agricultural worker, a smaller proportion of pre-pension age females said they planned to continue working. However, the de facto work roles performed by many older rural women in the private plot sector are not included in this analysis.

Another line of inquiry shows that whereas material motives ("a need for additional income") figured prominently in the decision not to retire among those workers in predominantly female occupations such as animal husbandry and field work, "social" motives ("a need for work," or "wanting to stay in the collective") characterized the decisions of agricultural specialists, administrators, tractor drivers, and mechanics. These are all predominantly male occupations in rural Russia.[24] Unfortunately, we cannot determine whether sex, status, and income differences are the motivating factors in these differing assessments of the work roles of rural old-age pensioners.

Overall, 29.9 percent of the RSFSR's female rural old-age pensioners remained in the work force, whereas 35.2 percent of all males did so. For every age cohort among those rural old-age pensioners over 60 years of age, the proportion of working females was from 4-11 percentage points lower than the figure for males. Among those female nonworking pensioners who expressed a desire to resume employment, 83.3 percent of those seeking to return to work only wanted part-time employment. Among those wanting to return to work at a new specialty, about half said they would prefer to do "piece work" at home.[25]

A 1974 study of urban female working pensioners during the first five years after they reached pension eligibility showed that most continue in their previous jobs or professions. A majority of the respondents (53 percent) said that their decision to postpone retirement until some later date was governed by material necessity.[26] The same data suggest that female working pensioners have a "future orientation" characterized by a certain amount of uncertainty and fear in contrast to the motivations of males. Presumably, this reflects what these women believe happens to 55-59 year old women who do not retire immediately. Such beliefs can tell us not only about perceptions, but also about the reality behind them.[27]

Research conducted in Moscow and Dnepropetrovsk in 1981 confirmed that material motives figure prominently in the work-retirement decisions of urban female working pensioners. In Moscow, the level was 46 percent, and in Dnepropetrovsk it was 72 percent.[28] An earlier study conducted in Leningrad in 1971 pegged 69 percent of all working pensioners as being motivated by material considerations, with only 31 percent of the respondents moved by social considerations.[29] Males were twice as likely to mention social factors in their decision to forego retirement than were females. The above-mentioned survey of the RSFSR confirms that social incentives play a bigger role in the work decisions of male working pensioners as compared to female working pensioners. This still holds true when age, education, and income differences between men and women of pension age are considered. Sex differences therefore qualify as a "primary variable" in any model of retirement-work decisions.[30]

This conclusion is reinforced by the fact that male-female distinctions regarding individual motives for staying in the work force hardly vanish when shortened day, reduced work week, work at home, or full-time work options are considered. On the average, full- or part-time female working pensioners mention "material considerations" 10-11 percent more often than men. The proportion of such replies for "at home" workers and for females working a reduced week was 14-22 percent of the total.[31] Nor did the branch of the economy in which they were employed make a major difference. Material considerations influenced 53 percent of the work decisions of female working pensioners in the service sector, and 63.2 percent of the decisions of those involved in industry. The comparable figures for male working pensioners were 41 percent in the service sector, and 36.1 percent in industry.[32]

These survey data show that Soviet female old-age pensioners are more likely than their male counterparts to choose retirement over continued employment, even when age, income, occupational, and other differences are taken into account. In contrast to the orientation of males, female old-age pensioners who chose to work are motivated more by perceived material necessity than by attachment to work roles. This can be explained either by basic differences in male-female work roles not captured by the occupational-income controls mentioned above, or by basic differences in male and female attitudes toward work. In either case, work roles appeal to only a minority of Soviet pension-age women, and then largely for instrumental purposes.

The data needed to determine whether material necessity is an objective factor in the decision of older Soviet women not to retire remains incomplete. However, material need is not a purely subjective motivation. Among all old-age pensioners working part time, over half of those involved in industry and consumer services have a per capita family income of less than 70 rubles a month. Of all nonworking pensioners who wish to work, 70 percent received a pension of under 60 rubles a month.[33] Many in both groups are older women.

The significance of these figures lies in the fact that, as Soviet economists have pointed out, one can live, though not well, on 70 rubles a month. One cannot subsist even minimally, they maintained, on 50 rubles a month, which is the officially recognized "poverty level" (pozhitochnyi minimum). Meanwhile, the average urban old-age pension for males and females in 1980 was only 70 rubles per month, according to unpublished figures compiled by the State Planning Commission.[34] On the average, urban females of retirement age probably received a lesser amount, owing to their overall lower wage levels.

Working female old-age pensioners do not necessarily attain economic equality with younger women. For example, whereas the average female "at home" worker (nadomnitsa) of pre-pension age earns 70–89 rubles a month for piece work, the average female nadomnitsa aged 55 or more earns only 30–49 rubles a month.[35] Similarly, an analysis of the range of occupations in which all male and female old-age pensioners are currently concentrated shows that the largest proportion of old-age pensioners is lacking in both prestige and remuneration. Unfortunately, the absence of combined age- and sex-specific data regarding Soviet occupations renders any precise analysis impossible. However, a certain amount of "downward mobility" seems to be associated with the status of male and female working pensioners in the contemporary Soviet Union.

The influence of material considerations on the decision of some older Soviet women not to retire suggests that many female Soviet old-age pensioners, like their American counterparts, still labor under the burden of an inequitable pension system.[36] Soviet pensions are tied to past earnings on a percentage basis, and despite the existence of "wage creep" in recent years, the pension-wage scale has not been modified since 1956. All old-age pensioners are thereby disadvantaged because the replacement value of even recent pensions never exceeds 50 percent of one's pre-pension earnings. Older women suffer the most as the income inequalities they faced while working mount with age and probable widowhood.

Historically, the earnings of Soviet females have been lower than those of Soviet males. A Western economist who specializes in Soviet labor and welfare economics estimates that in the 1956-75 period the average female worker earned three-fifths as much as her male counterpart. A 1976 Soviet source points out that female piece-rate workers earn only 86 percent as much as their male colleagues.[37] Thus it seems likely that working female pensioners receive lower pensions and lower wages than male working pensioners. They also bear responsibility for a disproportionate share of household chores—15-20 percent more than males, according to one noted Soviet economist.[38]

Family

The evidence presented in the preceding section suggests that the attraction of work roles for Soviet women of retirement age remains ambiguous at best—a kind of "roleless role." This holds true despite the fact that official calculations by the State Committee hold that four-fifths of all Soviet citizens of retirement age can be classified as "able-bodied," and that 86 percent of nonworking pensioners are physically capable of some sort of employment in the labor force.[39] However, according to Soviet surveys carried out in the 1970s, only 25-31 percent of the latter group of nonworking pensioners indicate any interest in reentering the work force.[40] In addition, female nonworking pensioners are only half as likely as males to display any inclination to return to the working world. Among old-age pensioners who work, women are twice as likely as men to anticipate eventual retirement (22 percent versus 10 percent), and they remain undecided about their retirement plans in only half as many instances (14 percent versus 30 percent).[41]

Can we therefore conclude that a majority of older Soviet women, shunning the continuation of work roles, eagerly embrace the role of the *babushka* as a positive alternative? Soviet survey data on perceptions of retirement roles among Soviet female old-age pensioners suggest that the *babushka* role is less attractive and less widespread than is commonly believed in both the United States and the Soviet Union. A 1973–74 survey of Soviet female working pensioners aged 55–59 revealed that 40 percent did not look forward with any anticipation to assuming *babushka* responsibilities when they retired. Another 40 percent were neutral on the issue, and only 20 percent replied positively.[42] One-fifth of the sample displayed a negative attitude toward assuming the kinds of homemaker responsibilities that traditionally accompany the *babushka* role.

Surveys of male and female old-age pensioners in the RSFSR indicate that older Soviet women do not consider "care of younger children" to be a major reason for leaving the work force. Among female nonworking pensioners, 7 out of 10 cited "poor health" as their chief reason for retiring. A similar proportion of female nonworking pensioners cited various medical reasons as the main factor in their decision not to seek employment after spending some time as retirees.[43] Even when controls were imposed for urban-rural residence and educational levels, there were no major differences in the responses of female nonworking pensioners.[44]

Another set of survey data also suggest ambiguous attitudes toward the *babushka* role among Soviet female old-age pensioners. A 1977–78 study carried out among women in Kiev by the Institute of Gerontology revealed that most female old-age pensioners, especially female nonworking pensioners, associate retirement with "increased leisure" or "time to look after oneself." Only about one in four linked retirement to "care of grandchildren," and fewer than one in six associated it with "helping with household chores."[45]

Interviews with Soviet gerontologists confirmed that the *babushka* role and multigenerational living arrangements might not be altogether desirable in the eyes of many Soviet old-age pensioners. Citing as yet unpublished survey results, these specialists indicate that among females over 55 living with their extended families, 29 percent of those aged 55–59 and 25 percent of those aged 60–64 expressed a desire to live apart from their offspring and run only their own households.[46] An unpublished report to the 1976 Soviet gerontological congress went even further, stating that half of all old-age pensioners wished to live apart from their children and 88 percent of the younger generation expressed a similar preference with respect to their parents.[47]

Anecdotal evidence points in a similar direction. As one woman complained in 1968, "my mother claims she's still a competent engineer at age 58, and she refuses to stay home and change diapers." One professional in her mid-60s said that she looked forward to the day "when I can stay at home and amuse myself with my grandchildren," provided that she could continue with part-time teaching, research, writing, and consulting. Even elderly coat check women (*garderobshchiki*) who need the income to supplement meager pensions often say that they would "go crazy with boredom" if they had nothing to do but look at the four walls of their apartments or simply stand in line for food all day. The presence of other *garderobshchiki* with whom to gossip and socialize, a warm room in which to spend cold winter days, access to shopping facilities, and the kind of companionship generated over the ever-bubbling tea kettle seem to be preferable to performing *babushka* duties, even for elderly women workers with low wages and no skills.

Other types of evidence suggest that the traditional components of the *babushka* role may be declining in importance in modern Soviet society. A Leningrad study from the mid-1970s reveals that, contrary to popular assumptions in the West, the *babushka* is no longer the chief workhorse of the modern urban household, even in multigeneration families. Soviet sociologists who have disaggregated the amount of time that families spend on various domestic chores have found that Soviet husbands outrank *babushki* in all tasks except food preparation. Meanwhile, Soviet wives, whether working or not, continue to bear the burden of most household chores.[48]

The role of the *babushka* as child-minder might also be disappearing on an aggregate level. This would deprive female old-age pensioners of the opportunity to fulfill the *babushka* role, even for those who desired to do so. In 1979, there were an estimated 8–9 million Soviet children, presumably of preschool age, being cared for by *babushki*. Most of these were concentrated in single-parent families headed by females.[49] The absence of age-specific data from the 1979 Soviet census makes it difficult to gauge exactly what kind of "*babushka* coverage" this figure represents. However, using U.S. Bureau of the Census data on Soviet population growth and age distribution, we can estimate that the Soviet preschool population included between 22 and 37 million boys and girls in 1979. For the total preschool population in that year, this would mean a national "*babushka* coverage" level of between 24 and 35 percent.[50]

This might be misleading because the continued presence of a disproportionate number of multigeneration families in the traditional Muslim cultures of Soviet Central Asia might inflate our estimates. Conversely, the rural outmigration of young families leaves elderly women with no families to look after, and might push the level of coverage downward.

However, similar levels of "*babushka* coverage" were found in the European, industrialized, urban areas of the Soviet Union, as typified by cities such as Leningrad. A 1973–74 survey of urban families found that grandmothers, or both grandparents, actively assisted in rearing first offspring in less than half of all cases. By the time the second child had appeared, the level of assistance had fallen to about a third.[51] A recent study based on 1979 census materials for Leningrad confirms these findings. Only about

33 percent of all Leningrad children aged three and under live with their maternal grandmother in the same household, and between 13 and 18 percent live with paternal grandmothers in similar circumstances. Thus the level of *babushka* coverage extended to between 46 and 51 percent of this group of preschool children. By the time these children had reached school age, however, the level of coverage dropped to 42 percent.[52]

Moreover, as retired Soviet women grow older, the *babushka* role may hold fewer and fewer attractions. For example, a 1979 study in the Latvian republic showed that while 56 percent of all female nonworking pensioners carried out *babushka* functions during the first five years following their retirement, the proportion of those so occupied aged 60 or older dropped to 40 percent.[53]

Structural constraints on the *babushka* role in contemporary Soviet society are growing irreversibly. By 1970, for example, the number of nuclear families in the Soviet Union exceeded the number of multigenerational families by about one-third. Similarly, the increasing tendency of generations to live apart and at some distance from one another, even when they still reside in the same city, makes child-rearing and child-minding increasingly difficult for older women. A 1980 study suggests that *babushka* assistance varies from a high of 64 percent in urban families when different generations live nearby—within 30 minutes traveling time—to a low of 25 percent when they live an hour or more apart.[54] The significance of such figures should not be underestimated. In Moscow, a trip from one end of a subway line to the other, or from the center the city to a suburb when a bus connection is involved, can easily consume an hour of one's time.

Based on the available data, it seems that caring for grandchildren as part of the *babushka* role is no longer important in the plans that older Soviet females make for their retirement years. Nor is it an especially important part of their lives once they stop working. However, the reality of Soviet family life—high labor force participation rates for women with young children, inadequate child care facilities, and minimal male assistance with domestic chores—means that many female old-age pensioners are still thrust into the *babushka* role, even if they do not particularly relish the idea. Over time, the reality of the *babushka* role seems to be declining, and will probably continue to do so because of the nuclearization of the family, population mobility, a lack of enthusiasm for the role, and the fact that fewer than half of all urban Soviet children of preschool age live in multigenerational families.

Interviews with Soviet gerontologists conducted in 1981 indicate that some are convinced the *babushka* role is somehow redeemable. Researchers at the Institute of Gerontology in Kiev have set themselves the task of "modernizing" the *babushka* role. Arguing that progressively higher levels of education will better equip each successive generation of older Soviet women to play a positive role in the upbringing of Soviet children, these researchers have proposed an educational program on child development and child psychology directed toward Kiev *babushki*. The purpose, as one informant put it, is to "update the convictions, stereotypes and ideas of today's *babushka* and to help her accept the values and convictions of the parents so as to minimize conflict within the family." These researchers also argue that in order to "save the *babushka*," they must learn more about the positive functions that such individuals actually perform in the contemporary Soviet family from the perspective of each generation involved. A pilot study is underway to determine not only which family functions are viewed positively, but also which ones serve as a cause of intrafamilial conflict. Plans are also underway to assess the positive aspects of the role of the *babushka* in the moral, social, emotional, and physical development of the child, using children cared for in state-run institutions as a control group.

These specialists see three structural alternatives for the *babushka* in Soviet society between now and the year 2000. For rural areas, given the apparently irreversible outflow of younger generations, one arrangement would be for the *babushka* to join her urban family members during the winter months when life in the village becomes difficult. There she could care for the children, help out with chores, and generally do what *babushki* have always done. In the summer months, she would return to the familiar surroundings of the village—to her house, her friends, and her small private plot, taking the children with her. All would presumably profit by a such an arrangement. In urban areas, two variants are possible. The first is the *prikhodiashchiiasia babushka*, or the dayworker-*babushka*. This would be an individual living apart from her family, but in the same city or district, coming over daily to help with child-minding, cleaning, and shopping. The second alternative, the *babushka-nadomnitsa*, is a variant of the "at home" role of some old-age pensioners. Here the grandmother, while living apart from her family, would take her grandchildren into her own home, and return them to their parents on the weekend. Each of these alternatives is presented as a normative model and a set of guidelines to guide policy decisions designed to eliminate the lack of norms among older retired Soviet women. Presumably, any of the three would fit well with the pronatal policies of the Soviet regime. While each could eliminate structural sources of loneliness and feelings of uselessness among older Soviet women, it remains unclear that even a newly constituted *babushka* role would reflect the preferences of older women themselves.

Conclusions

The classic Western assumption that, under Soviet socialism, older women fare well in the aging process because they opt for and are needed as *babushki* appears to find little confirmation in reality. Only a minority of female working pensioners in fact eagerly anticipate the *babushka* role. As mentioned above, the stereotype of older Soviet single women always living with their children and grandchildren is also misplaced. Between one-fifth and one-fourth of all Soviet women of retirement age live entirely alone, with neither spouse nor children.

This points to a situation where, as in the United States, the need for new and different role models for older women has taken on a new urgency. The forces of social and economic change to which Soviet gerontologists have just begun to turn their attention are already at work to render the status of the older woman in Soviet society increasingly fragile.

Meanwhile, the forces of modernization seem likely to render the traditional *babushka* of Russian and early Soviet society a vanishing breed. What will replace her is still unclear. Perhaps Tolstoy's famous description of families in the opening page of *Anna Karenina* is most apt. "Happy families are all alike; every unhappy family is unhappy in its own way." In any event, a basic problem for older women in Soviet as well as in American society is that the powers-that-be decide "for her, without her." Indeed, it might be the absence of a meaningful political role—or even the prospects of one—that constitutes the most important disadvantage under which older Soviet women continue to labor.

Notes

1. For the purposes of this essay, "older" and "aged" refer to Soviet women aged 55 years and over, unless otherwise specified. "Normal" eligibility for an old-age pension for Soviet women starts at age 55. For those working in hazardous occupations or raising large numbers of children, pension age is lower. Soviet Legislation Series, *Pension Laws* (Moscow: Progress Publishers, 1967), pp. 1–40.

2. Godfrey Baldwin, unpublished estimates, U.S. Department of Commerce, Bureau of the Census, May 1982.

3. T. H. Rigby, *Communist Party Membership in the Soviet Union* (Princeton: Princeton University Press, 1968), pp. 359–363 and 517; and Jerry Hough and Merle Fainsod, *How the Soviet Union is Governed* (Cambridge: Harvard University Press, 1979), pp. 312–314.

4. *Newsweek*, November 1, 1982, p. 56.

5. Matilda White Riley, "Old Women," *Radcliffe Quarterly*, June 1979, p. 7.

6. A. I. Chebotarev and E. G. Sachuk (1980), p. 402; and *Sovietskoe zdravookhranenie*, August 1981, no. 8, p. 17. By way of contrast, the latest census reports a population ratio that is 53.3 percent female to 46.7 percent male, with a preponderance of females by 17.6 million. This is high by comparison to other nations, where a 51.4 percent ratio is the rule. Overall, 15.5 percent of the Soviet population was of retirement age in 1970, and the share is scheduled to rise to 17.6 percent by 1990, and to 19.2 percent by the end of the century. *Radio Liberty Research Bulletin*, "First Results of the All-Union Census," May 4, 1979, p. 3; and U.S. Congress,

Joint Economic Committee, *Soviet Economy in a Time of Change* (Washington, D.C., 1979), p. 15.

7. U.S. Department of Commerce, Bureau of the Census, *Projection of the Population of the USSR, By Age and Sex, 1964–1985* (Washington, D.C., n.d.), pp. 13–15.

8. Stephen Sternheimer, "Soviet Retirement Policy and Working Pensioners: Fruitless Quest?," paper delivered at 12th International Congress of Gerontology, Hamburg, Federal Republic of Germany, July 1981, p. 6.

9. A. G. Novitskii and G. V. Mil', *Zaniatost' Pensionerov* (Moscow: Finansy i statistiki, 1981), pp. 68 and 99.

10. *Sovetskoe zdravookhranenie*, p. 17.

11. D. I. Valentei, *Semi'ia segodnia* (Moscow: Statistika, 1979), pp. 46–47.

12. Valentei, *Semi'ia segodnia*, pp. 44–45.

13. A. M. Rumiantsev et al. (eds.), *Sotsial'no- ekonomicheskie problemy gerontologii* (Tbilisi: Georgian Academy of Sciences, 1976), p. 130.

14. These interviews were conducted by the author in 1981.

15. Interviews, USSR, 1981, Institute of Sociology, Institute of Gerontology, Central Economics-Mathematics Institute, Center for Population Studies at moscow University, and Institute of Economics. The issue, of course, is complicated by declining male life expectancy, and the historical failure of male life expectancy to rise as fast as that of women in the USSR. Interestingly enough, the first Russian census found an almost equal proportion of males and females over 60—6.9 percent and 7.0 percent of the population, respectively. By 1979, almost a century later, the share of older males in the population had risen only slightly to 8.7 percent, while that of older females had more than doubled to 16.7 percent. Maksudov [pseud.], "Nekotorye prichiny rosta smertnosti v SSSR," unpublished m.s., Russian Research Center, Harvard University, October 1981, p. 8; and Stephen Sternheimer, "The Graying of the USSR and Quality of Life Issues," paper delivered at the American Association for the Advancement of Slavic Studies Annual Convention, Washington, D.C., 1982, pp. 46–47. Today, the gap between Soviet male and female life expectancy—almost 12 years—is the largest in the world.

16. Peggy Polk, "Soviets Prescribe Work for the Elderly," UPI dispatch, Moscow, May 1, 1976, p. 2.

17. Stephen Sternheimer, "The Graying of the USSR," *Problems of Communism* 31 (September-October 1982), pp. 84–87; and Stephen Sternheimer, "Retirement and Aging in the Soviet Union," paper delivered at the American Association for the Advancement of Slavic Studies Annual Convention, Philadelphia, 1979.

18. M. Sonin, "Obraz zhizni-trudovoi," *Nauka i zhizn'*, 1981, no. 9, p. 22.

19. A. Z. Majkov and A. G. Novitskii, *Problemy nepol'nogo rabochego vremeni i zaniatost' naseleniia* (Moscow: Sovetskaia Rossiia, 1975), p. 60.

20. E. I. Stezhenskaia et al., *Usloviaa zhizni i pozhiloi chelovek* (Moscow: Meditsina, 1978), pp. 21 and 27.

21. Bragrova, 1975, pp. 18–20.

22. Novitskii and Mil', *Zaniatost' Pensionerov*, pp. 206–107.

23. Novitskii and Mil', *Zaniatost' Pensionerov*, pp. 73–74.

24. Novitskii and Mil', *Zaniatost' Pensionerov*, pp. 118 and 140.

25. Novitskii and Mil', *Zaniatost' Pensionerov*, pp. 105, 120, 136, and 138.

26. V. D. Shapiro, "Otnoshenie zhenshchin-pensionerok k rabote na proizvodstve," in Z. A. Iankova and A. A. Basalai (eds.), *Sotsial'noe problemy ratsional'nogo sootnosheniia funktsii zhenshchen* (Moscow: Institute of Sociology, AN SSSR, 1980), pp. 58–60.

27. Shapiro, "Otnoshenie zhenshchin-pensionerok k rabote na proizvodstve," p. 61.

28. Interviews, 1981.

29. A. M. Rumiantsev et al., *Sotsial'no-ekonomicheskie problemy gerontologii*, pp. 41 and 45–46.

30. Novitskii and Mil', *Zaniatost' Pensionerov*, pp. 83–85.

31. Novitskii and Mil', *Zaniatost' Pensionerov*, p. 88.

32. Novitskii and Mil', *Zaniatost' Pensionerov*, p. 176.

33. Novitskii and Mil', *Zaniatost' Pensionerov*, p. 176.

34. Stephen Sternheimer, "The Graying of the USSR," pp. 85– 86; and Stephen Sternheimer, "The Graying of the USSR and Quality of Life Issues," pp. 36–43.

35. Novitskii and Mil', *Zaniatost' Pensionerov*, p. 195.

36. Deborah Ranker, "Women, the Losers in Pensions," *New York Times*, January 14, 1981.

37. Alastair McAuley, *Women's Work and Wages in the Soviet Union* (Boston: Allen and Unwin, 1981); and A. M. Rumiantsev et al., *Sotsial'no-ekonomicheskie problemy gerontologii*, p. 50.

38. M. Sonin, "Obraz zhizni-trudovoi," p. 22.

39. Novitski and Mil', *Zaniatost' Pensionerov*, p. 50; and A. M. Rumiantsev (ed.), *Tezisy dokladov "Sotsial'no-ekonomicheskie aspekty gerontologii* (Moscow: IMEMO, 1975), p. 79.

40. A. M. Rumiantsev (ed.), *Tezisy dokladov "Sotsial'no-ekonomicheskie aspekty gerontologii*," p. 13; and V. S. Kogan, *Ekonomiko-demographicheskii aspekt zaniatosti naseleniia v pozhilom vozraste. Abstrakt dissertatsii* (Moscow: MGU, 1973), p. 15.

41. V. S. Kogan, *Ekonomiko-demographicheskii aspekt zaniatosti naseleniia v pozhilom vozraste*, p. 15; and N. V. Panina, "Problemy sotsial'noi adaptatsii pozhilykh liudei," unpublished candidate dissertation, Moscow, Institute of Sociology, 1979, pp. 119 and 126.

42. V. D. Shapiro, "Otnoshenie zhenshchin-pensionerok k rabote na proizvodstve," pp. 62–63.

43. Novitskii and Mil', *Zaniatost' Pensionerov*, pp. 74, 96, and 133; and V. D. Shapiro, "Faktory zaniatosti pensionerov v obshchestvennom proizvodstve," unpublished candidate dissertation, Moscow, Institute of Sociology, 1979, table 88.

44. Novitskii and Mil, *Zaniatost' Pensionerov*, p. 134.

45. N. V. Panina, "Problemy sotsial'noi adaptatsii pozhilykh liudei," p. 86.

46. Interview, Kiev, 1981.

47. N. N. Pyzhov, "Obshestvenno-politicheskii aktivnost' pensionerov," unpublished candidate dissertation, Moscow, Institute of Sociology, 1980, p. 33.

48. Pyzhov, "Obshestvenno-politicheskii aktivnost' pensionerov," p. 33.

49. *Literaturnaia gazeta*, June 27, 1979, p. 13.

50. U. S. Department of Commerce, Bureau of the Census, *Projection of the Population of the USSR, By Age and Sex, 1964–1985*, p. 9.

51. V. V. Boiko, *Malodetnaia sem'ia* (Moscow: Statistika, 1980), pp. 160–61 and 205.

52. M. A. Klut, "Sovershenstvovanie metodov statistiko- demograficheskogo analiza zhizni tsikli cheloveka i sem'ia," unpublished candidate dissertation, Leningrad, LFEI, 1981.

53. *Literaturnaia gazeta*, June 27, 1979, p. 13.

54. N. V. Panina, "Problemy sotsial'noi adaptatsii pozhilykh liudei," p. 90.

11. Alcohol Abuse and the Quality of Life in the Soviet Union

Western specialists have had a remarkable record of success in quantifying and analyzing various aspects of Soviet economics that otherwise would have remained hidden behind a facade of incomplete statistics, propaganda clichés, and what Sovietologist Gregory Grossman has called "descriptive distortions." This expertise is becoming particularly valuable as we observe a trend toward more omission and concealment in officially published Soviet sources.

The remarkable achievements of Western Sovietology have not been uniform, but most aspects of the Soviet economy have been adequately researched. However, there remains one "last frontier" of research where our knowledge of quantitative magnitudes is rather scant—the general area that can be termed the "quality of life in the Soviet Union." This area encompasses a large number of phenomena such as age- and sex-specific mortality, morbidity, life expectancy, mental health, homicide, suicide, abortion rates, crime, corruption, the quality of the environment, drug abuse, alcoholism, and various economic facets of these phenomena, such as their effect on real income distribution.

The quantitative dimensions of some of these phenomena can be illustrated by an examination of incomplete mortality statistics. Between 1960 and 1980, the crude death rate in the Soviet Union increased from 713 to 1,033 deaths per 100,000, but these figures are only for two major causes of death—heart disease and cancer. The sizable unexplained residual amounted

This chapter originally appeared in *Soviet Politics in the 1980s*, Helmut Sonnenfeldt, ed. (Boulder, CO: Westview Press, 1985).

to 354 deaths per 100,000 in 1960, and dropped to a low of 287 in 1966, reflecting major improvements in medical services, particularly in the treatment of infectious diseases. Since 1966, the unexplained residual rose to 351 deaths per 100,000, and at present amounts to about one million deaths per year. In 1971–72, the last year for which age- and sex-specific mortality data are available, male deaths accounted for 63 percent of all unexplained deaths. Out of the total number of unexplained deaths of people 20–29 years old, 75 percent were males.[1]

The alarming size of the unexplained residual is particularly puzzling because there was a reduction in the incidence of most infectious diseases during this period. The unexplained residual includes infant mortality[2] and a host of other causes of death, such as accidents, homicides, suicides, and alcohol poisonings—that is, factors relating to the quality of life. Several loosely worded and undocumented statements by prominent Soviet demographers indicate that these causes account for about two-thirds of the unexplained residual.

Our inability to break down the unexplained residual into individual causes of death and analyze underlying factors is hardly surprising, for the secrecy shrouding these statistics can be compared only with the secrecy extended to Soviet military data. For most of the phenomena affecting the quality of life in the Soviet Union, we lack not only basic statistics, but also essential methodological and classificational data. In fact, it is not known what Soviet agency or agencies have responsibility for the collection and processing of these statistics, and there is some evidence that the responsibility for tracking social indicators was removed from the purview of the Central Statistical Administration and entrusted to the internal security organs long ago.[3] Alcohol abuse, alcoholism, and related social, health, and economic problems are some of the most important issues affecting the quality of life in the Soviet Union. Directly and indirectly, they explain a large portion of the Soviet Union's unexplained residual death rate.

Alcohol Consumption and Abuse

The magnitude and scope of alcohol abuse and the severity of its impact on Soviet society is unique in terms of the international experience. The main aspects of the Soviet Union's alcohol problem can be summarized by noting that in 1980 the consumption of all alcoholic beverages—vodka, cognac, wine, and beer—converted to pure alcohol was over 17 liters for every person 15 years old or older. Of this amount, *samogon*, or illegal home-distilled moonshine, accounted for about 3.5 liters, and homemade wine and beer accounted for another liter.[4] Soviet and émigré sources also report that large quantities of technical alcohol are stolen from work places. According to some estimates, this could add another liter to total per capita consumption levels. A large share of all technical alcohol consists of synthetic or poorly rectified ethanols that are highly toxic.

At this level of consumption, the Soviet Union ranks fourth or fifth among some 30 nations for which alcohol consumption data are available. The fact that nations such as France, Italy, and Portugal record higher levels of per capita consumption is somewhat misleading if we are inquiring into the overall pernicious social impact of alcohol abuse. As a rule, world experience shows that nations with high per capita consumption levels drink alcoholic beverages mainly in the form of wine and beer, while nations with relatively low per capita consumption levels drink mainly distilled spirits, i.e., strong beverages with an average alcohol content of 40 percent or higher. The Soviet Union is unique in this respect as it has a very high level of per capita consumption in the form of vodka and other strong beverages. With respect to per capita consumption of alcohol in the form of strong alcoholic beverages, the Soviet Union ranks first in the world. It should be noted that strong alcoholic beverages are more detrimental than wine and beer to the population's health and the social environment in contributing to mental disorders, chronic and acute poisonings, accidents, and deaths.

Another striking feature of alcoholism in the Soviet Union is the very rapid growth of consumption levels for persons 15 years old and older. From 1955–80, the consumption of all alcoholic beverages, including *samogon* and homemade wine and beer, increased by an average of about 4.5 percent per year. The consumption of pure alcohol in the form of state-produced alcoholic beverages grew even faster, at a rate of about 6.9 percent per year. Though accurate estimates are impossible to arrive at, it appears that the main factor contributing to the growth of per capita consumption was the rapidly growing incidence of drinking by women and teenagers. As the price of alcoholic beverages increased in 1981, sales declined in 1981 and 1982, thus constituting a reversal of a long-term trend. However, per capita sales of sugar, which declined in the 1975–79 period, began to increase in 1980. Because sugar is the main substance necessary for distillation and wine-making, one can assume that declining sales of state-produced alcoholic beverages were offset by a corresponding increases in *samogon* and homemade wine drinking.

Drinking and alcohol abuse in the Soviet Union are highly differentiated by region and nationality. In oversimplified terms, we can say that excessive drinking and alcoholism, with all of their adverse effects on health and productivity, are concentrated among the Slavic and Baltic nationalities—that is, among the peoples of the Russian republic, the Ukraine, Belorussia, Lithuania, Latvia, and Estonia. Consumption levels are also relatively high in the wine-producing republics of the Soviet Union—Moldavia, Armenia, and Georgia—but the adverse effects of alcohol abuse are less severe in these areas than in Slavic republics because a large share of all alcohol is consumed in the form of wine. In addition, people in wine-producing republics drink local, relatively mild wines, while wines exported to other regions of the Soviet Union are fortified with pure alcohol, which makes them much stronger and more toxic.

On the average, people of the Muslim cultural tradition in Azerbaijan, parts of Georgia, and most of Soviet Central Asia consume less than half as much alcohol as those in Slavic republics. Accurate breakdowns of alcohol consumption by ethnic group are very difficult to estimate, but pilot studies suggest that in the 1960s and 1970s regional differences were either stable or in some instances increasing. Such regional and ethnic differences are reflected in mortality, morbidity, and other "social" statistics. At least in part, they explain differences in birth and death rates among the various republics of the Soviet Union.

Much more research will be required before we can arrive at a complete picture of the impact of alcoholism and heavy drinking on health in the Soviet Union. According to numerous studies by Soviet demographers, statisticians, and medical specialists—which rarely provide us with overall national statistics and are poorly documented—heavy drinking is an important factor affecting Soviet mortality and morbidity levels. Heavy drinking can cause premature death from chronic poisoning of the liver and other vital organs; it can lead to alcohol psychoses and other mental disorders; and it contributes to infant mortality and deaths from heart disease. Unfortunately, estimates of alcohol-related deaths for these maladies are impossible to arrive at because of the paucity of Soviet data. According to numerous Soviet studies, heavy drinking accounts for from one-third to two-thirds of all deaths resulting from traffic, industrial, and domestic accidents; accidental deaths from fire, freezing, and drowning; homicides and suicides; and fatal poisonings. Mortality statistics for these catagories, known in Soviet demography as "accidents, trauma, and poisonings," are not generally available. However, using scattered data, it seems that in the late 1970s the total number of deaths resulting from these causes was between 370,000 and 400,000 persons per year, or between 140 and 150 per 100,000.[5] Alcohol abuse probably explains well over half of the total number of such deaths.

One of the most alarming causes of death in the Soviet Union, both in terms of absolute numbers and rates of growth since the mid-1960s, has been acute alcohol poisoning. Estimates based on Soviet forensic medical statistics indicate that the number of deaths caused by alcohol poisoning increased from about 12,500 in the mid-1960s to a staggering 51,000 in 1978. The latter figure translates into 19.5 deaths per 100,000, compared with a rate of about 0.3 for 19 nations surveyed in the 1970s.[6]

Death from alcohol poisoning is caused by the traditional Russian *opoi*— the rapid ingestion of a critical quantity of alcohol, usually on an empty stomach. It must be noted that the toxicity of alcoholic beverages differs depending on type. *Samogon* is more toxic than vodka, and wine fortified with poorly rectified alcohol is more toxic than naturally fermented wine. The rapid increase in fatal alcohol poisonings observed in the 1970s is probably explained by the lower quality and increased toxicity of alcoholic beverages produced in the Soviet Union. The use of synthetic alcohol in the production of beverages and the low quality of alcohol used in wine fortification have contributed to the number of poisonings. The increased consumption of various alcohol surrogates such as aftershave lotions, varnishes, cleaning fluids, and stolen technical alcohol, caused in part by higher prices for state produced alcoholic beverages, also contributed to the increased number of fatal poisonings.

Aside from medical and health problems referred to above, heavy drinking and alcoholism significantly affect labor productivity and the general performance of the Soviet economy. Shortages of certain labor skills, leniency toward drunkards on the part of managers, and the general relaxation of labor discipline in the 1960s and 1970s have extended the adverse effects of alcohol abuse to the Soviet work place. No overall statistics are available, but one should note that reports of drinking on the job or infringements of labor discipline rarely appeared in the Soviet literature on the subject during the 1950s. Frequent reports on extensive drunkenness in rural areas even noted that most drinking was done on holidays or upon completion of the harvest season. The situation began to change in the early 1960s, as reflected by an ever-increasing number of media and specialized reports that complained of drinking on the job, worker absenteeism due to drunkenness, and productivity problems resulting from the effects of earlier drunkenness. Managerial and supervisory personnel were not only allowing this, but were contributing to the problem by rewarding workers for special tasks with vodka or technical alcohol available in industrial plants.

No general statistical data on industrial accidents, worker absenteeism, or infringements of work discipline have been published in the Soviet Union for many years, but it is reasonable to conclude that the situation has significantly worsened since the 1960s and 1970s. Two prominent Soviet economists and labor specialists, S. Strumilin and S. Sonin, estimated that drinking and alcoholism reduced labor productivity by about 10 percent in the early 1970s.[7] We can surmise that because of increases in the per capita consumption of alcohol, the situation must have deteriorated further in recent years.

Heavy drinking and alcohol abuse significantly affect the social aspects of life in the Soviet Union. As is true with respect to other Soviet social problems, there are no summary data or overall statistics on the subject, but anecdotal evidence and media and specialized reports strongly suggest that drinking is a major cause of divorce in the Soviet Union, and that women in alcoholic families have more than the average number of abortions.[8] Soviet specialists repeatedly stress the high degree of correlation observed between violence and property crime and drinking.[9]

Sobering-up Stations and Drunk Driving

The impact of heavy drinking and alcohol abuse on everyday life in the Soviet Union can be illustrated by the widespread use "sobering-up stations," or *vytrezviteli*. Public drunkenness is controlled by the police, who regularly sweep the streets, picking up drunks and placing them in special sobering-up stations for overnight confinement. Upon their discharge, the culprits pay a fine and have their names and the charges against them reported to their employers. Sobering-up stations operate in virtually every city and town of any size. In the early 1970s, Leningrad had 20 sobering-up stations and Moscow had 29, one of which was for women.[10] In the mid-1960s, over 300,000 drunks, including 5,600 women, were confined each year. This amounted to about six percent of the adult population of Moscow.[11]

In 1979, between 12 and 15 percent of the Soviet Union's adult urban population, or between 16 and 18 million drunks, were processed through sobering-up stations.[12] To place these percentages in comparative perspective, only about 0.6 percent of the adult population of the United States—a nation that has a serious alcohol problem of its own—is arrested for drunkenness each year.[13]

Regardless of the high number of drunks placed in sobering-up stations, these figures identify only a fraction of the total number of habitual heavy drinkers and alcoholics in the Soviet Union. Some simply escape the attention of the police, and others, such as minors or soldiers, are confined in regular police stations rather than in sobering-up stations. A large group consists of heavy drinkers who, while in a state of inebriation, suffer accidents, are hurt in falls or fights, or who are in a comatose state caused by acute alcohol poisoning. These drunks are picked up by the police or by first aid teams and placed in special emergency wards. A study of a large sample of drunks conducted by two prominent Soviet specialists in the early 1970s showed that of the total number of people identified by the authorities as habitual drinkers or alcoholics, 14 percent were registered in various psychiatric clinics for alcoholics, 66 were registered through sobering-up stations, and 20 percent were identified by emergency medical facilities.[14]

We cannot know the degree to which this sample is representative or whether the ratios have changed over time, but it appears that in addition to the 16–18 million drunks placed in sobering-up stations each year, several million more urban adults, possibly as many as 6–8 million, must be considered habitual heavy drinkers or alcoholics. The extent of alcohol abuse in rural areas without sobering-up stations or medical and psychiatric treatment facilities cannot be measured. Given the alarmingly high numbers cited above, the misery and suffering of alcoholics and the misery that drinkers create for their relatives, neighbors, and coworkers is not difficult to imagine.

Another illustration of the impact of alcohol abuse on everyday Soviet life is the high incidence of drunk driving in the Soviet Union. Soviet authorities have been fighting drunk driving with increasing police patrols, stiff fines and penalties, and mandatory sobriety tests given to drivers of most state trucking enterprises prior to the onset of the day's work. But due to rising alcohol consumption levels and a rapid expansion of private automobile ownership, there has been an increasing number of traffic accidents involving drunk drivers. In 1983, V. Fedorchuk, the head of the Ministry of Internal Affairs (MVD), reported in *Pravda* that "over 800,000 drunken drivers lost their licenses in 1982." This translates into about 5.9 drunk driving arrests per million vehicle-kilometers. The U.S. figure was about 0.58 in the same year.[15] One should also note that in the United States, some 20 percent of all drivers are professionals—for example, truck, taxi, and bus drivers—while in the Soviet Union, professionals probably account for more than two-thirds of all drivers. One could assume that experienced professional drivers are less likely to be picked up by the police, and that as a result the actual number of intoxicated drivers per million vehicle-kilometers is higher than the above figures indicate.

Of course, not every intoxicated driver arrested by the police loses his license. Some might be driving without a license to be taken away, and some first offenders are placed on probation by the courts. According to one report, some 10,000 drunk drivers were apprehended in Latvia in 1970, and only 6,000 lost their licenses.[16] Applying the same ratios to the 800,000 figure given by Fedorchuk, we can estimate the number of drunk driving arrests in 1982 at about 1,300,000.

Causes of Increased Alcohol Abuse

The changes that have occurred in the Soviet Union's level of per capita alcohol consumption are complex multi-dimensional phenomena that would be difficult to explain even with the benefit of complete historical and socioeconomic data. Given the dearth of information on various aspects of alcoholism in the Soviet Union, the task is almost impossible. Nevertheless, we can list several causes of increased alcohol abuse in the USSR.

Since mid-1955, Soviet citizens have enjoyed a significant growth in real income, an even more rapid growth in money income, and a gradual decrease in the length of the workweek without a commensurate increase in the availability of income-elastic goods and services, residential housing, and the availability of entertainment or leisure facilities and activities. Thus drinking is increasingly becoming one of the most generally accepted ways of spending one's leisure time and one's discretionary income.

Drinking is a social activity, and to some extent, it is therefore self-generating. Drinkers introduce and often force nondrinkers to drink. The general relaxation of work discipline observed in the postwar period has made possible increased drinking during working hours, when the inducement by one's coworkers is particularly strong.

Increased drinking by women—a phenomenon that has been observed in a number of nations in recent times—is partly the result of demographic factors. Heavy war losses have created a serious and lasting male-female imbalance in the Soviet Union.[17] Thus it is not surprising that some 20 million women without husbands and families have, to one degree or another, taken to drink.

Another reason for increased drinking among women is related to state policy. As was pointed out above, drinking of strong alcoholic beverages is more detrimental to health than drinking wine or beer. Recognizing this fact, the authorities have purposely affected a gradual change in the mix of state-produced beverages, reducing the share of vodka and increasing the share of wine and beer. This was achieved by a variety of means such as the production of more wine and beer, price adjustments, and restricting the hours and number of outlets that sell vodka. This policy was successful, but only in the sense of reducing the share of strong beverages as a percentage of total sales. Between 1955 and 1980, the supply of vodka and other strong beverages increased 2.5 times; the supply of grape and fruit wine increased 10 times; and the supply of beer increased 3.5 times. As a result, the share of strong beverages was reduced from 78 percent to less than 50 percent.

One of the unexpected and unfortunate results of this policy was that women who traditionally prefer wine to vodka were encouraged to drink by the wider availability and lower prices of wine. The policy was also frustrated because wine prices are roughly proportional to alcohol content, and because wine industry and retail trade outlets expanded the production and sale of strong fortified wines in their attempts to respond to the demands of the drinking public. Thus most of these wines consumed had an alcohol content of between and 16 and 18 percent, while light and dry naturally fermented wines practically disappeared in the 1970s. Alcohol used in wine fortification is generally poorly rectified and relatively toxic. As a result, the switch from vodka to wine compounded the health problems associated with alcoholism.

A number of émigré and Western authors have accused Soviet officials of "forcing" or inducing drinking, echoing similar accusations levied by Soviet writers at the tsarist government. It is not likely that Soviet, or for that matter tsarist, officials have ever purposely pursued a policy actively encouraging drinking. However, the price of alcoholic beverages is inelastic, and this makes them an excellent product for taxation. From the 1930s to the present, the Soviet government has depended on alcoholic beverages for a large share of its budgetary revenues.[18] The production and sale of alcoholic beverages has been equally attractive to industrial and consumer trade networks. Thus the entire system, from the highest fiscal authorities to retail sales clerks, is vitally interested in maintaining and promoting the sale of alcoholic beverages. As a result, alcoholic beverages are always available in retail trade outlets and public dining facilities of the state distribution system, which is well known for its periodic shortages of most consumer goods.[19] Naturally, this has contributed to a general increase in drinking over the last 25 years.

A host of other factors have probably contributed to the Soviet Union's increasing levels of per capita alcohol consumption. These include rapid urbanization, which is often accompanied by loneliness and feelings of frustration on the part of newly arriving rural-urban migrants; lower career expectations caused by reduced upward mobility; and small but not insignificant changes in the age-sex structure of the population. Most important in this regard is that the adult male population, with its strong propensity to drink, is growing more rapidly than the adult female population.

Societal Costs and State Policy

A study by the respected economist B. Urlanis, which unfortunately lacks proper documentation, indicates the rough order of magnitude of the social costs of alcoholism in the Soviet Union.[20] In 1973, Urlanis reported at a major conference devoted to alcohol consumption problems that social losses associated with alcoholism and heavy drinking clearly exceed tax revenues and profits derived by the state from the production and sale of alcoholic beverages. If we accept his estimates as valid, this would mean that in the early 1970s the total social cost of alcohol abuse was 7–8 percent of the Soviet Union's "net material product," or national income. Taking into account the growing level of Soviet alcohol consumption, adverse changes in mortality associated with alcoholism, and the sluggish growth of Soviet national income, it seems that the total social cost of alcohol abuse rose to about 8–9 percent in 1980.

As the definition and the scope of the social costs estimated by Urlanis are unknown, intertemporal and international comparisons are difficult to interpret. Nevertheless, it is instructive to note that an earlier Soviet study estimated the "total losses in the national economy caused by alcohol abuse" at about 4.8 percent of the Soviet Union's national income in 1927–28.[21] Total losses due to alcohol abuse in the United States were estimated at about 3–4 percent in 1971, but it appears that the definition of such losses was much broader in the U.S. study.[22]

The historical record of organized public and state policies designed to control alcoholism and alcohol abuse in most societies is not encouraging, and moderately successful policies are often exceptions to the rule. Even so, Soviet anti-drinking policies have had a dismal record. It is hardly an exaggeration to suggest that the Soviet Union has never had a balanced or comprehensive set of policies for the reduction of alcohol abuse and alcoholism. In addition to the ever-present threat posed by the uncontrolled *samogon* market, the fiscal advantages derived by the state and by producers and distributors of alcoholic beverages continuously interfere with the recognized need to reduce alcohol production and sales. As a result, the authorities vacillate between the introduction of restrictive measure and the relaxation of controls. Perhaps the only sustained policy for which the authorities can be credited is the financial support of medical research on alcohol abuse combined with a continuous educational campaign, which might bear fruit sometime in the future. In all other respects, the Soviet Union's anti-alcohol policies are restricted to periodic and often rescinded increases in the price of alcoholic beverages, restrictions on retail trade outlets, and the imposition of increased penalties for drunkenness. In short, the growing social, health, and economic costs of increasing alcohol abuse in the Soviet Union suggest that these policies have failed.

Notes

1. *Vestnik statistiki*, 1967, no. 11, p. 92; 1969, no. 2, pp. 81–92; 1973, no. 12, pp. 79–83; and 1981, no. 11, pp. 70–77.

2. Christopher Davis and Murray Feshbach, *Rising Infant Mortality in the USSR in the 1970's*, U.S. Department of Commerce, Bureau of the Census (Washington, D.C., 1980), p. 95.

3. When in 1967, a conference of Soviet sociologists criticized the Central Statistical Administration (CSA) for having stopped collecting and publishing "moral statistics," the deputy director of the CSA responded that "moral statistics exist and are being continuously developed, however not in the CSA but other organs." A. Ezhov, *Vestnik statistiki*, 1968, no. 7, p. 29. The latter reference is a well-known Soviet euphemism for the Committee for State Security (KGB) or the Ministry of Internal Affairs (MVD). In recent years, it has become quite clear that all statistics and summary data on alcoholism and alcohol abuse are handled by the MVD.

4. General Soviet sources have not published any data on the production, sale, or consumption of alcoholic beverages since the mid-1950s. All statistics in this study were estimated by the author on the basis of data in industrial journals, retail trade statistics, émigré interviews and other sources, and are explained and documented in Vladimir Treml, *Alcohol in the USSR: A Statistical Study* (Durham: Duke University Press, 1982).

5. This paper precludes a reproduction of the long set of tedious calculations underlying these estimates. Soviet sources that provided the basic set of necessary data are A. Serenko, *Sovetskoe zdravockhranenie*, 1981, no. 8, p. 4; A. Serenko and V. Ovcharov, *Zabolevaemost', smertnost' i sredniia prodolzhitel'nost' zhizni naselenia SSSR* (Minsk, 1979), p. 25; and L. Velisheva and I. Serebrennikov, *Sudebno-meditsinskaia ekspertiza*, 1981, no. 3, p. 20.

6. Vladimir G. Treml, "Fatal Poisonings in the USSR," *Radio Liberty Research Bulletin*, no. 50 (3203), December 15, 1982, pp. 1–12; and Vladimir G. Treml, "Death from Alcohol Poisoning in the USSR," *Soviet Studies* 34, no. 4 (October 1982), pp. 487–505. Estimates for the mid-1960s are less firm than estimates for later years. It must be added that these figures cover only deaths from the ingestion of alcohol-containing fluids. There are also a large number of poisonings from other toxins related to alcoholism. For instance, some 6,300 people died from drinking vinegar concentrate in 1978. Soviet medical authorities report that vinegar is a popular poison in suicides and also frequently ingested by alcoholics, either by accident or as a "hangover" remedy. It is impossible to estimate the total number of deaths from vinegar poisonings associated with alcoholism.

7. S. Strumilin and S. Sonin, *Ekonomika i organizatsiia promyshlennogo proizvodstva*, 1974, no. 4, p. 38.

8. Iu. Lisitsyn and N. Kopyt, *Alkogolizm* (Moscow, 1978), pp. 127–133.

9. A. Gertsenson (ed.), *Alkogolizm—put' k prestupleniiu* (Moscow, 1966). It is difficult to deny the correlation between crime and alcohol abuse that has been observed in most societies. At the same time, Soviet studies on the subject appear to simplify complex issues with declarative statements describing most crimes as caused by drinking. Surely, one would expect to find a high correlation between crime and alcohol abuse in a society in which 80–90 percent of the adult population drinks, many to excess. The assumption that inebriated perpetrators are more likely to be apprehended by the police than sober ones throws some doubts on the validity of crime statistics. It seems that the well-established link between violence, crime, and alcohol are used as an educational tool in anti-drinking campaigns, without a serious study of the causes of crime and alcoholism in Soviet society.

10. The Leningrad number is based on listings in the 1973 city telephone directory. The number of stations in Moscow was given in M. Keller and V. Efron, "Alcohol Problem in Yugoslavia and Russia," *Quarterly Journal of Studies on Alcohol* 35 (1974), pp. 267–268.

11. *Politicheskii dnevnik, 1964–1970* (Amsterdam, 1972), p. 50; and D. Fedotov (ed.), *Alkogolizm i toksomanii* (Moscow, 1968), p. 15.

12. In all probability, these numbers include repeaters. P. Dudochkin, *Nash sovremennik*, 1981, no. 8, p. 136. Dudochkin was later criticized for using inflated statistics. D. Vikotrov, *Literaturnaia gazeta*, August 4, 1982, p. 12. However, his percentages appear to be consistent with other evidence. Thus 10.1 percent of the adult population of Piatigorsk was arrested for drunkenness in 1975, and 11.6 was arrested in Leningrad in 1979. V. Dorofeev, *Literaturnaia gazeta*, March 31, 1976, p. 13; and "Soobshcheniia iz SSSR," *Edinenie*, October 10, 1982, p. 4.

13. *Statistical Abstract of the United States, 1982–1983* (Washington, D.C.: Government Printing Office, 1982), pp. 27 and 182.

14. Lisitsyn and Kopyt, *Alkogolizm*, 1978, p. 91.

15. The number of total vehicle-kilometers driven was estimated on the basis of the Soviet Union's stock of trucks, buses, and passenger automobiles, and the average number of kilometers driven in each category. Some estimates (e.g., trucks in transportation organizations, taxis, buses, and automobiles for private use) are fairly firm, while others are less accurate. Therefore, the overall figure of 221 billion vehicle-kilometers is subject to some error. The data for the United States are from *Statistical Abstract of the United States, 1982– 1983*, pp. 27 and 619.

16. ABSEES. *Soviet and East European Abstracts Series 2*, no. 3 (January 1972), p. 14.

17. In the late 1950s, the ratio of women 20 years old and older to men of the same age group was about 1.4, excluding the Central Asian republics.

18. In the 1960s and 1970s, the excise taxes on alcoholic beverages and other income derived from the production, export, and sale of alcoholic beverages were generating from 10–12 percent of all state budget revenues.

19. Radio Liberty conducted a survey of some 700 recent Soviet émigrés concerning the availability of basic foods and beverages in the USSR in the early 1980s. According to this survey, vodka was by far the best supplied commodity in state retail trade. Ninety-six percent of all respondents reported that vodka was always available. Bread was available without interruption according to 83 percent of the respondents. RFE-RL, "Food Supply in the USSR: Evidence of Widespread Shortages," *Soviet Area Audience and Opinion Research*, AR 2-82 (April 1982), pp. 1–2 and 34.

20. B. Urlanis, *Ekonomika i organizatsiia promyshlennogo proizvodstva*, 1974, no. 4, p. 49.

21. Urlanis, *Ekonomika i organizatsiia promyshlennogo proizvodstva*, p. 49. Urlanis refers to a 1929 study by E. Deichman, who estimated total losses at 1,270 million rubles. The estimate of Soviet national income for 1928—26,442 million rubles— is from A. Vainshtein, *Narodnyi dokhod Rossii i SSSR* (Moscow, 1969), p. 96. Vainshtein estimates national income using current Soviet methodology, but without reference to excise taxes. Including the latter would probably lower the percentage of losses due to alcohol abuse to about 4.3 percent.

22. National Institute on Alcohol Abuse and Alcoholism, U.S. Department of Health, Education and Welfare, *Alcohol and Health: New Knowledge* (Washington, D.C., 1974).

12. Aspects of the Quality of Rural Life in the Soviet Union

The following investigation of the quality of rural life in the Soviet Union originates from the assumption that living conditions in Soviet villages and hamlets are considerably different from those in Soviet cities. The idea that rural life has its distinguishing features needs no elaboration. Marx had great contempt for the "idiocy of rural life," but the history of ideas offers many examples of a more positive attitude toward rural lifestyles. Rural life has often been seen as beneficial to the soundness of mind and body.

Russian villages have always been a popular subject for social scientists, writers, and those involved in public affairs. Russian *mir* and *obshchina* (village communes) are still the subject of intense debates about societal development. The most recent example of this debate is a discussion by Danilov and Altrichter about how the Soviet system changed rural institutions and how much it was itself transformed by rural tradition. On the other hand, some have an image of the Russian countryside as the home of uncountable Oblomovs who do nothing but deplore the mud of their thoughts and emotions, not to mention the Russian *bezdorozhnost'* (the time of year when rural roads become unpassable because of pervasive rain and mud). But if Oblomov was a typical rural inhabitant, Turgenev's Khor was another—the incarnation of a self-assured, sound Russian peasant from whom an urban hunter could always draw wisdom on life and society.

Such differing approaches to the quality of rural life still exist in the Soviet Union. On the one hand, the official Soviet goal is to extinguish the differences between rural and urban life by lifting rural conditions up to urban standards in line with the assumption that urban standards are superior. Another tendency is to see rural life as a kind of punishment. This is consistent with the traditional tendency to exclude people who do not live up to the expectations of Soviet society from urban life. On the other hand, Soviet writers such as V. Rasputin and V. Soloukhin glorify rural life and juxtapose it with urban decay and what they see as the deteriorating mores of Soviet society. For the representatives of the "village prose," "human goodness, respect for the elderly and diligence all originate in the countryside."[1]

It remains unclear to what extent the internal fabric of rural life and the spiritual superiority that Rasputin and others associate with it originates from the external environment of the Soviet countryside, and to what degree Rasputin's heroines are endowed with something special that a male urban dweller could never acquire. However, it seems apparent that according to official Soviet ideology, the mental and emotional capacity of mankind can only improve in relation to the environment. This environment should be urban and industrialized, indicating an advanced level in the development of productive forces.

In attempting to assess the quality of rural life in the Soviet Union, we will therefore not consider the spiritual values of undisturbed Siberian villages concerned with subsistence farming, but try to describe what opportunities the contemporary Soviet countryside offers rural inhabitants to advance emotionally and mentally. How do rural inhabitants organize their leisure time in the Soviet Union? Can one go to the movies in the Soviet countryside? Can one read books? And can one leave the countryside if one wishes to do so? In answering such basic questions about rural life in the Soviet Union, the following will avoid comparative measures, for no other industrialized nation has a comparable rural population or a similar percentage of its work force involved in agriculture.

When judging the level of "culture" in the Soviet Union, one should keep in mind that a minimum exposure to books, newspapers, and Soviet culture in general might be preferable to some people. To be left alone is sometimes considered to be an important part of the quality of one's life. However, there is no evidence that many people understand rural life as a refuge from the demands of Soviet society or a withdrawal from participation in the destruction of the environment. We can therefore assume that more culture—more books, more movies, and more opportunities to take advantage of art and participate in sports—is better than less culture.

Mobility in the Soviet Countryside

Accessibility to rural centers or nearby towns has always been of great importance to rural settlers and the development of rural life in the Soviet Union. An interest in the quality of rural transportation is shared by urban authorities in need of agricultural products. The better the quality of communication between cities and villages, the better and the more timely the provision of food to urban areas. Better links between countryside and town also increase one's chances of selling privately produced goods on urban markets. The supply of rural stores depends on unhampered traffic, and individual opportunities to look elsewhere for inspiration and entertainment correlate with the quality of rural transportation. Not surprisingly, the quality of rural transportation is often the object of both official and private criticism in the Soviet Union. Rural roads are poor, and public transportation from village to village is almost nonexistent. Twice a year, large parts of many rural areas experience the well-known *bezdorozhnost*, when all rural traffic ceases. The effects of the *bezdorozhnost'* have been documented in the well-written accounts of V. Sergeev.[2]

Only 85 percent of all rural *raion* (district) centers and 78 percent of all central farms in the Russian Soviet Federated Socialist Republic (RSFSR) were served by all-weather roads in 1980. The situation is even worse if we include the many small villages and hamlets normally included in a large Soviet farm. Only one-fifth of the roads that link outlying areas with farming centers can be used in any weather.

The need for more on-farm roads in the Soviet countryside can be measured by comparing the official norm, which is based on the total amount of agricultural land, with the number of actual roads in each Soviet republic. The norm is three kilometers per 1,000 hectares. Certain republics have a "surplus" of roads, but 192,000 kilometers of road are "missing" in the RSFSR alone, and when the less developed republics of Central Asia are included, only 60 percent of the Soviet Union's needs are satisfied. Understandably, wealthier agricultural republics such as Moldavia, Estonia, and Georgia have a much higher road density than poorer Soviet republics such as Uzbekistan and Kazakhstan.[3]

The importance of roads for increasing agricultural production was recognized in the 11th Five-Year Plan (1981–85). The amount of money allocated to rural road improvement was 40 percent higher than in the previous plan. Improved rural roads have a beneficial impact on the quality of rural life because access to secondary education and better medical care is made easier. At the same time, however, as the quality of the rural road system improves, many rural workers use the opportunity to move to urban areas.

Creating better opportunities for rural inhabitants to share the cultural amenities of rural centers or cities is far from the goal of the Ministry of Transportation, which is responsible for four-fifths of the USSR's total road length. The ministry is mainly interested in recouping lost products and the more effective use of machinery.

Soviet roads are deficient, and private means of transportation are scarce as well. The proverbial German sugarbeet grower who drives a Mercedes is beyond the imagination of the typical Russian *kolkhoznik* (collective farm worker). The number of privately owned cars that exist in the Soviet countryside is difficult to calculate. Soviet sources indicate that one out of 14 rural workers has a vehicle at his or her disposal.[4] We know from Soviet statistical yearbooks that there are 72 motorcycles and 214 bicycles per thousand rural inhabitants. Other sources indicate that roughly every fourth family has some means of transportation.[5] Commuting to far-off places for work or pleasure is neither customary nor easily accomplished. The following sections therefore analyze how people spend their spare time without leaving their place of residence.

Leisure Time in the Soviet Countryside

At present, about 97 million Soviet citizens live in rural settlements, which Soviet sources merely define as not being cities or towns. During the years 1981–84, the rural population of the Soviet Union decreased by only 1.5 percent (from 36.6 to 35.1 percent). This was noticeably less than during earlier periods. Of the Soviet Union's 97 million rural inhabitants, 64 million are considered "agricultural." During the period from 1960–80, the number of people actually employed in agriculture declined from 25.5 million to 21.6 million, which is still 20 percent of the Soviet work force.

The amount of free time at the disposal of these people varies between men and women and is dependent on seasonal considerations. Soviet surveys indicate that women normally have less free time than men, which is no surprise given the modest degree of mechanization of house work and the likely engagement of women in private agriculture. The time budget in Table 12.1 indicates that women in the Stavropol region devote roughly 20 hours a week to leisure, and that half of the total is spent on activities that one might call "cultural." However, the priorities revealed in Tables 12.1 and 12.2 have to be taken with a grain of salt, for the way in which rural inhabitants spend their free time depends on what is available. If there is nothing that they can do but play dominoes, they will do just that regardless of what they would rather be doing. They live as probably no one else at the mercy of their employer, the *kolkhoz* (collective farm) or the *sovkhoz* (state farm), which might be either poor or wealthy and might not be inclined to spend money on cultural pursuits. If the Soviet state budget does not include allocations for a cultural center in the region in which they work, they can hardly demand one, and cannot possibly rectify the situation by themselves.

Such factors devalue Soviet time budgets as an indicator of the preferences of rural inhabitants in the Soviet Union. Their stated preferences can only serve as a guide for evaluating the opportunities that exist for spending leisure time in the Soviet countryside. Yet the prevailing assumption is that the more opportunities that exist and the better their quality, the higher

TABLE 12.1
Spare Time of Peasant Women in the Stavropol Region

Activity	Hours per Week	Percent of Total
Child Rearing	1.10	6.0
Public Work	0.42	4.0
Learning	4.40	25.0
Cultural Activities	5.50	31.0
Television	4.05	21.8
Movies, Theater, Concerts, Radio	1.10	6.0
Reading	0.35	3.2
Artistic Hobbies	0.56	5.0
Hospitality	1.24	8.0
Walking as Recreation	0.49	4.0
Passive Recreation	3.09	17.0
Total	18.40	100.0

Source: S. F. Frolov and G. G. Markova, "Izpol'zovanie svobodnogo vremeni kilkhoznikami," in Sotsiologicheskie issledovaniia, 1980, no. 1, p. 109.

the quality of rural life. The sequence of priorities identified in Table 12.2 is radio and television, reading, clubs and movies, artistic hobbies, and sports.

Television and Radio

In 1983, the television networks of the Soviet Union reached 88 percent of the population. Radio transmissions reached 98 percent of the population and covered the entire territory of the USSR.[6] Most likely, the 32 million people who cannot receive television (12 percent of the population) live in the countryside. In 1983, 84 out of 100 rural families had a radio and 83 had a television set. More than two million televisions are sold in the countryside every year, and 400,000 of them are color sets. This means that during the last decade, 20 million rural families acquired a new television. If all of those sets are still functioning, there should be a set in each rural household that can receive television signals. In addition, roughly two million radios are bought each year.[7]

Obviously, there is no shortage of television sets in the Soviet countryside. However, the evidence points to drastic differences in the availability of

TABLE 12.2
Spare Time of Workers and Peasants in 1963-64

Activities	Workers		Peasants	
	Men	Women	Men	Women
Hours of Sparetime				
(per working day)	4.0	2.3	3.45	2.70
Child Rearing	0.2	0.1	0.00	0.08
Learning	0.4	0.2	0.09	0.14
Public Work and				
Artistic Activities	0.1	0.2	0.21	0.15
Sports	0.2	0.0	0.14	0.05
Reading	0.7	0.4	0.41	0.67
Radio and				
Television	0.7	0.3	1.40	0.97
Clubs and Movies	0.5	0.3	0.20	0.30
Passive Recreation	1.2	0.8	1.00	0.36

Source: Berezhnoi and Ovchinnikov, "Opyt issledovaniia izmenenii v strukture svobodnogo vremeni kolkhoznikov," Nauchnye doklady vysshei shkoly. Filisofskie nauki, 1966, no. 5, pp. 21-27.

television programming. In November 1977, the Central Committee and the Council of Ministers published a joint decree, "On the Further Improvement of Cultural Services to the Rural Population," containing a long paragraph on the need to improve rural television communication. Republics and smaller administrative units were allowed to spend more money on the enlargement of rural networks than was originally planned. Collective farms were encouraged to use their own money for such purposes.[8] Nevertheless, the impressive figures on televisions sold in the Soviet Union obscure regional differences in Soviet television coverage, and might also indicate that a frequent replacement of equipment is necessary.

Very few studies are available on the extent to which rural inhabitants turn to television or really like the programs they watch. Most people watch television simply for diversion or entertainment. Such attitudes are little appreciated by officials or interviewers conducting surveys on popular attitudes toward television. The summary of one of these surveys contained the demand for more programs on "civic duties, family life, and on norms for behavior and reality." Even if the peasants in this study failed to respond as they should, the reviewers certainly knew how they ought to.[9]

Literature

The Soviet Union claims to have a booming publishing industry and an eager reading audience. People who read in every possible situation are a common theme of photograph collections depicting the contemporary Soviet Union. But what chances actually exist for the rural population to quench its thirst for literature?

In 1983, there were 96,900 libraries in rural areas—a figure that has remained constant during the early 1980s. They hold 825.4 million books and journals, and the number is constantly increasing. In 1975, there were 673.6 million rural libraries. In the same year, rural libraries lent some 60 million readers about 1.2 billion books and journals. The average rural library had about 600 visitors.[10]

In 1983, there were 58,700 agricultural units in the Soviet Union, and there were 41,963 *sel'skij sovet* administering roughly 500,000 rural settlements.[11] Therefore, almost one out of every five villages should have a library. Alas, this is only statistical logic, for we do not know the precise population structure of each settlement. Many hamlets might not qualify for a library, whereas in large villages or rural centers more than one library might exist, particularly as *kolkhozi* and *sovkhozi* are encouraged to maintain their own libraries.

A survey conducted in the non-black earth zone found that many families had a substantial number of private books. Sixty-five percent of the respondents claimed to have more than 50 books, and 10 percent said they had more than 100 books. Although people frequently ask that more books be made available, half of all the books contained in official libraries have never been requested—yet another example of nonaligned supply and demand in the Soviet Union.[12] Another survey reported that only seven percent of the people sampled had their own books.[13]

Most officials regard rural libraries as an instrument to foster political agitation and increase vocational qualifications. This is one of the reasons why library holdings fail to match the interests of potential readers. A tractor driver who demands Lenin's works or a brochure on a new harvester is indeed difficult to imagine.

A rare survey on rural book purchasing that classified the respondents by age indicated that people between the ages of 17–24 and 30–39 are the most active book buyers, whereas people over 60 are the most reluctant.[14] This helps us to identify which age groups have surplus income to spend in the Soviet countryside.

Another problem characteristic of many rural settlements is a lack of library personnel. Most librarians tend to gravitate toward the cities despite the fact that rural employment entitles them to free housing and other benefits under the terms of a 1977 decree that also promises rural *kul'turno-prosvetitel'naia* specialists a five-year, interest-free loan of 1,000 rubles.[15]

Clubs and Movies

Next to watching television and reading, the average *kolkhoznik* most likes to visit the nearest "rural club," in most cases to see a movie. Soviet clubs, or in some cases "houses of culture" or even "palaces of culture," have nothing in common with Western connotations of the word "club." Rural clubs are rather the center of political and cultural activity in rural areas. A 1975 *Pravda* article explained that a decent rural club should have a concert hall, a library with a reading room, music classrooms, a sports complex, and hobby rooms.[16] This was the dream of the 1970s based on the realities of the 1960s, when the average rural club amounted to little more than a stuffy, sparsely furnished room decorated with some slogans and a few agricultural posters, often without heat in the winter.[17]

Since the 1960s, the number of rural clubs has increased even as the number of rural settlements has declined. In 1983, there were 118,300 clubs in rural settlements, while in 1965 there were only 111,300. During the last five years, the number of rural clubs has remained constant, but their quality has improved.

The above-mentioned 1977 decree stated that rural clubs had serious deficiencies and admitted that many clubs failed to live up to the demands of rural workers. Equipment, furniture, musical instruments, and "technical means" of propaganda were in short supply. All agencies having to do with the quality of rural clubs were therefore asked to improve the situation, particularly by erecting new *dom kultury* (houses of culture) and repairing older buildings in a timely and proper fashion.[18]

Surveys of visitors to rural clubs indicate that young people attend most often. Adults, not to mention elderly people, seldom frequent clubs. Older people tend to find their way to rural clubs only to participate in political events.[19] The typical visitor is under 23 years of age, and goes to the village club to dance and see movies. Not surprisingly, movie performances are the focus of the attention of rural clubs—much more so than orchestras or stereo equipment for dancing events. Ninety percent of all clubs organize movies that must be paid for. One such club documented 97 performances in 100 working days.[20] Soviet statistics indicate that the number of rural moviegoers declined slightly during the last decade. There were 1.8 billion rural moviegoers in 1970 and only 1.4 billion in 1983. This decline can be explained by decreases in the Soviet Union's rural population and the number of rural settlements, though declining movie attendance has been reported in urban areas as well.

The average rural person goes to the movies about 15 times a year. This is an incredibly high figure that represents a frequency of moviegoing unparalleled in any other nation. The actual frequency must be even higher as not all of the Soviet Union's roughly 100 million rural inhabitants are potential moviegoers. Regional and seasonal differences are beyond our assessment, but it seems safe to assume that one's chance of seeing a movie is a function of distance, weather, and road conditions. It also seems likely that the quality of the movie and the copy actually shown is similarly determined.

Artistic Hobbies and Sports

Soviet folklore ensembles dance and sing all over the world, offering proof of how much the Soviet state cares for the cultural heritage of rural Russia. Some of their shows are of rural origin, and some of the actors might have been born in a village, but for the most part they are well paid professional performers whose ties to the countryside might best be symbolized by a *dacha* (summer home). Of more importance to the daily life of Soviet villages is how the rural squaredance develops or how the local choir fares.

How is Soloukhin's white-shirted local accordion player doing today? As Soloukhin himself lamented, he wants to have a Sony radio and a stereo for dancing at the club, and he wants to replace his accordion with an electric guitar. As regards his white shirt, it has always been fictitious. Even today, the Soviet countryside has not been sufficiently supplied with detergents to keep anyone's shirts white.

Information on rural and urban artistic hobby groups (*kruzhki*) have not been released since 1976. In 1975, there were 388,007 rural groups out of a total of 585,000. This amounts to about 4.9 million rural hobbyists out of a total of 8.9 million.[21] In 1983, there were 717,000 groups (23,000 less than in 1980), or about 12 million participants.[22] If we assume that villages still account for more than half of the total as they did in 1975, we can conclude that one out of every 12–15 villagers takes part in one of the *kruzhki*. Table 12.3 shows the number of *kruzhki* in the Omsk region in 1969 and 1970.

Soviet time budgets indicate that rural people spend very little time on sports. One survey reported that Soviet villagers spend an average of 0.02 hours (or 1.2 minutes) per week on physical activities. This adds up to one hour of physical activity every two months. Evidently, the morning exercise of the rural teacher made it into the survey.

Contrary to this dim picture, in 1984 *Ekonomicheskaia gazeta* reported that the chairman of a trade union committee in Belorussia boasted of having 12 different sports sections with more than 350 people actively

TABLE 12.3
Changes in the Cultural Activities of Rural People in the Omsk Region

Indicators	1969	1970
Number of Artistic Groups (per 1,000 inhabitants)	4.5	7.5
Number of Participants in Artistic Groups (per 1,000 inhabitants)	49	104
Number of Readers (per 100 inhabitants)	52	61
Number of Movies Attended Annually	38	33

Source: P. P. Velikii, "Sotsial'no-kul'turnaia deiatel'nost' sel'skogo naseleniia," *Sotsiologicheskie issledovaniia,* 1982, no. 4, p. 107.

involved. Six hundred people were identified as *znachkisti* (medal bearers), having earned the GTO award (Ready to Work and to Defense), and 100 were qualified sportsmen. Unfortunately, it remains unclear how many villages the chairman supervises or how large they are.[23]

Regardless of such attempts to show that rural workers are dutifully involved in *fizkultura* and sports, the situation is not encouraging. This is because, first, rural inhabitants exhibit a strong disdain for unnecessary physical exertion and a traditional antipathy to changes in traditional leisure habits imposed from the outside. Second, close limits are set on outdoor recreational patterns as a result of the very nature of agricultural labor and the Soviet climate. A severe winter stretches from October to April, and during the summer months work occupies most of one's time. Third, the general poverty of the Soviet countryside and its lack of good roads has limited the possibilities of constructing sophisticated sports facilities or organizing regular physical education programs.[24] Beside these factors, it would take an affluent society—which the Soviet Union is not—to equip the Soviet countryside with gymnasiums, soccer fields, and swimming pools.

Conclusions

Given the fact that the Soviet Union is by many accounts an advanced, industrialized nation, and considering that the Soviet communist party and government have always been in favor of "culture"—whether this is taken to mean going to the ballet or the use of a handkerchief—one would expect the quality of cultural life in the rural Soviet Union to be better than it actually is. A genuine rural culture does not seem to have emerged in the Soviet Union. Carved spoons or embroidered peasant shirts are nowhere to be found, and no one turns to the countryside to relax by square dancing or listening to the wisdom of a new generation of Khors. Of course, the urban hunters who could talk to a peasant such as Khor have vanished as well. To be called a peasant or a *kolkhoznik* is a derogatory remark frequently used in Soviet cities.

Indeed, it seems that Soviet villages show signs of negative selection. Those who are mobile, energetic, and young enough attempt to migrate to the cities. As for those who remain in the countryside, rural socialization processes have hardly fostered their personal initiative. A peasant who has been told for 50 years how to plant his crops is not likely to develop the idea of a chess tournament on his own. He is even less inclined to do so when recalling those times when peasant customs were officially regarded as "superstition" or incompatible with the new times. In addition, for the greater part of Soviet history, life in the countryside was a struggle for survival and a decent standard of living. People who struggle for survival rarely think about libraries or setting up a village choir. Cultivating a private plot or escaping to the city is a much safer bet.

The Soviet village of the 1980s might well have the time and material resources to be concerned with cultural activities, but the heritage of the Soviet past has combined with modern developments so that most people's free time is now spent working for a new television set or a car to drive off to the movies. On the other hand, the opportunity to escape an environment that one believes to be an uninspiring burden could well be interpreted as bettering the quality of life of those who escape, even if this means a further decline in the cultural condition of those who remain.

Notes

1. V. Rasputin, "Den'gi dlia Marii," in *Vniz i vverkh po techeniu* (Moscow, 1972), p. 211.

2. V. Sergeev, "Ekhal muzhik po doroge . . ." in *Zhurnalist*, 1981, no. 4.

3. E. Clayton, "Rural Infrastructure in the Soviet Union," conference paper to be published; quoted by permission of author.

4. A. V. Voronsov, "Razvitie dukhovnykh potrebnostei kolkhoznogo krest'ianstva Nechernozemnoi zony RSFSR," *Sotsiologicheskie issledovaniia*, 1980, no. 3, p. 84.

5. *Narodnoe khoziaistvo SSSR v 1983 godu* (Moscow, 1984), p. 443.

6. *Ezhegodnik bol'shoi sovetskoi entsiklopedii* (Moscow, 1984), p. 82.

7. *Narodnoe khoziaistvo SSSR v 1983 godu* (Moscow, 1984), p. 441.

8. *Sobranie postanovlenii Pravitel'stva SSSR*, 1977, no. 29, stat'ia 184, pp. 634–640.

9. E. V. Vasil'evskaia, "Sel'skii telezritel', etgo zaprosy i stepen'ikh udovletvorenii programmami televedeniia," *Izvestiia Sibirskogo otdeleniia AN SSSR, seriia obshchestvennykh nauk*, 1969, no. 2, *vypusk* 3, pp. 113–116.

10. *Narodnoe khoziaistvo SSSR v 1983 godu* (Moscow, 1984), p. 506.

11. *Narodnoe khoziaistvo SSSR v 1983 godu* (Moscow, 1984), p. 11.

12. Voronsov, "Razvitie dukhovnykh potrebnostei," p. 87.

13. L. I. Lobanova, "Kul'turnoe obsluzhivanie sel'skikh zhitelei Nechernozem'ia," *Sotsiologicheskie issledovaniia*, 1982, no. 4, p. 102.

14. *Sobranie postanovlenii Pravitel'stva SSSR*, 1977, no. 29, *stat'ia* 184, p. 639.

15. I. P. Tikhonova, "Kto chitaet knigi na sele? Opyt sotssiologicheskogo issledovaniia sprosa knigi," *Knizhnaia torgovlia*, 1967, no. 2, pp. 32–33.

16. *Pravda*, September 5, 1975, p. 3.

17. A. S. Duchal, "Izmenenie struktury rabochego i svobodnogo vremeni krest'ian za gody Sovetskoi vlast," *Voprosy filosofii*, 1965, no. 4, p. 79.

z18. *Sobranie postanovlenii Pravitel'stva SSSR*, 1977, no. 29, *stat'ia* 184, p. 637.

19. V. P. Odinsov, "Klubnoe ovsluzhivanie naseleniia," *Sotsiologicheskie issledovaniia*, 1976, no. 1, p. 122.

20. Odinsov, "Klubnoe ovsluzhivanie naseleniia," p. 122.

21. *Narodnoe khoziaistvo SSSR v 1975 godu* (Moscow, 1976), p. 701.

22. *Narodnoe khoziaistvo SSSR v 1983 godu* (Moscow, 1976), p. 515.

23. *Ekonomicheskaia gazeta*, March 1984, p. 13.

24. J. Riordan, *Sport in Soviet Society: Development of Sport and Physical Education in Russia and USSR* (New York: Cambridge University Press, 1976).

About the Contributors

Robert Belknap received his Ph.D. from Columbia University and is currently a professor of Russian at Columbia. He has worked on a wide range of topics relating to Russian literature, and his most recent paper was on the rhetoric of Dostoyevsky's last inspirational speeches.

Mark G. Field, a professor of sociology and codirector of the Russian Studies Institute at Boston University, received his Ph.D. from Harvard University. Dr. Field has published over 100 papers on Soviet society, medicine, psychiatry, and comparative health systems. He is the author of *The Social Consequences of Modernization in Communist Countries* (1976).

Horst Herlemann, the editor of this volume, received his Ph.D. from the Ruhr Universität Bochum. He is now an associate professor of political science at the Universität Würzburg. Dr. Herlemann has written extensively on various aspects of Soviet domestic policy and the political culture of communist systems.

Friedrich Kuebart received his Ph.D. from the Ruhr Universität Bochum. His present position is senior research associate at the Comparative Education Research Unit, Ruhr Universität Bochum. Dr. Kuebart has written articles and books on various aspects of Soviet education and the history of Soviet studies in Germany.

Mervyn Matthews teaches Soviet studies at the University of Surrey in Guildford, England. He received his Ph.D. from Oxford University. He is the author of *Class and Society in Soviet Russia* (1972) and *Privilege in the Soviet Union* (1978), and his most recent work is entitled *Poverty in the Soviet Union* (1986).

Henry W. Morton, a professor of political science at Queens College, City University of New York, received his Ph.D. from Columbia University. In recent years, his primary research concern has been Soviet urban and housing problems, and his most recent book, which he coedited with Robert C. Stuart, is *The Contemporary Soviet City* (1984).

Anna-Jutta Pietsch received her Ph.D. from the Freie Universität Berlin. She is now a research associate at the Osteuropa-Institut of the Universität München. Dr. Pietsch has written several articles and books on various aspects of Soviet domestic and economic policy.

Gertrude E. Schroeder, a professor of economics at the University of Virginia, received her Ph.D. from The Johns Hopkins University. She has published extensively on the Soviet economy, in particular on economic reform, labor, and living standards. Dr. Schroeder's most recent work is entitled *Soviet Economic Problems: System vs. Progress* (forthcoming).

Stephen Sternheimer, an analyst with the Central Intelligence Agency, received his Ph.D. from the University of Chicago. His research has focused on Soviet foreign and domestic policy, with special emphasis on social policy. Dr. Sternheimer's most recent work, which appeared as part of a report prepared for the National Council on Soviet and East European Research, is entitled "The Role of Imported Technology in Soviet R & D" (1986).

Wolfgang Teckenberg, who received his Ph.D. from the Universität Köln, is currently an associate professor at the Institut für Soziologie of the Universität Heidelberg. He has written numerous articles and books on various sociological problems, particularly those relating to the social structure of the Soviet Union and Germany.

Vladimir G. Treml, a professor of economics at Duke University, received his Ph.D. from the University of North Carolina. He has written extensively on input-output analysis, the economics of alcoholism, and foreign trade. Dr. Treml is currently working on a book about alcoholism and the quality of life in the Soviet Union.

Index